Hypnocounseling:
An eclectic bridge between Milton Erickson and Carl Rogers

by
Hugh Gunnison

Crown House Publishing Limited
www.crownhousepublishing.com

Published by
Crown House Publishing LLC
6 Trowbridge Drive, Suite 5
Bethel, CT 06801
www.crownhousepublishing.com

©2004 by Crown House Publishing LLC
First published in 2003 by
PCCS Books Ltd
Llangarron, Ross-on-Wye, Herefordshire, HR9 6PT, UK

© Hugh Gunnison 2003
Reprinted 2010 and 2011.

All rights reserved.
No part of this publication may be reproduced, stored in a retrieval system, transmitted or utilized in any form by any means, electronic, mechanical, photocopying or recording or otherwise, without permission in writing from the publishers.

A CIP catalog record for this book is available
from the British Library

13 digit ISBN: 9781904424499
10 digit ISBN: 1-9044249-X

LCCN: 2004106203

Cover illustrations © 1987 from *Psychotherapy: The Listening Voice-Rogers and Erickson* by Richard Leva. Reproduced by permission of Routledge/Taylor & Francis Books, Inc.

Contents

FOREWORD	i
PREFACE	iii
NOTE TO THE READER	vii
ACKNOWLEDGEMENTS	viii

CHAPTER 1: ROGERS AND ERICKSON	1
Impact on Counseling	1
Origin and Development of Values	4
Person-Centeredness	6
The Self as a Tool	13
The Importance of Caring and Respect for the Client (Positive Regard)	15
The Importance of Empathy	16
Genuineness, Communication, and Self-Hypnosis	16
The Use of Metaphors	20
On Growth, Self-Actualization and the Unconscious (Nonconscious)	23
Rambles at Random and Implications	27
CHAPTER 2: THEORY	29
Carl R. Rogers and Theory	33
The Propositions	36
Milton H. Erickson: Tentative Assumptions	44
A Short Course in Epistemologies	47
CHAPTER 3: MYSTERIES FROM PHYSICS	57
A New Oxymoron: Ordered Chaos — Complexity on the Edge of Chaos: The Story of Nonlinear Emerging Systems	58
Quantum Chaos: A Footnote	64
Quantum Mechanics: a.k.a. QM; a.k.a. Quantum Theory; a.k.a. The Copenhagen Interpretation; a.k.a. The Newer Physics	65
The Principle of Complementarity	68
The Uncertainty Principle	70
Choice — Free Will	75

CHAPTER 4: HYPNOSIS AND HYPNOCOUNSELING — 81
- Hypnosis — 81
- Definitions — Hypnosis — 86
- Hypnotic Phenomena — 87
- Definitions — Hypnocounseling — 89
- Implied Directive Language (IDL): The Core of Hypnocounseling — 91
- Hypno-Suggestive Language Patterns of Hypnocounseling (IDL) — 92

CHAPTER 5: ECLECTICISM — 105
- Definitions and Discussions — 105
- R.R. Carkhuff, *et al* — 110
- The Core Conditions (A Certain Type of Relationship) — 110
- The Three Phase Counseling Process — 123

CHAPTER 6: STRATEGIES — 129
- Surrogate Self — SS — 130
- Fantasy Relaxation Technique — FRT — 136
- Fantasy Door Approach — FDA — 142
- Dials, Meters and Gauges — DMG — 149

CHAPTER 7: HYPNOCOUNSELING AND BRIEF THERAPY — 157
- Brief Therapy — BT — 158
- BT Assumptions — 159
- *Examples of BT Questions* — 162
- Creed of a Counselor — 168
- Hypnocounseling and A Surrogate Self (SS) as a Scaffolding for Brief Therapy: An Example of Mix and Match — 173

NON CONCLUSION — 179

APPENDICES — 181
- Appendix A — A Script for FRT — 181
- Appendix B — A Script for FDA — 186
- Appendix C — 'Reaction to Gunnison's article on the similarities and differences between Erickson and Rogers' by Carl R. Rogers — 190

REFERENCES — 195

INDEX — 205

Foreword

I have a strong disagreement with practitioners who call themselves 'client-centered or person-centered' while feeling free to add interventions, techniques or directiveness to their work with clients. These additions inevitably compromise the client's absolute authority and the therapist's absolute trust — core concepts of person-centered theory. Although we have the right to 'borrow' from theoretical systems in finding our own best way to counsel, I appreciate the integrity of those who acknowledge the influences. It is drastically different for practitioners to say their practice is *informed* by person-centered values than it is to call themselves person-centered.

In this book, Hugh Gunnison does exactly that. The very title of the book states clearly that his personal approach to counseling relies significantly on the philosophies of Carl Rogers and Milton Erickson. He does not use the title of Person-Centered Counselor or Hypnotherapist. He calls his carefully wrought system *Hypnocounseling*.

The book, though rich in information, is delightfully easy to read. Gunnison's style is conversational and personal, filled with rich metaphors and examples of the theoretical points he is attempting to drive home. Sometimes the writing is even hypnotic! Once the reader becomes familiar, for example, with the concept of hypno-suggestive language, it is easy to identify throughout the book. Also reflective of some of the techniques of Hypnocounseling, Gunnison invites readers to focus on the issue he is exploring, check out their feelings about what he is saying, make their own choices and look more deeply into self; much as he would do in a counseling or teaching situation. Although he does it subtly, readers get a sense of the technique as well as the experience of his model of counseling. I always look for the integration of process and content, and have rarely seen it done so effectively as here. If, as he says, he will use this book as a text for counseling students, it will be both theoretical and experiential.

Gunnison's look at the biography, theory, and therapeutic intentions of Rogers and Erickson is very engaging, and provides some fine examples of 'biography as theory'. He makes a very strong case for the danger of constructing dichotomies, and demonstrates his own preference for making connections rather than focusing on differences. In chapters six and seven, Gunnison provides rich examples of some strategies and interventions taken from his practice of Hypnocounseling and Brief Therapy. This section brings to the surface differences between Rogers, Erickson, and Gunnison and their work — as well as similarities. Part of the challenge for the reader lies in identifying those differences, a provocative project indeed.

There are some very special reminders in this book about the sacredness of the therapeutic relationship, the exquisite respect for the person of the client, new discoveries in physics and their implications for the field of human development, and the privilege and responsibility of working in the field of counseling. There is opportunity to enhance one's personal and professional awareness, especially in the chapters on 'Strategies' and on 'Hypnocounseling and Brief Therapy'. The breadth of scholarship in these pages, beautifully integrated with compassion for the human condition, promises a rich read for all.

Peggy Natiello
Sedona, Arizona.
March 2003

Preface

> *I shall be telling this with a sigh*
> *Somewhere ages and ages hence;*
> *Two roads diverged in a wood, and I —*
> *I took the one less traveled by,*
> *And that has made all the difference.*
> Robert Frost

In certain ways this work might resemble a travel journal. It is a kind of written geography of mental wanderings that serves as memoirs of my development as a counselor and the inner journey I have taken.

'Hypnocounseling,' (Gunnison, 1989, 1990a, 1990b, 1990c, 1991a, 1991b) represents a metaphor of my learning, my experiences, and a record of my continual search for and twists on the road not traveled on the way to my becoming a counselor. I believe that each of us from beginning counselor to seasoned practitioner looks for less traveled paths that make all the difference. Our fingerprints and signature are inked indelibly on our works. Our experimenting with different models and theories, our exploring of personal values and beliefs result in our approach, that eventually becomes 'our way.'

For over twenty-five years I have been a counselor and have taught courses in counseling and therapy, and yet what I have learned about people has not come as much from the literature or research as it has from the students and clients who have sat with me. I owe them much.

I have written my share of articles for professional journals; however, this book represents a first for me. Writing articles seems so different from writing books. Articles tend toward pithiness. Their length requires that they be specific, directional, and possibly a bit dull; however, this book, as I envision it, opens up many possibilities. I feel like the client who first walks in to see a counselor or the practicum student who presents an initial tape to supervisors: scared, confused, wondering what will happen, unsure, yet vaguely excited and hopeful. I feel vulnerable toward you, the reader. I feel naked in a sense, for you read and evaluate me, right now. I visualize this book as a funnel through which I pour the learnings and experiences of my students, my clients and me. Although I want to personalize this book making it as informal as possible, engaging, and challenging as if we two conversed together, I am aware that certain sections may not lend themselves to a comfortable intimacy.

Your reading should enhance and enrich your understanding of another perception of counseling, as the writing of this book has stimulated and challenged me to clarify and explore my understandings and state them as clearly as I can.

I believe this book can provide support and reinforcement for existing beliefs of the reader as well as sponsoring ideas and techniques that may be new. I visualize *Hypnocounseling* as a primary text in courses on hypnosis and counseling or as a secondary text for beginning students in the helping professions, as well as a 'stretch,' challenge, and fresh approach for practising counselors, psychotherapists, and social workers.

Since Hypnocounseling depends so much on the sensitive use of language, you will probably notice my dependence on General Semantics as well as my occasional use of E-Prime language (Bois, 1966; Bourland, 1966; Johnson, 1946; Korzybski, 1941), especially when referring to human behavior. E-Prime of writing avoids the use of the verb 'to be' (excepting auxiliary forms). It seems to me this creates language and understanding that result in a more functional, nonlinear, and process-oriented style. Use of 'E-Prime' results in a language style less absolute, all inclusive or permanent than forms of the verb 'to be' seem to generate (personal communication and lectures, Dr. William Fox, Professor, St. Lawrence University).

Notice your own reaction to the verb 'to be' when you say, 'I *am* depressed.' Now, say, 'I depress myself,' or 'I feel depressed.' Do you sense a felt shift in your internal processing? The statement 'I am depressed' forms a declaration. It seems to convey the impression that I *equal* depression, that I seem only depressed, nothing else. In fact, I believe I exist as a whole person with many parts, not only depression, but also excitement, joy, sadness, hope, etc. 'He *is* bad' has many peculiar if not inaccurate meanings. 'Is' can get us into trouble too. It assumes an independent existence out there in the external world. To say, 'He is bad' can result in the meaning of 'all' and thus closes off the subject. 'He is bad' and 'that's the *all* of it.' He comprises nothing else but 'bad.' When I say, 'When *he* screams at his kids that way, *I feel frustrated* and *damned uncomfortable.*' Here I refer to his behavior and how I react to it. In addition, I have separated the person *(he* is *bad)* from the behavior that frustrates, and I have been operational about the process. It seems clearer, more accurate and more descriptive than simply to describe the above situation as, 'He is bad.' The argument holds that words such as forms of the verb 'to be' are not 'bad' of themselves, but rather the uses we make of them may be unclear and unhelpful.

Furthermore, I appreciate a special quote from O'Hanlon and Weiner-Davis that permeates Hypnocounseling, '. . . the creative and mindful use of language is perhaps the single most influential indirect method for creating contexts in which change is perceived to be inevitable' (1989, p. 60).

Can you make meaning of this, of the importance of language, especially how you internally talk to yourself, as well as the way you hear others' language?

Carl Rogers remains a primary mentor and stimulus for me, and Milton H. Erickson and his utilization approach has fast become another. Although I never had the opportunity to meet Erickson, his death has meant I have had to construct an idea of this man through his audio/video tapes, his writings, and the seminar-workshops, talks and writings of his family, colleagues, and former students. However, this book will not attempt to rehash Rogers' or Erickson's work, but rather will tentatively describe adaptations, examples and broadening implications of their messages as each contributes to form my foundation for Hypnocounseling.

This writing represents a different kind of eclecticism. Rather than selecting, combining and drawing upon the major theories in counseling, I choose to focus on strategies or techniques drawn from counseling and therapy 'schools' at first presumed foreign to Erickson and Rogers. Hypnocounseling, the merging of Rogers' person-centered and Erickson's utilization approaches, can be viewed as an adjunct or catalyst to be used with the strategy or technique that best seems to fit the client. After all, in Hypnocounseling we shall learn that the client is invariably at the center of the counseling process. The argument will be presented that Rogers' person-centered approach together with Erickson's utilization approach can serve as a template or map, broad and wide enough to provide journey directions for most clients.

While each counseling encounter has its own uniqueness as expressed in different problems, contexts, issues, and resolutions, the undergirding process, the process-stages of counseling remain essentially the same, and this process has been described in the work of Carl Rogers and that of R. R. Carkhuff and his associates. Thus, this book will represent an attempt to merge the philosophies of the *utilization* and *person-centered approaches* and how they fit within Carkhuff's process model to form Hypnocounseling.

Hypnocounseling shall stand for the use of (1) Ericksonian hypno-suggestive language (Gunnison, 1990; Lankton and Lankton, 1983; O'Hanlon and Martin, 1992; O'Hanlon and Weiner-Davis, 1989) in conjunction with (2) Rogers' (1957, 1962, 1985, 1986b) *person-centered,* highly facilitative therapeutic relationship.

Unlike hypnotherapy, Hypnocounseling does not have as its goal the elicitation of trance or deep hypnosis nor does it represent a primary strategy. Hypnocounseling can become a powerful adjunct, catalyst or support for the counselor's primary strategy whatever it might be (Adlerian, cognitive behavioral, Freudian, Gestalt, Jungian, psychodynamic, Rational Emotive Therapy (RET), Reality Therapy (RT) or any of the brief therapies).

In addition, Hypnocounseling becomes an excellent eclectic bridge for the various approaches. In this book, the primary strategy I have chosen for our example is solution focused brief therapy (deShazer, 1985; Cade and O'Hanlon, 1993; O'Hanlon and Weiner-Davis, 1989) dictated by the moment-by-moment changes and needs of the client. Client behavior, direct and/or indirect verbal and nonverbal communications, may mean modifying and mixing several strategies. For example, Hypnocounseling might be used more effectively with Gestalt Therapy, RT or RET, rather than with brief therapy. I must trust the lead of my client.

The definition of Hypnocounseling can set the chapter organization of the book. In the first chapter I examine the utilization approach of Erickson and how it compares with the person-centered approach of Rogers. After a brief stroll through the fields of theory (Chapter II) and Mysteries From Physics in Chapter III, I review Hypnosis and Hypnocounseling in Chapter IV. Chapter V represents an attempt to explore such issues as eclecticism, counseling process, and facilitative, therapeutic relationships. In Chapter VI, I explore specific Hypnocounseling strategies. Brief descriptions are followed by client-counselor dialogues and two of the strategies are placed in Appendices that can be read or taped for counselors' trial use with themselves and/or their clients. The last chapter, Chapter VII, consists of client/counselor interactions demonstrating solution-oriented brief therapy as the primary strategy combined with Hypnocounseling.

I now realize that the process of getting started in writing a book differs only in degree, not in kind, from getting started in teaching a class. The way I begin sets the tone. One of my early discoveries concerned a realization that I probably could teach counselors[1] very little but could 'learn' them a lot. I came to realize that when I tried to 'teach,' students seemed passive and reactive to whatever I did or said. I had a mental image of a hole in the top of their heads into which I poured 'knowledge' and then from the tap or spigot in their mouth I got back, in the form of tests, the information originally poured in, in a kind of mental circulation mostly from me and rarely from them. As I twisted the verb 'to learn' I found greater comfort in believing I could 'learn' them something. This put the greater emphasis on them. The grammatical misuse of 'learn' seemed to assume the student was being proactive and doing something, taking responsibility for learning and so I'll promise to teach you very little but I sure hope I can 'learn' you something.

Why not take a few moments now to ponder the implications of 'teach' and 'learn' if you haven't done so? You may wish to go back to a time when you can recall 'being taught' and then to a time when you 'learned.' Do you sense a difference in the lasting results?

[1.] Throughout, I shall use the term counselor to mean therapist, social worker, advisor, or anyone who works closely with others in a helping capacity; and this easily could include teachers. In addition, I will use the feminine-masculine pronouns in alternation so as to avoid the awkward he/she, him/her forms.

Some years ago, I recall a student in a first class of Techniques of Counseling saying that he wanted to learn about the 'role' of a counselor. I responded with my hope that we could learn how the person becomes a counselor and that roles, techniques, seem to miss the mark. What I have continued to learn has convinced me that effective professionals are able to bring themselves, their authenticity, and their valuing processes to counseling and that has made a significant difference. My assumption still holds, that counselors in their training and practice will continually re-examine their own beliefs, values, and self concepts.

In a culture fixed on 'pat' and predictable answers it seems difficult to give an honest answer, from 'I am fixed and certain about my beliefs' to 'I am open to many possibilities.' Do you sense the difference? The difficulty in these questions is that we all want to be open, not rigid. I am asking you to test your degree of openness to many of the suggestions and possibilities in this book. What a difference between, 'I am certain about my beliefs' and 'Right now I'm relatively certain; however, with new data, reevaluation and reexploration, I can change'.

NOTE TO THE READER

Parts of this book differ greatly from one another. Some sections are designed for the 'beginning student' in the helping professions (counseling, psychotherapy, and social work) while other parts may assume a knowledge or background base that goes beyond the introductory levels.

My goal has been to whet your curiosity, to challenge your assumptions, and to expose you to questions, and ideas that very well may become issues in your future.

I might have written this book in a concrete, repetitive, and drilling-style, suitable only for the beginning student. I have learned over the years that students do like to be challenged and do relish considering diverse ideas, as well as exploring new and different beliefs and assumptions. Hypnocounseling is a supplementary text, designed to build upon the basics. The intent throughout is 'brightening up' rather than 'dimming or dumbing down.'

You may find yourself choosing to skip whole sections at a time and then returning to them if you are so inclined. Use your own discretion as to how you read this book because this happens to be the major point in what this book is all about; learning to be the authority for your own living. You might question the assumptions and beliefs. You could be on the lookout for what might appear as indoctrination. Or be on the lookout for the road(s) not taken and why not? Look what it did for Robert Frost.

Acknowledgements

First, I wish to thank my wife, Patricia, who stood by me. She showed her usual positive and encouraging characteristics that are so necessary in an endeavor such as this. She, too, was working on a book.

An editor is the most important part of successfully publishing a book. I want to thank my editor, Pete Sanders, of PCCS Books. Pete's endurance, input, and patience were truly appreciated. He led the way. In addition, I owe much to Dr. Suzanne Moore, USN. She had a deep and abiding awareness of the works of both Rogers and Erickson and helped so much in the later renewing and polishing of Hypnocounseling.

I must thank St. Lawrence University Presidents Frank Piskor, Lawry Gulick, and Dan Sullivan for their support and acceptance of my teaching, my often unusual ideas and the experiment in beliefs and values that went on during their tenures. Had it not been for Dr. William T. Elberty, Chair of the Department of Geography at St. Lawrence University and his providing feedback, heated discussions and office facilities, this book might not have taken shape.

Dr. (Fritz) T. F. Renick deserves much praise. He was a former professor of mine at Syracuse University and then became the head of the Graduate Counseling and Development Program at St. Lawrence University. As a teacher, colleague and friend, Fritz invariably encouraged my 'far out' ideas; challenging, questioning, supporting but never judging. It was he who constantly challenged me to explore different paths, different ways of looking at things. He remains a model to me of respect, genuineness, and integrity. Fritz created that psychological climate in which I flourished.

I owe so much to Carl Rogers, a friend and colleague. His writings, thoughts, and presence were exhilarating and reassuring.

While I never had the chance to meet Dr. Erickson in person, I did learn of him through his work, as well as from lectures, programs, writings, and conversations with the following: Joseph Barber, Stephen Gilligan, John Grinder, Carol Lankton, Stephen Lankton, William O'Hanlon, Ernest Rossi, and Jeffrey Zeig. I am indebted to each of them.

This part becomes very difficult. There were many friends, former students, and colleagues who rooted for me and were in my camp, backing me up, inspiring and giving comfort. Sadly I do not have the space to mention all of their names. Representatively, I will mention Jeff Lazovik, a special colleague, who was with me at the center of my work — prodding, reviewing and often cajoling me into taking a different tack or approaching things from another vantage point. He kept me on my toes.

The Lea R. Powell Institute for Children and Families at Alfred University invited me to present a week-long workshop on Hypnocounseling. I used the text as 'lesson plan' and blueprint. I wish to thank Dr. Jay Cerio, Director of the Lea R. Powell workshop as well as the counselors, psychologists and doctoral students for their exceptional feedback and recommendations.

I am grateful to the typists and readers who gave of their time, energy and patience: Ms. Faye Martin and Ms. Bonnie Enslow, typists. Readers were: Mr. Al McAllester, Ms. JoAnn Elberty, Dr. T. F. Renick, Professor Emeritus; Dr. William T. Elberty Jr., Geography; Dr. Albert Glover, English; Dr. Al Romer, Emeritus Professor of Physics; Ms. Jan Lambertz and Mr. Rance Davis, Counseling Center; Ms. Anne Townsend, Director of Student Activities, all of St. Lawrence University; Mr. Jeff Lazovik, SUNY Potsdam; Dr. Harold Munson, University of Rochester. I owe special thanks to a former academic and now 'reformed' artist, writer, and motorcyclist, my cousin Herb 'Gunny' Gunnison. Hardly a page went unmarked or untended. I appreciate the meticulous and critical comments which jarred me into a continued reexamination of my ideas, my goals and my writing.

I cannot forget my 'Irish' benefactor, Jake Dillon, who provided me with general support, but more than that, encouraged me to continue writing and resubmitting my manuscript.

And finally, thanks must go to Darlene Leonard of the St. Lawrence University Library Archives for handling the transatlantic electronic transactions and the many PDFs that went back and forth between Canton and Ross-on-Wye.

Chapter 1
Rogers and Erickson

A tree that ran till the span of a man's arms
Grows from a tiny tip;
A terrace nine stories high
Rises from hodfuls of earth;
A journey of a thousand miles
Starts from beneath one's feet.
                              Lao-Tzu

What is the most rigorous law of our being? Growth. No smallest atom of our moral, mental or physical structure can stand still a year. It grows — it must grow; nothing can prevent it.
                              Mark Twain

IMPACT ON COUNSELING

To say that Carl R. Rogers has had a significant impact on counseling has become an understatement. Smith (1982) surveyed clinical and counseling psychologists to learn their primary theoretical orientation. While only 9 per cent of the respondents reported allegiance to the person-centered approach, they ranked Rogers at the top of the list of those psychologists who had the greatest impact on the field of counseling and psychotherapy. The apparent discrepancy might be explained away by Rogers' adamant insistence that there should not be a 'school' of person-centered therapy. He opposed the formal institutionalizing of his approach by discouraging the formulation of standards, credentialing, licensing or sponsoring institutes. Erickson, too, decried the rigidity and channeling resulting from 'theoretical schools' and neither sought to be a leader-guru of a movement nor desired to found a 'school' of therapy. The deliberate absence of formal dogma is theoretically consistent with Rogers' and Erickson's nondirective counseling.

Perhaps Rogers' courage, endurance, and stamina represented personal characteristics that took him through the 1930s, 1940s, and the 1950s; years of lonely struggle with the psychiatric establishment. Prior to

Rogers, psychology conformed to the disease model of medicine and psychiatry, and Rogers, virtually alone, struggled and battled with these bastions of the status quo. Because of Rogers, medicine and psychiatry did not gain a monopoly on the research and knowledge of the human condition nor a stranglehold on counseling and psychotherapy.

Rogers, in those early days, opened up the counseling-therapy process to public scrutiny and to the scientific method. In 1938, he was the first to 'wire-record' a therapeutic hour and also became one of the first to film a counseling session (Evans, 1975). Rogers devoted years to developing and carrying out research methods designed to study the efficacy of his unique approach to counseling and therapy. He told me of the honor and appreciation he felt when the American Psychological Association elected him as one of its first three recipients of the Scientific Achievement Award.

Counseling and therapy had hitherto been a private and secret process, open only to the elect few. Rogers attempted to demystify the practice of counseling, and through his observation and research it became possible to infer that constructive counseling and personality growth and change might not have to depend solely on formal professional training or on special knowledge or techniques. In fact, most humans who could create a therapeutic climate probably could become excellent helpers. These ideas seemed contentious and emotional. How could individuals who had studied long hours, memorized incredible amounts of material, worked diligently at constructing research questions and designs and written countless tests and papers suddenly accept that all of this might not make that much difference in terms of helping people?

There is existing evidence that effectiveness in counseling appears to be unrelated to professional training (Dawes, 1994; Peterson, 1995). College professors in many disciplines were compared with professionally trained counselors. Cases were randomly assigned to the 'untrained' professors and the 'trained' counselors. With all their expertise and training, the counselors did no better in outcome measurements than did the professors (Strupp and Hadley, 1979). Similar research studies showed that the professionals and the 'paraprofessionals' did not differ in their counseling effectiveness, that the effects of training showed little difference (Berman and Norton, 1985; Lambert, Shapiro and Bergin, 1986). Even the experiences of the therapist seemed unrelated to effectiveness (Stein and Lambert, 1984; Truax and Carkhuff, 1967). Sadly, psychotherapy is not alone. For example, teachers were also shown to demonstrate a wide discrepancy between their training and their effectiveness — no matter how measured (Aspy, 1969; Combs, 1965; Pierce, 1966).

The striking conclusion of all of this is that the *interpersonal relationship*, the therapeutic climate, stands as the fundamental variable that must be present if learning, growing, and changing are to occur and both Rogers and Erickson spent their professional lives stressing this critical importance.

Many years ago, as a hospital corpsman in the military service, I studied traditional hypnosis with a psychiatrist. The process involved talking in a low monotonous voice and continually repeating suggestions (which seemed more like condescending commands), all the while swinging an object (preferably shiny) in front of the subject's eyes. I grew increasingly disenchanted and uncomfortable. I came to view this form of hypnosis, in some respects, as demeaning and disrespectful to the client. The hypnotist became the authority, rarely taking into consideration the perceptual field and uniqueness of the client. It seemed as if the hypnotist operated from his or her map of the world and expected the client to obey.

Some years later I discovered hypnosis through the works of Milton H. Erickson. Although the subject matter still concerned the use of hypnosis, clients were treated from value and belief systems entirely different from those to which I had previously been exposed. Erickson's work came as a breath of fresh air and the similarities between his utilization approach and Rogers' person-centered approach excited me. These observations led me to write a paper about the parallels between these two psychotherapists (Gunnison, 1985a).

Dr. Rogers wrote a response to my paper (see Appendix C) on the parallels between Erickson's and his own work: 'I am profoundly impressed by the similarities that Gunnison found between my work and that of Milton Erickson' (Rogers, 1985, p. 565), yet Rogers claimed only a slight personal acquaintance with Dr. Erickson when both were undergraduates at the University of Wisconsin. Rogers had not read any appreciable portion of Erickson's writings and to his knowledge Erickson had not had personal contact or familiarity with Rogers' writings. He explained, 'I mention these things to indicate that whatever similarities exist developed quite independently — certainly not out of close contact or through knowledge of each other's writings. The similarities are therefore real and not simply derivative' (Rogers, 1985, p. 565).

While reading Erickson's writings and attending courses, lectures, and seminars given by his former students and colleagues, I became intrigued by common threads of assumptions, attitudes, and beliefs regarding the human condition as well as certain processes in counseling and therapy. It was as if I were reading Rogers. So much of what Erickson addressed could also have been stated by Rogers (Gunnison, 1987; Leva, 1987).

I became impressed by Erickson's daring individuality. It seemed to me that Erickson's work existed as an exquisite example of experiential and personal learning. His skills, breadth of knowledge, sensitive astuteness, and creativity resulted in his being called Mr. Hypnosis (Weitzenhoffer, 1976). He became the leader and first president of the American Society for Clinical Hypnosis and the founder and editor of its journal.

It seemed that he could put conventional theories aside and begin creating a model of human internal processing through open and wide-ranging observation both of self and others. He took a very radical position. He and Rogers moved in parallel directions. Both might appear as rebels in their profession because of their unique beliefs and methods of approaching the therapeutic process. Each shared a similar curiosity which Rogers described as the immediate experience of the observer. For Rogers (1980), the starting point of science occurs at the moment of concentrated and focused observation. Erickson probably could not have agreed more wholeheartedly.

Zeig (1980) writes that, 'It is not hyperbole to state that history will demonstrate that what Freud contributed to the *theory* of psychotherapy, Erickson will be known as contributing to the *practice* of psychotherapy' (p. xix). The Lanktons (Lankton and Lankton, 1983) use another analogy: '. . . Erickson's influence is thought by many to equal Freud's. Whereas Freud can be thought of as the Einstein of theory, Erickson will likely be acknowledged as the Einstein of intervention' (p. 6). In the mid-1980s Zeig (1985b) reports that 'Ericksonian methods may be the fastest growing field of psychotherapy in the western world' (p. 31).

Erickson described the utilization approach as '. . . *patient-centered* and highly dependent on the momentary needs of the individual' (italics added, Erickson in Erickson and Rossi, 1979, p. 14). The utilization approach focused on the person, utilizing and activating unconscious resources and learning that already existed within rather than being imposed from without.

Like Rogers, Erickson focused primarily on the person, and his utilization approach directly and indirectly paralleled the person-centered approach of Rogers. In fact, Erickson and Rossi (1979) commented on this parallel: '. . . our approaches might appear similar to the *nondirective client-centered approach* of Rogers' (italics added, p. 51). Erickson continually emphasized the past learnings, resources, world views, and perceptions of clients.

Erickson's use of hypnosis became quite radical in its own right. He urged us to consider people at both levels, the conscious and the unconscious. He went to both levels for the source of his interventions. This also becomes a cornerstone of Hypnocounseling. It was a fascinating departure, because instead of becoming the authority (advising and attempting to change clients from without) Hypnocounseling now focused on the client as the core and, therefore, the foundation of what can take place in subsequent counseling sessions.

As practitioners this requires interacting with our clients by encouraging them to become their own authorities, their own experts. Implicit in this may be found a revolutionary shift in direction of our values regarding our clients' trust, understanding, respect, confidence and belief in them and who is in power and control.

ORIGIN AND DEVELOPMENT OF VALUES

'The child is father of the man' wrote the poet laureate William Wordsworth, and the childhood experiences of Erickson and Rogers are inextricably intertwined with the shaping and the creation of the histories of their values. Each grew up on a farm. Each became deeply influenced by the natural growth processes they witnessed daily, 'the experiences that permeated their values, the optimistic and positive joy in life and in the simple ever changing world around them. Both emphasized and sensed the uniqueness of each living thing and prized above all those differences' (Gunnison, 1985a, p. 563).

It is well known that Erickson was struck by polio in adolescence, but few may be aware that as a young child Rogers was seriously ill as well. He tells how, 'As a boy I was rather sickly and my parents have told me that it was predicted I would die young' (, 1980, p. 89). Viktor Frankl (1965) argues that suffering can stretch, enrich and motivate the human and, perhaps, the early years of pain and suffering somehow deepened Erickson's and Rogers' values of sensitivity and appreciation of growth and of change.

Erickson also learned that he was not expected to live very long. At the age of 17 when Erickson had his first bout with polio, he overheard the doctors telling his parents that their son would probably be dead in the morning. Erickson believes he lived because he felt such incredible anger toward doctors insensitive enough to tell a mother her son would be dead the next morning. In his partial delirium he had his mother move the mirror-dresser across the room so the angle would reflect the sunset through the west window of the other room. He said, 'I was damned if I would die without seeing one more sunset. If I had any skill in drawing, I could still sketch that sunset' (Erickson and Rossi, 1980, Vol. 1, p. 111).

I admire such courage, that when all seemed doomed he still had the choice as to how to react. My guess is that some readers will recall a time in their own lives when they had similar experiences.

I recall Viktor Frankl discussing his bare existence in the death halls of Hitler's Germany. He realized one night that when all choice seemed taken away he still had the *choice* as to how to react to that.

Erickson saw the vast sunset covering the sky and blocking out everything else, including a fence and a large boulder. After his autohypnotic experience of the intense sunset, he lost consciousness for three days. When he recovered, he made his career choice. It was following that intense close-to-death experience that Erickson realized, 'I no longer had the strength to be a farmer, but maybe I could make it as a doctor' (Erickson and Rossi, 1980, Vol. 1, p. 112).

These life experiences may have led to the development of those values which other authors have found noteworthy.

> Milton Erickson had a clearly defined value system. Evident in his work are: the strength of his convictions about the integrity of each human being; the importance of the family; the necessity of strong and close relationships with others; and the positive internal potentials of each person. (Yapko, 1985, p. 280)

> Values have been described as an enduring filter through which subjective experience is created, interpreted and reacted to. (Yapko,

1985, p. 273)

The values of the man Erickson *[Rogers]* underlie the psychiatrist Erickson *[psychologist Rogers]*. [Italics added] (Yapko, 1985, p. 268)

PERSON-CENTEREDNESS

Due to change and growth certain reptiles regularly shed their skins. I have been impressed with how Rogers remained flexible in the shedding of the various labels of his work, from client-centered therapy, to nondirective counseling, to student-centered teaching and group-centered leadership. Yet, the impact of Rogers' work, and the growing application and extension of client-centered therapy to many other arenas and situations in the 1970s, caused Rogers to shed the term 'client-centered'. He chose the seemingly more inclusive and appropriate label, 'person-centered' (Rogers, 1980, pp. 114–15).

I strongly agree with Brodley's (1986) attempt to distinguish between client-centered and person-centered counseling when she writes:
> I think it would clarify this situation to classify a therapy practice as a *person-centered therapy* whenever a therapist is trying to work from the basic hypotheses; the inherent growth principle and the major attitudinal conditions for constructive change. [Italics added] (p. 2)

In another article, Brodley (1988) further expands on the distinction:
> The theory of therapy can be filled in (in attempts to build client-centered therapy) *but not added to*. No principles which are contradictory to or not contained implicitly within the conditions can be added and still call the therapy 'client-centered.' But there can be *contradictory* and *additional theoretical elements* and the resulting therapy be considered a person-centered therapy. [italics added] (p. 2)

Brodley (1988) describes Hypnocounseling as a person-centered not client-centered therapy:
> There are many, not one, person-centered therapies ... Examples of person-centered therapies that are now in existence are: the client-centered experiential therapy of Laura Rice; the experiential therapy of Gendlin; the pre-therapy of Garry Prouty; person-centered Gestalt therapy; person-centered psychodrama; N. Rogers' expressive therapy; *Hypnocounseling*; the person-centered therapy of Maria Bowen; etc. [Italics added] (pp. 2, 3)

Hypnocounseling is based on (1) the facilitative and therapeutic climate and the growth principle of Rogers (1985) and (2) the hypno-suggestive language and utilization approach of Erickson (Gunnison, 1990b). Nevertheless, I agree with Brodley that Hypnocounseling is fundamentally a person-centered approach since major emphasis is placed on Rogers' facilitative, therapeutic climate and on his principle of inherent growth. In addition, while I concur with Brodley when she asserts that Hypnocounseling is a person-centered not client-centered therapy, I would go further and suggest that the 'person-centeredness' of Hypnocounseling can be more accurately described as eclectic.

I am reminded once again that, although he developed a rigorous theory, Rogers warned repeatedly of the dangers of over-theorizing, that theories can develop into absolute creeds and become highly rigid. He emphasized the importance of setting theory aside and letting the person emerge. In a class discussion at St. Lawrence University in 1978, he urged us to be there fully and authentically for our clients and that 'the person becomes your theory.' He went on to tell us that what he had 'ultimately learned about people was from people.'

Similarly, Erickson advised against limiting our approaches because of fealty to a theory, a method, a school, or a mentor. Instead, he suggested that we learn and observe as widely as possible, practicing only those techniques and skills that allow us to express ourselves authentically. In a lecture Erickson reminded the audience, 'Remember that whatever way you choose to work must be your own way, because you cannot really imitate someone else. In dealing with the crucial situations of therapy, you must express yourself adequately, not as an imitation' (Haley, 1967, p. 535).

Secter (1982) once queried Erickson as to where and how he obtained his psychiatric knowledge. 'From patients,' he responded. Erickson felt that theory was restrictive, stifling and could trap both patient and therapist (Zeig, 1980). Stern (1985) paraphrased the contents of a personal communication with Erickson:

> ... each patient is unique and no single theory will fit everyone. That is why, he said, he developed a new theory for each person... Erickson knew that the procrustean myth not only referred to someone with a rigid view, but that the result of that rigidity was Procrustes' own demise. Erickson was a modern-day Theseus who took great pleasure in slaying theories in their own procrustean beds. (p. 79)

Rogers (1977) echoes Erickson's concern for authenticity:
> There is one *best* school of therapy. It is the school of therapy you develop for yourself based on a continuing critical examination of the effects of your way of being in the relationship. (p. 185)

Bozarth and Brodley (1986) describe the major misunderstanding of Rogers' person-centered approach as being the confusion between 'the way of doing' rather than 'the way of being' (p. 268).

Erickson wrote, 'In therapeutic approaches one must always take into consideration the actual personality of the individual ... Therefore, the more fluidity in the hypnotherapist, the more easily you can actually approach the patient' (Rossi, 1980, Vol. 4, p. 78). Erickson emphasized the ideas of flexibility, indirection, permissiveness and unique differences (Zeig, 1982, 1985). How apt all of these characteristics seem in terms of Rogers' description of the effective counselor-therapist.

Rogers (1961) discussed the process of effective counseling as involving 'a change in the manner of the client's experiencing . . . *a loosening* of the *cognitive maps* of experience' (italics added, p. 64). Note Erickson's parallel remarks: 'Patients have problems because their conscious programming has too severely limited their capacities. The solution is to help them break through the limitations of their conscious attitudes to free their unconscious potential for problem solving' (Erickson, Rossi and Rossi, 1976, p. 18).

The utilization approach of Erickson has been described as '. . . *patient-centered* and highly dependent on the momentary needs of the individual' (italics added, Erickson and Rossi, 1979, p. 14). Like Erickson, Rogers had a realistic, yet positive and optimistic view of the potentials of the human being. In one of his most familiar and oft-quoted statements, Rogers (1980) described the two major tenets of a person-centered approach:

> . . . Individuals have within themselves *vast resources* for self-understanding and for *altering their self-concepts, basic attitudes and self-directed behavior;* these resources can be tapped if a *definable climate of facilitative psychological attitudes* can be provided. [italics added] (p. 115)

I am convinced that Erickson's reaction to the Rogers' quote (and the included italics) would have been strongly supportive. Not only did Rogers and Erickson believe in the inherent growth principle and the high-trust interpersonal climate, but also that individuals invariably have choice.

Rogers' idea of 'a definable climate of facilitative psychological attitudes' became so crucial to the person-centered, utilization approaches and to Hypnocounseling that an acronym (PEGS) was developed. In classes at St. Lawrence we began to talk about P standing for Positive regard, E for Empathy, G for Genuineness (congruence) and S for Specificity of expression (concreteness). Soon PEGS became a special formula and one to which we would return continually.

This '*definable climate of facilitative psychological attitudes*' (PEGS) is so crucial that it will be further developed in Chapter 5, through the summary of research findings done many years ago by Robert R. Carkhuff and his students and associates at the University of Massachusetts.

A primary assumption in Hypnocounseling as well as in the person-centered and utilization approaches shows itself in the belief and trust in freedom, that clients can choose and can choose responsibly. The concepts of choice and freedom serve as a concrete foundation in the structure of Hypnocounseling

By freedom I mean the act of identifying alternatives, choosing among them and then acting responsibly on that choice. By 'responsibly' I mean being aware and then accepting the consequences of one's actions, actions beneficial not only to self, but also to others (or at least not harmful to others). Parenthetically, responsible choice also can mean accepting consequences of acts neither good nor beneficial. This puts a heavy weight on us. No longer can we get into the 'blame game,' nor play the 'victim,' shifting and excusing our actions. Too often, counselors hear, 'Well, I really can't help it because_____.' In effect these clients seem to be telling us that they are excused, not responsible, and are saying, 'I am a victim and I can't help it.'

Without the assumption of responsible choice on the part of the counselor, there lies little hope for client commitment, change, and growth. More than that, clients can indirectly learn to *depend* on the counselor to make their choices, to advise and guide them. Unbeknown to us, one of our great traps happens when we allow clients to depend upon us. When this occurs, we choke off growth, we banish autonomy, and above all, we have let the person down. Moreover, some clients still believe they come 'for counseling' to be told what to do, what 'choices' to make and how to resolve their issues.

I recall one young man almost demanding I tell him what to do. I simply told him that the issue was too personal and private and that I couldn't possibly tell him what he should do, but that I truly believed he had the wherewithal to choose for himself and that I would be there with him. I remember telling him a story about a little boy who went to the wise man on top of the mountain for advice. The wise man said, 'I cannot die for you, therefore I cannot live for you. You must live and choose for yourself.' (This 'story' came to me 'out of the blue' and once again reinforced my belief in the counselor's trance which we will cover later.) I felt I had tried, but to no avail. I referred the young man to a counselor who I knew would be more comfortable in giving advice. At the same time, this counselor was noted for his sincere concern and desire to help.

I have learned that when clients' values and belief systems widely differ from my own, referral is in order. It seems to me that it becomes critical for counselors to become increasingly sensitive and aware of their changing limitation, and to be aware of referral as a most powerful and helpful counseling tool they can have at their disposal.

I believe this is a critical point in counseling. As we consider the assumption of responsible choice the question becomes: 'Do I believe clients can learn to make choices that are responsible, i.e., the consequences are beneficial to self and others?' If, as a counselor, I advise and choose for them I take away a great deal of their potential personal power?

At first, Rogers' nondirective stance and Erickson's directive approach may appear as a blatant contradiction. However, upon further consideration this contradiction lessens and becomes a difference more of degree than of kind. For example, as I listen to clients comment on their self-beliefs, I often hear a link with their behavior.

Cl (Client): Ah, yeah, I sometimes don't like myself... (pause).
C (Counselor): Sort of — well, right now not much of a friend to yourself, is that it, Carol?
Cl: Yeah, and I keep putting myself down. Keep thinking I'm kind of a failure. [THIS INTERNAL PROCESSING IS BEHAVIOR, TOO.]
C: And all those put downs of yourself sure don't help you feel any better, or do they?
Cl: No, and so I don't bother going out much or doing my work. I pretty much stay in my room. [NOW THE BEHAVIOR IS PROJECTED OUTWARD INTO DOING NO WORK AND STAYING IN THE ROOM.]

In this interaction the belief about self triggers the behavior of what is internally spoken and then translates to external behavior in this client's world. In addition, the vicious cycle continues. Does the counselor break it or does the client? Does the counselor 'direct' the client by pointing this out?

Although I generally prefer to have clients learn to discover their own process of problem solving, I am not averse to describing what I believe is going on. Notice my response to Carol:

And so not going out, staying in your room and not doing your work are a series of actions that sure prevent you from feeling good about yourself, is that it?

This interchange contains an indirect suggestion and the counselor *directs*, when he or she says:

It must really hurt, not liking yourself' or '... well right now not much of a friend to yourself?' or '... these put downs of yourself sure don't help you feel any better.'

Here, the counselor subtly connects with the client in a less 'directive' manner and, hopefully, deeper feelings and clarification result. Thus, the objective neutrality wrongly projected onto the term 'nondirective' results in not only a misunderstanding but also an unhelpful illogic. We cannot help but direct; the question becomes how and for what purposes?

In fact if you were to go back to my counselor responses, you would notice that in each case it could be said that I 'directed' the client to her perceptions: 'not much of a friend,' 'those put downs of yourself.' In being as empathic as I can, my empathic statement *redirects* the client's focus.

In 1977 Rogers spoke of being *facilitative* rather than *nondirective*, and I feel more comfortable with this term. The use of *facilitate* results in a more accurate description of the counseling process which might be described as facilitating clients by helping them *direct* themselves to deeper levels of authenticity and congruent self-awareness and ultimately doing this by themselves.

Unfortunately, the term 'nondirective' became equated with the client-centered approach and that label, with all of its varied meanings, evolved into a millstone for Rogers that became increasingly difficult to shake. In fact, Rogers rarely used the term in his later years. 'Nondirective' techniques meant 'reflecting the client's feelings' or even more of a distorted caricature, repeating 'the last words the client has said' (Rogers, 1980, p. 139). I often carry this further. How can I stand in front of a class or sit with a client and act in a nondirective way? Here 'nondirective' has the meaning of neither influencing nor affecting another. My very presence has an influence. Imagine the effect should I turn my back to the class? I cannot help but not communicate. For me, 'nondirective' came to mean my own ability to be less directive or less intrusive, to allow as much freedom, as much room for individuals to go about making their own choices and decisions. Nondirective refers to an attitude (value) on the part of the counselor. It represents strongly held beliefs that clients must direct themselves; that constructs such as self-direction, self-regulation must come from the client; and that the counselor's task must be to facilitate these and *not assume* what may appear to be helpful or 'best' for clients.

Perhaps the greatest misunderstanding arose when counselors began to follow too rigidly and slavishly the meaning of the nondirective stance. This often resulted in technique-by-the-numbers-oriented counseling rather than person-centered counseling. Once again, counselors focused on what they should say, focused on the technique rather than focusing on the person. Interestingly, there have been times when my sense of helping and empathy have somehow signaled within me 'permission,' perhaps, to give some information, support, even an answer. I must do it with respect and tentativeness, trying to give the power and choice back to clients. I wish this issue were clearer. It isn't; and I have to trust my own sense of our relationship as well as my own belief that my clients can see through me (transparent) and learn that I trust them to direct themselves and I will share this with them.

Being directive sometimes implies manipulation and, perhaps it is. It took some time for Rogers (1977) to realize how 'directive' his presence was in the therapeutic relationship and what a powerful impact it had. Since there was no longer a belief in neutrality, per se, Rogers truly wanted to *empower* his clients. I shall never forget his telling one of our classes that, 'If you want power, give it away.' Richard Farson (1975) went so far as to suggest that Rogers had not sensed, nor appreciated, how political his approach had become, how much latent power was in his respectful and caring interactions.

Direction and manipulation can be perceived as the heart of communication.

> Manipulation has a negative connotation. However, as communication analysts such as Watzlawick point out, it is impossible not to manipulate [direct]. Interpersonal exchange is predicated on manipulation. Manipulation is unavoidable; the issue is how to manipulate constructively and therapeutically. (Zeig, 1985b, p. xv)

Likewise, Erickson directed (manipulated), he avoided lecturing or interpreting and the guiding he did invariably moved the patient inward and forward.

We might reflect at this point on the very delicate implications of nondirective counseling. Why is the term 'nondirective' less accurate than 'facilitative' or 'nonimposing'? When we consider the possible differences between 'directive' and 'facilitative' we challenge the assumptions underlying both process words. The concept of 'manipulation' may be viewed differently as a result.

Whatever the counselor does affects the client. Take a few moments to ponder the impact of counselor responses to different client statements. The counselor's response will serve to direct the client in varying directions.

    Cl: Last night my dog died.
    C: How did it die?

The client now moves back to process internally that unexpected question, and the interaction changes direction. Notice the different responses the counselor might make and how, in each, the client would change direction:

    Cl: Last night my dog died.
    C: Yeah, I lost a dog, too, and I found it important to get another quickly. You know the old saying when you're thrown from a horse, get right back on?
        or
    C: That's too bad, but everything living must die.
        or
    C: What did it die of?
        or
    C: How old was it?
        or
    C: Did you take it to your vet?
        or
    C: Sad! It must hurt to lose a pet, almost as if a member of the family had died.
        or
    C: Oh, that's too bad; however, it's not a catastrophe, and you'll have to learn to move on.

In each response the counselor suggests a direction the client might pursue. You might wish to reflect on similar interchanges. How would you react to each of the counselor's responses? Which do you find most helpful? To approach counseling as 'nondirective' not only detracts but also, it seems to me, becomes a real contradiction and an impossibility in the counseling process. I like to talk of 'nonimposing' counseling. It seems much more descriptive of Rogers' process than does nondirective.

As with the person-centered approach of Rogers, Erickson's utilization approach *centered* on the patient, utilizing and activating unconscious resources and learnings already within rather than imposing them from without (Erickson, Rossi and Rossi, 1976; Zeig, 1985a). Erickson said, 'Who is the important person in a therapeutic situation? Is it the therapist? . . . I don't think the therapist is *the* important person; I think the patient is *the* important person in this situation. I think, too, that the patient should be given the opportunity to dominate in any way . . .' (Rossi, 1980, Vol. 4, p. 78). 'Utilization basically suggests that techniques are best derived from the patient than from the therapist . . . His orientation was to strengthen what is right with the patient rather than analyzing deficits' (Zeig, 1985b, pp. 37–8).

In a dialogue with Erickson, Rossi (Erickson, Rossi and Rossi, 1976) observed that:
> 'Patients keep pulling at the therapist for the cure, the magic, the change, rather than looking at themselves as the change agent. You are continually putting the responsibility for change back on the patient.' Erickson replied: 'On to them always' (p. 27). And it is hard to imagine Rogers disagreeing with any of this.

I cannot imagine a more 'person-centered' observation than this one by Erickson (1980a):
> The therapist's force should not be a proselytizing of the patient with his own beliefs and understandings. No patient can really understand the understandings of his therapist nor does he need them. What is needed is the development of a therapeutic situation permitting the patient to use his own thinking, his own understandings, his own emotions in the way that best fits him in his scheme of life. (Vol. 4, p. 223)

THE SELF AS A TOOL

When Rogers proposed the growth principle, he had spent many years studying the therapeutic climate that elicited this growth process. He approached '. . . the phenomena with as few preconceptions as possible, to take a naturalist's observational, descriptive approach . . . I used myself as a tool' (Rogers, 1961, p. 128) and this is precisely what Erickson did.

In his study of hypnosis Erickson also used himself 'as a tool,' spending countless hours as a young man observing and reflecting on experiences in self-hypnosis and learning to relieve his own pain by focusing on relaxation, heaviness, fatigue, dissociation, and so forth (Rossi, 1980); he learned through his own exceptional capacities for observation and introspection.

It was fascinating to me to learn of the history of those 'countless hours' that Erickson spent experimenting with hypnosis. Because of his handicaps such as dyslexia, arrhythmia, color blindness, tone deafness — as well as two separate battles with polio, he explored and lived in a very different world and his inner journeys were filled with excitement as he learned from a first-hand view what human uniqueness and difference mean.

As a boy, Milton felt hurt when his grandfather made it clear that he would not believe nor accept that the young man's potatoes grew equally as well even though they were neither planted during the 'proper phase of the moon' nor with their 'eyes' planted 'up.' The young Erickson was learning of human rigidities and 'blindness' that he was to encounter the rest of his professional life. Two other learning incidents from Erickson's early life describe the blinding-light-of-insight he experienced.

Erickson's dyslexia prevented him from differentiating an 'm' from a '3.' As his teacher tried to help by tracing the figures with his hand, Erickson described a genuine perceptual alteration; a flash of light suddenly disclosed the difference between the 'm' and the '3.' 'The m was standing on its legs and the 3 was on its side with the legs sticking out' (Erickson and Rossi, 1980, Vol. 1, p. 109). This phenomenon is not unlike the Gestalts' insight.

A similar flash of insight occurred in early high school when Erickson discovered, in an instant, how to pronounce the word 'government'. His teacher Miss Walsh can be credited for introducing the idea of breaking things down into their smallest learning parts. By using the name of a fellow student, La Verne, Miss Walsh taught him how to pronounce 'government.' She had him pronounce gov-La Vernement, then asked him to omit the La of La Verne. Again he experienced the blinding flash of learning. Here, we have an example of 'chunking' things down as currently borrowed and developed by brief therapy and Neuro-Linguistic Programming (NLP) (Bandler and Grinder, 1979, 1982; Grinder and Bandler, 1981).

He would later argue that the presence of intense light or visual hallucination that blots out all other perceptions of reality provides evidence for a spontaneous autohypnotic state. Erickson believed that frequently there occurs a distinct connection between 'altered states' and significant learning, a statement of profound implication not only for counseling, but also for teaching and indeed any truly creative effort.

There remains little question that Erickson's childhood experiences with autohypnotic phenomena sparked a lifelong interest in hypnosis. Yet one other experience as an undergraduate at the University of Wisconsin seems worthy of mention. Ronald Havens (1985) mentioned that, at the end of Erickson's sophomore year, Erickson attended a demonstration of hypnosis by the famous American psychologist Clark L. Hull, and that this may have been the beginning point of Erickson's illustrious professional career. He was so excited by this chance demonstration that he spent the following summer hypnotizing everyone who cooperated.

During the following fall, Erickson presented his findings and conclusions in a seminar on hypnosis taught by Clark Hull. Erickson's experiences and his conclusions were in direct conflict with Hull's. Hull's conclusions, which have since formed the modern scientific view of hypnosis, were based on an objective, experimental and standardized approach. Erickson's experiences taught him of the uniqueness of each individual, of the richness of the subjective world and led him to conclude that people had to be respected and treated as human beings not as objects in a scientific lab.

This, to me, shows the basic courage and integrity of Erickson. Like Rogers, he dared question the authorities and the professional establishments, stuck by his guns and created another perspective that viewed the person as a unique individual to be treated with respect. This disagreement with Hull spurred Erickson's interest in research and writing. 'Both he and Rogers were able to look at different ways of "seeing" themselves, others and the relativity of different world views' (Gunnison, 1985a, p. 562).

When we accept the challenge to 'see' ourselves, others and the relativity of different world views this often adds to our lives, affects our work, relationships and dreams.

THE IMPORTANCE OF CARING AND RESPECT FOR THE CLIENT (POSITIVE REGARD)

Unconditional positive regard (love) came to represent a core condition in the therapeutic relationship (PEGS). When clients felt appreciated and prized as people, when they felt warmth and trust, and, above all, when they did not feel judged or continually evaluated by their counselors, change and growing became real possibilities. 'It means that he prizes the client, in a nonpossessive way' (Rogers, 1961, p. 62).

Haley (1967) described a similar deep caring in Erickson's work. Erickson spoke of working with a client whom he felt had little chance for successful change. Nevertheless, despite the poor prognosis, Erickson kept the doubts 'to himself and he let [the client] know by manner, tone of voice, by everything said that he [Erickson] was genuinely interested in him, was genuinely desirous of helping' (Haley, 1967, p. 516). The technical and methodological brilliance of Erickson sometimes can overshadow the therapeutic relationship he emphasized and created with his patients. 'It is all too easy to focus on things like Erickson's breathing rate or his use of peripheral vision at the expense of appreciating the intensity of the relationship he had with his patients, which microscopic analysis cannot define any more than one can analyze and define "love"' (Yapko, 1985, p. 268).

Erickson's writing summarizes the importance of the uniqueness of the person and the therapeutic relationship:

> . . . the technique for the induction of hypnotic trances is primarily a function of the interpersonal relationships existing between subject and hypnotist. Hence, hypnotic techniques and procedures should vary according to the subject, circumstances, and the purposes to be served'. (Rossi, 1980, Vol. 4, p. 28)

Erickson's basic trust in people came through in his belief and respect in the competence of people to work out things in their own lives. He believed that his patients had the natural desire '... to acquire mastery, to obtain understanding, to have fun, to have certainty, and to have immediate results' (Lustig, 1982, p. 459).

THE IMPORTANCE OF EMPATHY

Empathy, along with genuineness, unconditional positive regard (PEGS), and a trust in the potential of the person all together came to represent that 'definable' climate so critical in Rogers' work (Rogers, 1957). Empathy becomes a crucial condition. 'It means entering the private perceptual world of the other and becoming thoroughly at home in it . . . you lay aside your own views and values in order to enter another's world without prejudice' (Rogers, 1980, pp. 142–3).

Laying aside my own views is like imagining I have a screen door that I can move aside so that you come through — not blocked or influenced by the screen door (my views). Many of us may recall people who empathize this way. Perhaps you do this with your friends, family, your clients?

Erickson also stressed empathy particularly in the preparation phase of his approach; the most important factor appears as '... sound rapport — that is a positive feeling of understanding and mutual regard between therapist and patient' (Erickson and Rossi, 1979, p. 1). Erickson believed that 'an attitude of empathy and respect on the part of the therapist is *crucial* to ensure successful change' (italics added, Erickson and Zeig, 1980, p. 336). Erickson amplified the concept of rapport that developed out of a *genuine* acceptance of the other (italics added, Erickson and Rossi, 1979). A powerful kind of empathy developed as Erickson would use the patient's own vocabulary and frames of reference (pacing and matching) to form the interpersonal connection (Grinder and Bandler, 1981; Grinder, DeLozier and Bandler, 1977). 'Meet the client at his or her model of the world' (Lankton and Lankton, 1983, p. 12).

GENUINENESS, COMMUNICATION, AND SELF-HYPNOSIS

Genuineness or congruence must stand as another basic condition within the person-centered climate. For if realness does not exist in the relationship, then toxicity and distrust may develop. Lankton and Lankton (1983) expanded on counselor-therapist genuineness by adding, 'The Ericksonian hypnotherapist must have a personal manner that gives credibility and potency to his or her interventions. It can be called congruity, sincerity, or confidence' (p. 133). Rogers (1986a) senses a kind of genuineness in Erickson when he observes,

   It seems strikingly clear that for Erickson, too, therapy was a highly personal affair, a deeply involving experience different for each person. He thought about his patients, he reacted to them in very personal ways — challenging, abrupt, patient, soft, hard — always being himself in the interest of the client. He sometimes took individuals into his home, or used pets or told of his own life — doing whatever would keep him in close personal touch. (p. 132)

For the counselor-therapist, genuineness means being fully there with the client, sharing clear and transparent communication. 'Sometimes a feeling "rises up in me" which seems to have no particular relationship to what is going on. Yet I have learned to accept and trust this feeling by my awareness and to try to communicate it to my client' (Rogers, 1980, p. 14). This experience on Rogers' part may be akin to what Erickson would describe as autohypnosis, an altered state of consciousness. In fact, Rogers actually uses the words 'altered state of consciousness' in his writings.

Interestingly, Rogers (1985) discovered another important characteristic of the growth-promoting relationship (in addition to genuineness, positive regard and empathy) that I will quote at some length:

> But recently my view has broadened into a new area which cannot be studied empirically. When I am at my best as a group facilitator or a therapist, I discover another characteristic. I find that when I am closest to my inner, *intuitive self,* when I am somehow in touch with the unknown in me, when perhaps I am in a slightly *altered state of consciousness* in the relationship, then whatever I do seems to be full of healing . . . There is nothing I can do to force this experience, but when I can relax and be close to the transcendental core of me, then I behave in strange and impulsive ways in the relationship . . . But these strange behaviors turn out to be *right,* in some odd way. At those moments it seems that my inner spirit has reached out and touched the inner spirit of the other. [Italics added] (Rogers, 1985, p. 565)

At this point I believe Rogers (1985) describes, almost mystically, a therapeutic trance, an altered state that he has found profoundly beneficial in the counseling process.

He continues:
> I realize that this account partakes of the mystical. Our experiences, it is clear, involve the transcendent, the indescribable, the spiritual. I am compelled to believe, that I, like many others, have underestimated the importance of this mystical, spiritual dimension.
>
> In this I am not unlike some of the more advanced thinkers in physics and chemistry. As they push their theories further, picturing a 'reality' which has no solidity, which is no more than oscillations of energy, they too begin to talk in terms of the transcendent, the indescribable, the unexpected — the sort of phenomena which we have observed and experienced in the person-centered approach. (p. 565)

While Rogers describes this altered state in terms of 'mystical,' 'transcendent,' 'spiritual,' I would counter that his descriptions also speak to those experiences I label as the therapeutic trance (autohypnosis).

Rogers adds:

> I have come to value highly these *intuitive* responses . . . In these moments I am perhaps in a *slightly altered state of consciousness,* in dwelling in the client's world, completely in tune with that world. My *nonconscious* intellect takes over. I know much more than my conscious mind is aware of. I do not form my responses consciously, they simply arise in me, from *my nonconscious* sensing of the world of the other. [Italics added] (Rogers, 1985, p. 565)

The uses of 'intuitive,' 'full of healing,' 'slightly altered state of consciousness,' and 'nonconscious' mean to me that Rogers speaks of a process that is at the core of Erickson's work. Erickson so accepted and trusted his own unconscious as well as that of his patients that he became totally in tune with their worlds.

Rossi (1980) reports how Erickson,

> . . . is always in complete rapport with the patient. He is never dissociated and out of contact with the patient. Autohypnotic trance usually comes on spontaneously and always enhances his perceptions and relations with the patient. Trance is an intensely focused attention that facilitates his therapeutic work. (Vol. 1, p. 117)

All of this reinforces my conjecture that Rogers and Erickson both utilized the trance state to move more deeply and therapeutically into the encounter. Zeig (1982) felt that Erickson was so in touch with his own inner experiences and so *trusted* the 'wisdom of *his* unconscious' that he became capable of incredible understandings of his patients' worlds. I believe Rogers writes about the same phenomenon in his own experiences.

When I am most effective in counseling, the client appears enlivened, interested and self-motivated. Clients begin to answer their own questions and rediscover hope. In other words, they begin to take responsibility for the consequences of their actions. They choose to take responsibility for themselves in ways that are exciting and, to me, almost poignant, as when a green shoot appears from cold damp earth and my garden shows life. To me, counseling and gardening share similar processes of magic and excitement.

But what am I doing? What am I doing differently that brings on this apparent success? I do believe that at those times I am truly with my clients. Indirectly and sometimes directly they tell of my empathy and respect for them. Yes, I believe that Rogers' 'definable climate of facilitative psychological attitudes' (PEGS) are operating here, yet there is something more, as both Rogers and Erickson imply.

I often wondered about the origins of those sudden flashes of insight and connection. It was as if for a moment the client's pain, confusion, problems, and solutions became starkly clear. I also noted that this experience was rare, came spontaneously and could not be pushed even though I tried intellectually and effectively to bring it about.

Let me digress a little. I struggled with learning about process. The more I struggled the more I pushed process away. Slowly I began to hear my own admonition; 'trust the process' as well as the warning of Barry Stevens (1970), 'Don't push the river; it flows by itself.' I think there develops a kind of mental letting-be sense, a special kind of patience, which I find difficult to draw upon and yet in the counseling or therapeutic trance its presence can be clearly felt. Oddly enough I hadn't a clue until I read of Erickson's experiences.

Erickson's early life, so taken up with autohypnotic experiences, served as a rich foundation for all of his later work. His unusual ability to go into a trance became increasingly a major part of his therapy.

Responding to a question by Rossi:
Do you tend to go into autohypnosis now when you work with patients?
E: At the present time if I have any doubt about my capacity to see the important things I go into trance. (Erickson and Rossi, 1980, p. 116)

Erickson would go into trance by observing in detail each movement, cue and sign, and helped by listening to his own rhythmical voice. I can identify. I relax myself by quietly counting down (a strategy that we shall explore later), and allow myself to let go.

As I observe and listen to my client, my perceptual field narrows into what Erickson called a kind of 'therapeutic tunnel vision.' What I sense is the client; everything else becomes extraneous and at that moment I have learned to utilize this powerful and intense state. It is as if I can almost feel my own blinders, perceptions, melt away, slide away as if a part of me temporarily leaves.

I have come to call this phenomenon the 'therapeutic trance'; this can be viewed as a therapeutic hypnotic state of the counselor wherein we allow ourselves to go into an altered state and where another powerful connection with the client takes place. To repeat what Rogers (1985) has written about his own altered states in counseling, 'At those moments it seems that my inner spirit has reached out and touched the inner spirit of the other' (p. 565), a rich and therapeutic connection.

It is as if you and I were to clear the noise-wax from our ears and wipe or wash away the cloud-film in our eyes. It is as if we had a screen around us and we could choose to take that screen away. In many ways I consider this opening-up-process to be a very vulnerable act on our part. We also banish our own internal babble, or dialogue and become fully present for and with our client. And this cannot be forced. To me, it is a kind of letting go and letting be — a kind of therapeutic trance, that you and I can enter. I want to repeat that, in this state, I am like a tabula rasa. I am no longer thinking of anything except listening and observing my client. I am not analyzing. I am not theorizing. I am not jumping ahead to strategies or solutions. I am not wondering about us or where we're going or how we're doing. I am not worrying about what to say next. This passive and receptive mode cannot be forced; however, it remains for me the essential mental state that begins my counseling.

I repeat a quote that at this point seems so very relevant and appropriate:

> I have come to value these *intuitive* responses ... In these moments I am perhaps in a *slightly altered state of consciousness*, in dwelling in the client's world, completely in tune with that world. My *nonconscious* intellect takes over. (Carl Rogers, 1985)

The first counseling professor to have an impact on my learning was a mentor, colleague and friend — Fritz Renick. He compared the therapeutic encounter to a walk to an abyss, standing before it, wondering if he dared leap into the other person's world. Sometimes he chose not to, for many reasons: his own insecurity at the moment, perhaps his needs for control or simply fear. When he chose to make the leap, to be there fully with the other, it seemed to him as if he were letting go of his own anchors and allowing himself to be swept into the current of the person across from him. I often recall this process description because it so clearly portrays my own experience. Again, I argue this represents the therapeutic trance, the altered state in which I think I do my best work.

I hope this resonates with the reader's experience — the notion of a therapeutic trance, a state of autohypnosis. Do you know what I mean? In all of this, the counselors' psychological health — the importance of being grounded and in the process of growing — is of critical importance.

THE USE OF METAPHORS

One of the strategies of Erickson's utilization approach involves the use of metaphors. These stories and anecdotes serve as the tapestry upon which are woven the themes that utilize the patient's experiences, resources, and mental maps. From these metaphors the unconscious mind can draw its own conclusions and meanings by utilizing its own resources stored there in a lifetime of memories and experiences.

Rogers, on the other hand, shared Erickson's belief in the power of metaphor yet differed in its use. He (Rogers, 1985) generally became encouraged when clients would resort to figurative language or metaphor because they often could express themselves much more coherently and deeply than through an exact and literal language:

> So when a client begins to speak of 'this heavy bag that I carry around on my back' or speaks of the fear of 'walking into darkness — out of light and into the darkness,' I feel sure that progress will be

made and I am eager to respond on the metaphorical level... I do use my own metaphors in some intuitive responses, however, and this seems close to Erickson's approach. (Rogers, 1985, p. 566)

I prize Rogers' (1961) exquisite story from his youth used to illustrate the growth tendency.
> I remember that, in my boyhood, the bin in which we stored our winter's supply of potatoes was in the basement, several feet below a small window. The conditions were unfavorable, but the potatoes would begin to sprout... But these sad, spindly sprouts would grow two or three feet in length as they reached toward the distant light out of the window. The sprouts were, in their bizarre, futile growth, a sort of desperate expression of the directional tendency... But under the most adverse circumstances, they were striving to become. Life would not give up, even if it could not flourish. (p. 118)

Erickson's use of anecdotes, puns, metaphors, stories, and jokes has become legendary (Rosen, 1982). His figurative language suggests open-endedness. It encourages patients to utilize their unconscious mind and search through the vast storehouse of learning, resources, and experiences. Erickson utilized patients' maps, experiences, and perceptual fields by the wording and phraseology of his stories that appeared relevant and appropriate and thus let the unconscious take over. For example, with a florist, Erickson used a metaphor of the tomato seed in process of becoming a fruit-bearing tomato plant (Haley, 1967). The patient, then, heard the general contextual meaning of a tomato seed in 'process of becoming' at the conscious level, yet the words and phrasing had unique associations that went beyond the general context (Erickson, Rossi and Rossi, 1976). 'In this his interspersal technique, Erickson inserted words and phrases that indirectly stimulated deeper focusing on the patient's experiences and interests. Through the scattering of indirect suggestions, the unconscious was put to work' (Gunnison, 1985a, p. 563).

Just the other day, using Hypnocounseling with a 13-year-old young man, I learned of his interest and expertise in auto mechanics. When I talked about 'an auto inspection, checking his timing, changing the oil and filter,' he was quick to respond and connect in fruitful ways. The metaphor access can be extremely powerful.

I like the metaphor of the bucket. We each have a psychological bucket and when it is 'full' it gives us a feeling of well-being, a sense of psychological health. We learn to keep our buckets 'full' if we choose to help another. When our buckets are empty, we begin to be toxic. We cannot give in helpful ways if our buckets are empty. We must learn what we must do, what and how we think, to keep them full.

I remember those cold blustery mornings when I walked to the warm office in the Geography House to write this book, carrying my winter walking stick or crook (a broken hockey stick). My dear old friend Tugs, a Golden Retriever, lumbering on, sprinkling yellow dye on white snow banks and doing lots of nose-down sniffing, led the way. Just a gentle touch with my 'crook' encouraged him to get his nose up and continue to lead the way along the walk and then turn in at a certain path which took us to the door. Tugs knew as did Erickson's horse in the story that follows.

Gordon and Meyers-Anderson (1981) report a favorite metaphor, a story drawn from Erickson's youth. A riderless horse appeared one day in the Erickson farmyard. No one could identify the owner. Undaunted, Erickson volunteered to find its home and mounted the horse. As he approached the main road, he slackened the reins and waited to see in which direction the horse would lead. Erickson intervened only when the horse would wander off the road. After progressing in this fashion for about four miles — sometimes slowly and sometimes quickly — the horse turned into a farmyard. The surprised owner asked Erickson how he knew where the horse belonged. 'I didn't know. The horse knew. All I did was keep him on the road' (p. 6). What an extraordinary process description of counseling and therapy! What an exquisite description of the utilization and person-centered approaches, observe, observe; listen, listen!

Notice Rogers' (1985) comparisons with Erickson in this concluding quote:

> If in our work we both rely on the fundamental directional tendency of the client-patient, if we are intent on permitting the client to choose the directions of his or her life, if we rely on the wisdom of the organism in making such choices and if we see our role as releasing the client from constraining self-perceptions to become a more complete potential self, then perhaps the differences are not so important as they might seem. (p. 566)

The discussion thus far has focused on Erickson's work through the lens of Rogers' person-centered approach. However, the process could easily have been reversed. Gunnison and Renick (1985b) describe the subtle and hidden Ericksonian patterns inevitably present in much of conventional counseling and therapy. More specifically, Lankton and Lankton (1983) describe and discuss the Ericksonian hypnotic patterns observable in Rogers' work in the film *Gloria*. What appear as two very divergent positions, upon further inspection, evolve into interesting connections and similarities.

While differences in approaches exist, Erickson and Rogers had similar beliefs and goals for their clients-patients: the utilizing of directional tendencies, the evoking of 'the wisdom of the unconscious' and 'the wisdom of the organism.' Rosen (1979) described this as '. . . a typical Ericksonian paradox. The master manipulator [facilitator] allows and stimulates the greatest freedom' (p. xiii). Moreover, each did this so genuinely, humanely and uniquely.

ON GROWTH, SELF-ACTUALIZATION, AND THE UNCONSCIOUS (NONCONSCIOUS)

In 1959, Rogers offered his explanation of 'A Theory of the Fully Functioning Person' (Rogers, 1959, pp. 234–5). Even though Erickson does not lay out formal theoretical statements, I believe he clearly states an assumption that parallels Rogers. I find Erickson's views on the healthy personality most clearly described in his discussion of the unconscious.

What emerges as the goal(s) or outcome(s) of our counseling? What do we envisage for our clients? What do we propose to do *to* our clients or, for that matter, *with* our clients? How we answer these vital questions becomes a most significant basis of our personal counseling approach. When examining these issues for myself I have found a little-known book *The Therapeutic Relationship: Foundations for an Eclectic Psychotherapy* by C.H. Patterson to be valuable.

I recall how excited I felt when first reading Albert Szent-Gyoergyi's (1974) article entitled 'Drive In Living Matter to Perfect Itself.' I had just been working on Rogers and Erickson's views on the unconscious and growth. Here, a research biologist, twice awarded the Nobel Prize, poetically describes a 'drive' toward perfectionism. By perfectionism he does not mean a perfect state outside of life itself, but rather the optimum in the organism's potentiality. By 'drive' he does not mean to find an explanation by substituting a label, but rather to connote a process of growth (syntropy) he has postulated in living matter, just as 'real' to him as its opposite, entropy. Entropy, the tendency of organized forms to gradually disintegrate into lower forms of organization, has a respectable place in science; however, Szent-Gyoergyi stated that science has now begun to focus more and more frequently on the process of syntropy — one more map to give us a richer and wider perspective.

When re-examining values regarding self and others, the following questions arise:
1. Do I believe I have a tendency toward growth?
2. Am I aware of taking care of myself physically, emotionally and intellectually day by day?
3. Am I treating myself with respect and with care?
4. Am I filling my bucket?
5. Can I honestly say that I try to do the same for others in my life?

In their words and actions both Rogers and Erickson emphasized the internal motivation and processing within people: Rogers in his growth-formative tendency and Erickson in his view of the unconscious. Both believed in the individual's potential toward growth. Rogers (1961) stated it explicitly:

> There is one central source of energy in the human organism. This source is a trustworthy function of the whole system rather than of some portion of it; it is most simply conceptualized as a tendency

toward fulfillment, toward actualization, involving not only the maintenance but also the enhancement of the organism. (p. 123)

I have heard answers to the goal(s) question in counseling that speak to: total growth, unlearning bad habits, reduction of symptoms, improving social functioning and intrapsychic growth, adjustment to society, insight, self-awareness, raising of self-esteem, personal meaning in life, rational thinking. Each of these goals seems positive and credible, yet the question I would ask is, 'Do these goals come from the client or the counselor?' Even more important would be which approach one finally chooses, which ultimately goes back to our attitudes, values, and beliefs regarding the human condition.

My bias dictates a goal of counseling for me that moves in the direction of growth, self-realization, or in A.H. Maslow's sense, 'self-actualization.' (I prefer the participle form 'self-actualizing' because it implies openness, movement and process, an ongoing process that resides inherently in the organism. 'Self-actualization,' the gerund form, seems to denote an end point, the top of the mountain, completion as it were.)

We can be mindful of Goldstein's (1939) meaning when he created the term 'self-actualization'. 'An organism is governed by a tendency to actualize, as much as possible, its individual capacities, its nature in the world' (p. 196). Furthermore, this goal-concept has been viewed as biologically based and inherent in the species. Combs, Richards and Richards (1976) describe Donald Snygg's sense of this as man's basic need, a '. . . biologically grounded force in each of us by which we are continually seeking to make ourselves ever more adequate to cope with life' (p. 57).

Rogers (1959) found it critical to describe growth or self-realization as:
> . . . the inherent tendency of the organism to develop all its capacities in ways which serve to maintain or enhance the organism . . . It should be noted that this basic *actualizing tendency* is the only motive which is postulated in this theoretical system. [Italics added] (p. 196)

In addition, a point not to be overlooked emerges. I believe that the actualizing tendency occurs in all living organisms. However, growth potential might be limited, modified or changed when severe organic and/or psychological trauma exist. Even under the most dire circumstances, however, the organism still reaches toward its upper limits, its relative potential (reminiscent of the 'spindly potato sprouts' found in Rogers' potato-bin metaphor).

You very well might ask, 'What about the criminal, the killer, etc.?' In aberrant cases the actualizing tendency may take on warped and destructive dimensions since the individual's perceptual field may not have included routinely experienced PEGS and, instead, may have included psychological trauma and deprivation. The actualizing tendency from within propels the individual in directions that mirror deprivation. It may very well be that psychological trauma and deprivation may distort the life experiences and limit perceived choices of the person so that antisocial and self-destructive behaviors occur.

As a counselor, I trust and depend upon this natural tendency which, when intact, propels the person forward in constructive directions. As mentioned earlier, each of us brings to counseling a set of beliefs that results from the enculturation-socialization process that takes place over our lifetimes.

We might also reflect on these so-called 'nature of man-/woman-kind' beliefs:

Do I believe some groups of humans are inferior?
Do I believe that people are basically ignorant, dependent and evil?
Do I believe people need to be told what to do and how to act?
How you respond to these beliefs will determine, to a large extent, how you interact with clients.

Some believe people are basically evil and can't be trusted, or believe there is only one right way and their job is to bring people to that view for their own good. (Note the usage of the verb 'to be' in these examples.)

Beahrs (1982) discusses Erickson's concept of the unconscious not as the fearful, boiling cauldron of untamed energy of Freud, but rather as a source for growth, as a repository of all past learning and experiences. Erickson further elaborates, 'In hypnosis we utilize the unconscious mind. What do I mean by the unconscious mind? I mean the back of the mind, the reservoir of learning. The unconscious mind constitutes a storehouse' (Rossi, 1980, Vol. 3, p. 27). Erickson and Rossi discuss another dimension of the unconscious (Rossi, 1980, Vol. 1):

Rossi: You really believe in a creative unconscious?
Erickson: I believe in a different level of awareness.
Rossi: So we could say the unconscious is a metaphor for another level of awareness, a meta-level?
Erickson: I can walk down the street and not have to pay attention to the stop light or the curb, I can climb Squaw Peak and I don't have to figure out each step.
Rossi: Those things are being handled by other levels of awareness. (pp. 119–20)

Sacerdote (1982) expands on this and writes of Erickson's concept of the unconscious as being closer to Jung's *archetype,* the unconscious having 'attributes of basic wisdom which include the capacity of the body's organs and cells for producing physical and mental healing.' Gilligan (1982) discussed Erickson's notion that 'Unconscious processes can operate in an intelligent, autonomous, and creative fashion ... People have stored in their unconscious all the resources necessary to transform their experience' (p. 89). Thus, the therapeutic task might become one of arranging conditions (climate) and accessing resources that facilitate and elicit this unconscious processing, another central foundation in Hypnocounseling.

We now have a wider and enhanced picture of the unconscious. It emerges as a nonFreudian construct in its definition and becomes more than just a storehouse of memories and experience. As ever-widening new experiences occur, the unconscious is continually expanding and becoming enriched. Memories, in the unconscious, are also undergoing continual change. Memories might be said to be viewed as being constantly reconstructed in the interest of the present. Naturally, this brings into question the assumption of 'accurate memory' that the courts have been wrestling with for years. In sexual abuse cases, hypnotically recalled memories have been used in the courts. Yet recent evidence and memory redefinitions have riled the waters.

Briefly, we know that hypnosis can be used to help retrieve memory, but accurate memory is another thing. I can clearly recall a huge apple tree endowed with magnificent curling limbs that my cousins and I suddenly transformed into ships' crow's nests or saddles for riding horses or dragons. This magical tree became a transformed 'jungle gym.' However, when I recently revisited this apple tree it seemed disappointingly plain and small and not how I remembered it.

What would be accurate memory and how would we know? My memory must always remain a figment of the intervening filters of my life's experiencing in the interim. There is an important difficulty here (and difference of views) concerning the issue of accuracy of memory. In addition, the concept of the unconscious translates and expands to mean creativity and a capacity for inner wisdom and healing. Erickson (Haley, 1967, 1973, 1985) saw the unconscious as the core or center of the person (not unlike Rogers' 'self') and significantly emphasized the positive power of the unconscious.

Rogers (1985) used the term 'nonconscious' in a way which I see as identical to Erickson's. Using a biofeedback metaphor, Rogers (1985) writes of the nonconscious mind at work:

> If you ask me to raise the temperature of the middle finger of my right hand, my conscious mind is completely baffled. It cannot possibly do it. Yet if you show me a needle that indicates the temperature of that finger and ask me if I can make it move upward, I find that I can do it. How do I make all the analyses and discriminations necessary to accomplish this end? It is completely inexplicable if we limit ourselves to the conscious mind. But the *nonconscious organic mind* is quite capable of the task. [Italics added] (p. 566)

I value the use of the term 'nonconscious' by Rogers because it avoids the inevitable semantic 'red flag' that the word 'unconscious' elicits. I guess I have become tired of the tedious task of explaining the difference between the Ericksonian and the Freudian 'unconscious.' The Freudian 'unconscious' has a very different connotation than does Erickson's 'unconscious.' The Freudian unconscious was viewed as a boiling caldron of repressed material — woe be to us should it get out of control.

I believe that Erickson would have found the concept of the 'nonconscious' mind congenial, and, furthermore, Erickson might have identified with the biofeedback example as well. I am hard-pressed to find any significant difference here. It is clear to me that when Rogers thinks about moving a needle upward, he alters his state from a conscious level to 'another level' similar to Erickson and Rossi's earlier example of the creative unconscious — the moving of the needle by 'another level of awareness.' The moving needle example might also be explained by Sacerdote's (1982) description of Erickson's unconscious as having a kind of basic wisdom as well as the capacity of the body to produce mental and physical healing.

Erickson also felt strongly about the growing process inherent in the unconscious as the following quote attests:

> Life isn't something you can answer to today. You should enjoy the process of waiting, the *process of becoming what you are.* There is nothing more delightful than planting flower seeds and not knowing what kind of flowers are going to come up. (Rosen, 1979, p. xii)

RAMBLES AT RANDOM AND IMPLICATIONS

To assume that each of us has a tendency to grow and to evolve toward ever greater levels has fascinating implications.

In the spring I place tomato plants in my garden at the back of the house. These small, green and eager plants, I trust, will grow. However, I must be responsible *to* them (not responsible *for* them) — by providing a growing *climate* for tomatoes. My trust lies in their potential and their natural tendency to grow toward rich, fruit-bearing plants. In a person-centered and utilization approach this metaphor could easily be used in describing the assumptions we have regarding humans.

For example, note the significant shift in meaning when I substitute the prepositions 'for' and 'to.' I am responsible *to* clients, responsible *to* them by providing them with the therapeutic climate (PEGS) that can evoke their instinct-like tendency to grow. I am not responsible *for* them, only they can be responsible *for* themselves. They live their lives. They must choose and act in ways that are beneficial *for* themselves and *to* others.

A belief in the growth principle must take into account trust and faith, which perhaps represent the cornerstones of the person-centered and utilization approaches. As I expand the belief that my client-person can be trusted to live a human life with its trials, joys, decisions, and a myriad of experiences that lead to autonomy and will choose to take responsibility *for* her own life and to become responsible to others in caring and respectful ways, then I become freer to help. As I believe that she can grow in directions that move her closer to the fullest possible realization of her potential, only then can I let go to help her help herself.

Implicit in this faith emerges a belief that the client can be trusted to take care of himself and this belief has a significant impact. Burnout significantly diminishes as my faith and trust in the client increases. Again, I must be responsible *to* him not *for* him. When I leave my office, I must close the door and not mentally take him home with me, worrying or anguishing over his pains or dilemmas (emptying my bucket). When I am with him, I will be there fully; however, I cannot help him if I am stressing myself in his absence. While difficult, I still believe this to be learnable.

I wonder how much counselor burnout occurs from just such situations? Practitioners can feel obligated to take on the responsibility for people, to fix them up, to take care of them? If so, I wonder what message the person receives. She might not feel trusted, might feel incapable of taking care of herself and might begin to feel even more inadequate and incompetent. How would we feel if the shoe were on the other foot?

Taking responsibility for clients can become a dangerous trap. For the beginning counselor it becomes a fear of doing harm. In my student days as a counselor I remember feeling 'terrified' of doing or saying the wrong thing to my clients. It seemed as if I believed I had a much greater impact on clients than really existed. As I began to learn to listen without imposing and to care without conditions, I also learned to appreciate and trust my clients' abilities to take charge of their own lives. Also, how can I hurt another when care, empathy, and genuineness are being conveyed? This may not be a curative, yet it cannot really harm. I have learned over the years that when this high-trust climate occurs, the magic of personal growth begins.

Chapter 2
Theory

Every theory is a self-fulfilling prophecy that orders experience into the framework it provides.
                                   Ruth Hubbard

No theory is good except on condition that one use it to go on beyond.
                                   André Gide

Early on, I recalled being shocked, overwhelmed by all of the models, theories, and approaches in counseling each of which purported to be the one right way. Hardly a year goes by without additions of many new therapies or approaches. In fact, recently I read that probably 1000 counseling-therapy theories and approaches exist today.

I began this section with trepidation. Part of me wanted to ignore this section on theory since Erickson represented an atheoretical, if not anti-theoretical position and Rogers continually cautioned us of the potential dangers of the overuse of theory. However, I do believe theory can help explain and illuminate practice — theory and practice can be enjoined. I chose to start with Rogers because, to me, he has produced one of the finest statements of theory.

The following remains as a brief summary of what I believe to be a fascinating and consistent statement of a remarkable theory yielding researchable hypotheses. We should begin by stating the premise that Rogers (and Erickson) represent the 'growth network' in the human sciences. Interestingly, Rogers' emphasis on growth and psychological health has come on the scene rather belatedly. Prior to Rogers, human behavior was studied and examined through the spectacles of pathology; the human being existed in degrees of pathology or, at most, free from symptomatology. That said little about the upper limit of the person; each of us stands for a lot more than just absence of symptoms. If we view the person from the vantage point of psychopathology, the essence of that person becomes degrees of illness or symptoms. However, viewing the person from the position of health may dramatically change our perspective. 'The point of view becomes the point of view.'

There is, however, a danger of constructing dichotomies that I want to avoid. For example, in this case the pathological vs. the healthy can imply an either/or, black/white situation. I am struck by how often we (me too) trap ourselves between the 'warring' camps of dichotomies. Now as we reframe this, notice how transforming a dichotomy to a continuum changes our point of view sometimes quite dramatically. Each practitioner can place themselves and their 'point of view' on the continuum of pathology (disease) on the one hand, and health (growth) on the other.

Pathology   Health
_____

Interestingly, the pendulum keeps swinging. Currently, counseling and therapy once again emphasizes the swing back to diagnosis, treatment plans, and pathology. Nevertheless, I still view my client as being temporarily '*stuck,*' not as diseased. Of course this goes against the current trend in the field.

Rogers was not the only person beginning to challenge the more conventional view of psychology. In its search for status, psychology took on the mantle of 'science' and in the nineteenth through mid twentieth century this mantle borrowed from classical Newtonian science. Observable and measurable human behavior, alone, became the *summum bonum* of psychological study. Along with this view of 'scientific' psychology the parallel process of reductionism occurred. It seemed fitting that a study of the human should result in reducing human behavior to its most irreducible part (the reflex arc, wherein 'survival' responses are hard-wired and automatic) just as the atom was the irreducible part in the physical world.

The idea of reductionism meant continually explaining even the most complex behavior in terms of this basic part, the reflex arc. But what of the whole, you might ask? Somehow something seemed disquieting about all of this. While psychology worked toward objectivity, while reductionism legitimately served as an heuristic device and the mechanistic, cause-and-effect determinism of classical science was upheld, the person got lost in the process. Those delicate and complex thoughts, emotions, and feelings, those parts that make us so human, were caught and separated out in the filters of classical science. Thus a major paradigm shift began and we shall examine this more thoroughly in Chapter 3.

In a sharply focused article of some years ago, Gordon W. Allport (1962) wrote of three models in psychology which helped me to clarify many of the confusing issues in counseling. First, he described the person as a *reactive being* (classical behaviorism). Here the position, so similar to the classical Newtonian view of science, portrayed us as primarily reactive to external stimuli, creatures of nature whose behavior was determined and objectively predictable. We became robots intent on reducing drives, intent on avoiding any form of imbalance and intent on focusing only on external behavior. In this model our subjective and private worlds, even our consciousness, became unreliable and, preferably, disregarded.

Allport's second model described the person as a *reactive being in depth*. In this view, akin to the psychoanalytic (Freudian) and psychodynamic approaches, we were viewed very similarly to 'the reactive being' with the 'depth' aspect a significant addition. This model also focused on the reactive parts of us, the restive forces within us involuntarily striving toward balance and homeostasis. Instead of external stimuli as the principle causative agent, in this approach the name 'depth' psychology not only seemed to fit, but also gave the 'depth' portion meaning to the *unconscious*. In both models we humans became associated with determinism of past experiences and their 'shapers.' Little that we could call positive choice remained available. This model presents what seems to be a kind of hopeless view of mankind with little room for choice, change or transformation.

In the third model (humanistic psychology) Allport described the person as a *being-in-the-process-of-becoming*. This model, a reaction to the first two, projected hope; concepts of psychological health, and a process of ongoing dynamism. I argue that it demonstrated a fundamental belief in the individual, a focus on proaction instead of reaction, a concentration on the concepts of wholeness and nonlinearity, a sense that we have choice and that we can be responsible for our choices. By and large this third model was considerably more optimistic and extended the boundaries of our behavior beyond simply normalcy and adjustment. It is to this last model that Rogers' person-centered and Erickson's utilization approaches belong.

I remember many years ago being berated that something I had experienced was, 'All in your head.' The implication was that what I had experienced existed only in my head and did not match 'reality' which alone comprised the external world. Actually, I must conclude that my detractor's (critic's) experience of the event was different from mine, which said little about the event, but almost everything about us as observers of the event and what went on in *our* heads.

In a sense most everything we think, feel, and perceive occurs in our heads and in the internal processing in which we engage. Epictetus' (first century AD) admonition echoes down through time; that the external event or situation doesn't disturb us, but rather we disturb ourselves by our perceptions and thinking about it. Shakespeare's Hamlet may have put it even more succinctly; 'Nothing is either good or bad, but thinking makes it so.' (I choose to make this pronouncement the *verbal logo* of Hypnocounseling.) And it becomes fascinating to realize that within our cerebral convolutions vast panoramas take place; internal plays, dialogues, feelings of joy, ecstasy, pain, and hurt boil together side by side; time and reality are constructed and stretched in seemingly endless variation — what a wonder, this process of becoming!

To be fair, there are probably few people who steadfastly hold to any one of these positions, but rather increasingly eclectic thinking may be the rule. In a very special book, A. H. Maslow's (1971) *The Farther Reaches of Human Nature*, this kind of synergizing or merging of what initially appeared as contradictory systems is described. Many call Maslow the father of the 'third force' which represented the so-called humanistic psychologies. Perhaps Maslow has been best known for his pioneering studies of the healthy personality (self-actualizing people). At any rate, he borrowed the prefix 'epi' which means 'beyond' or 'building upon.' Maslow described his position as being both epi-Freudian and epi-behaviorist. This might be seen as a form of synergy, the combining of an apparent dichotomy or contradiction into a larger concept (humanistic psychology). Maslow believed his humanistic psychology would fall like a 'house of cards' without the building blocks of behaviorism and Freudianism. This can be perceived as eclectic process thinking, as well.

You and I wear spectacles with lenses ground and polished by our lives. These lenses have been warped, cracked, and mended by our experiences, especially with others. When I look at you through my spectacles I find a reflection from my value-lenses. I cannot see you as you exist in yourself. I can only see you as I construct or create you out of my life's spectacles. You then become my representation, my construction of you.

At this point I ask the reader to pause with me and reflect on the above implications. You exist for me only to the degree that I can bring meaning to the sensations I pick up from you. Perhaps our total view of reality equates to one great big projection of ourselves into the 'stuff' out there in the external world.

As you probably have guessed, this idea did not emerge full blown as a revolutionary, new thought. No, Maslow stood on the shoulders of the great thinkers from the two traditions and 'stepped up' into humanistic psychology. It excites me to trace apparent 'new' concepts back into their philosophical roots.

I recall a little-known work by Hans Vaihinger entitled *The Philosophy of 'As If'*. After blowing the dust off its cover, I began to read and became excited by his major premise which is that we live in a world of fictions, out of these fictions we select our truths; for example, I live '*As If* I had choice. It becomes obvious that rarely does there occur something so startlingly new, so revolutionary, that it has no antecedence. Likewise, the actualizing or growth tendencies of Maslow, Rogers, Erickson *et al.*, as well as Allport's conceptualization of 'being-in-process-of-becoming,' do not exist without precedent. For example, Aristotle toyed with the principle which became known as 'entelechy.' He discussed concepts of potentiality and realization. The traditional illustration of this has the acorn potentially realizing itself as an oak tree. The acorn has within it the ground plan for becoming the strong, well-formed oak tree. Developmentalists such as Erik H. Erikson (1968) have labeled this as the epigenetic principle, meaning that:

> ... anything that grows has a ground plan and that out of this ground plan the parts arise, each part having its time of special ascendancy,

until all parts have arisen to form a functioning whole. (p. 92)

Thus the principle of entelechy simply stands for the 'telos,' the end point or goal of the acorn; the purpose of the growing acorn to become the well-formed oak tree. Epigenesis, however, represents the genetic structure, the blueprint in the acorn or human egg, which contains the ground plan for the end product of growth and development.

CARL R. ROGERS AND THEORY

Rogers (1959) believed that the best theoretical paper he had written regarding his approach came to be published by Sigmund Koch in the monumental series *Psychology: A Study of a Science*. Rogers argued that he worked harder on this theoretical formulation entitled, 'Therapy, Personality and Interpersonal Relationships as Developed in the Client-Centered Framework' than anything he had written before or since. Rogers later stated:

> It is in my estimation, the most rigorously stated theory of change in personality and behavior which has yet been published (p. 135)
> ... yet is the most thoroughly ignored of anything I have written. This does not particularly distress me, because I believe theories *too often become dogma*. (Evans, 1975, p. 137)

Nevertheless, this meaty and thorough statement, I believe, has not been read or understood by enough of his critics. The chapter resulted from a request by the American Psychological Association to Rogers to prepare a systematic statement of his theory according to a specified outline.

In his introduction, Rogers describes some crucial attitudes that flavor his theoretical statement. These attitudes serve as critical foundations for understanding his views of research and theory. He believed, for example, that research and theory represent attempts to order significant experience. Research must not become esoteric, 'It is the persistent, disciplined effort to make sense and order out of the phenomena of subjective experience' (Rogers, 1959, p. 188). In addition, Rogers felt strongly that science begins at the most basic level of awareness, natural observation. To observe carefully, to think clearly and creatively, and to ask the critical questions exist at the heart of science. The costly laboratory and the high speed computer are no more science than are chemistry, physics, or biology (the *results* of science). Science *represents a process*, a *method of inquiry* not a bucket of content.

> Science is built up with facts as a home is with stones. But a collection of facts is no more a science than a heap of stones is a house. (Jules Henri Poincaré)

For Rogers, science must begin primitively as an emerging method of inquiry, a process speculative, filled with errors and crude measurement. It must also appear open, developing, restless, dynamic, and changing. Rogers cited the process utilized by the Curies as they discovered radioactivity. The Curies saw spoiled photographic plates, an observation of a dynamic event due to any number of causes. Their speculative and creative thinking led them to create or construct hunches or rough hypotheses. Crude experimentation slowly led to the paring down and the confirming of their hypotheses. Rogers believed this to be the level of scientific inquiry of much of psychology, particularly in the development of personality.

Rogers believed in the subjective experience. We live in our personally subjective worlds and make our external observations from that private subjective source. He believed that there may be an objective truth out there, but that he could never know it '. . . all I can know is that some statements appear to me subjectively to have the qualifications of objective truth' (Rogers, 1959, p. 192). He went on, 'In relation to research and theory, for example, it is my subjective perception that the machinery of science as we know it — operational definitions, experimental method, mathematical proof — is the best way of avoiding self-deception' (Rogers, 1959, p. 192). And yet, there arises a caution. This, too, coincides with a subjective stand. Rogers pointed out that had he lived two centuries earlier or two centuries later, a different pathway to truth probably would have seemed equally, if not more, valid. These attitudes, and an openness to change, form the anchors to Rogers' theory and research.

Rogers described his theory as the '*if-then* variety,' involving no intervening variables. *If* certain conditions exist (independent variable), *then* a process will occur (dependent variable) which includes certain characteristic elements. For example, *if* facilitative conditions (high PEGS), are perceived by clients *then* certain growth processes will occur.

The theory statements of Rogers have strong *phenomenological*[1] underpinnings quite similar to the definitions of both Snygg and Combs (Combs, Richards and Richards, 1976). And these growth processes represent operational definitions, or constructs, of what the actualizing, psychologically healthy person is becoming. For me, they have served as 'sign posts' or clues to successful counseling. Even if only one or two changes occur in the direction of health, I am appreciative, since small

---

[1.] Since the suffix 'logy' could mean, 'the study of,' we might infer that *phenomenology* is the study of phenomena. In our particular case of counseling and Hypnocounseling we refer to *phenomenology* as the study of what and how people perceive the phenomena in their world (from their internal frame of reference). Rather than imposing our view, or our meaning, in phenomenological counseling we go to the person's perceptions of experience. As Patterson (1985) suggested, 'Phenomenology assumes that although a real world may exist, its existence cannot be known or experienced directly. Its existence is inferred on the basis of perceptions of the world' (p. 411). Put another way, you become the measurer of your world. You and I are continually constructing our realities. This becomes an *internal-framing-of-reference-model* concerned with the exploration of the internal meanings (to us) of the experience. Thus in phenomenology, the behavior becomes a function not of the external world but rather our internal representations of it.

steps presage a long and rich journey.

Combs, Richards and Richards, (1976) summarized a short story, 'A Day's Wait,' by Hemingway. A young boy became very ill and a physician was called in. The examination showed a temperature of 102°. The parents, after being told of this, provided medication ordered by the doctor. Later, the father asked the son if he would like a story read to him. The child, now pale and looking rather strange, tells the father he may leave the room if he wants to. Others attempting to visit the lad hear the same message. Confused by this, the father returns to the boy's room and finds him staring around the room in a peculiar fashion. The father retakes his son's temperature and calmly explains the results which had not yet changed — 102°. Then, the child asks: 'At about what time do you think I will die?' The father is caught off guard, and explains that people don't die from a temperature of 102°. The young boy continues, insisting that in school he learned that boys and girls in France die from temperatures of 44° and he has 102°. Only after careful explanation of the difference between Centigrade and Fahrenheit, did the little boy begin to change his perceptions. What we believe to be true will depend on the way in which observations and meanings are organized and the point from which they are made.

> Reality is what we take to be true.
> What we take to be true is what
> we believe.
> What we believe is based upon
> our perceptions.
> What we perceive depends upon what
> we look for.
> What we look for depends upon
> what we think.
> What we think depends upon
> what we perceive.
> What we perceive determines
> what we believe.
> What we take to be true is
> our *reality*.
> (Zukav)
>
> Round and round the prickly pear at 5 o'clock in the morning,
> (with apologies to T. S. Eliot)

I can know clients from an externally framed reference by observing their behavior (factual, things-and-events level). For example, we might notice a man standing very stiffly in a corner of the room. He has a frown on his forehead. He appears to be holding his breath. We can observe all of this and can make some assumptions as to what's going on from our point of view (the external point of view). We might think he's angry with someone or afraid of something. Each of these ideas would be inferred from the external frame of reference, but if we use empathic inference by listening beyond his words to his deeper feelings and internal frame of reference, we move closer to him and to much more helpful solutions. Now we can learn his perception from *his* point of view; this is the phenomenological stance.

THE PROPOSITIONS[2] (ROGERS, 1951, PP. 483–524)

I have found these statements of Rogers to be invaluable as a blueprint of his theory and as an excellent chart to follow as I begin my journey into the inner world of my client. Of course, you, the reader, have choice as to whether or not you will read the propositions (or, for that matter, read this book). If you do choose to look them over, you might enjoy discovering how many of your own examples you can come up with that would illustrate the propositions.

I. I LIVE IN A PRIVATE AND EVER-CHANGING WORLD OF EXPERIENCE (PHENOMENAL FIELD) AND I AM AT THE CENTER OF IT (P. 483)
You and I live in a private world of experience and our perceptions of it continually change. These experiences, for the most part, probably exist at our subconscious, preconscious levels and consist of everything going on in us: physiological, mental, affective processes, sensory experiences, and motor activities. Being at the center means we can only know and symbolize from our own experiences. We become alone with our experiences; no one else can experience our worlds as we do. Through our transforming of our experiences (symbolizing) we bring them into conscious awareness and in awareness lies choice.

Remember not to forget that in our 'continually changing world of experience' (our experiential or phenomenal field) only a small portion of that ongoing experience is *consciously* perceived. The vast majority of processes, visceral and sensory, are taking place at the preconscious and/or nonconscious levels. Generally, we are not aware of the processes at these levels, e.g., the processes of eye-focusing, digestion, heart functioning, breathing, blood circulation, oxygen exchange, etc.

II. I REACT TO THE WORLD AS I PERCEIVE IT AND I AM MY OWN 'REALITY CREATOR' (P. 484)
You and I do not react to an absolute reality; rather, we continually *construct* our individual realities from our internal frame of reference. Interestingly, two people watching the *same* political TV broadcast may *experience very different reactions*. One sees a positive, honest, and credible leader while the other might see a dishonest, arrogant braggart. Each reacts to the reality perceived.

[2.] Rogers, C. R. (1951). *Client-Centered Therapy.* Boston: Houghton Mifflin.

III. MY WHOLE BEING REACTS AS AN ORGANIZED WHOLE TO THE WORLD. I DO NOT REACT IN JUST SINGLE PARTS OF ME (P. 486)
We react in a whole, goal-directed response at the micro-cellular level all the way to the fully conscious affective-cognitive level. I do not just feel 'sadness.' I react as a total organized system with a change in physiology such as tears or a sensation of an ache. I might even demonstrate breathing or pulse-rate changes. Intellectually I may see, hear or feel the sad event and give it symbolization in affective language such as 'sadness.' In other words, we behave as a total organized system and a change in one part produces changes in other parts.

IV. YOUR BASIC TENDENCY IN WHATEVER YOU DO IS TO ACTUALIZE, MAINTAIN, AND ENHANCE YOURSELF IN YOUR WORLD AT THAT MOMENT YOU ARE EXPERIENCING IT (P. 487)
I view this as the pivotal proposition. It serves as the fundamental assumption in the person-centered approach. This is the one great need that motivates us. It appears as an inherent directional tendency toward maturation as we define it for each species. This tendency, providing it has not been destroyed by severe organic or psychological traumas, provides us with the foundation upon which counseling can take place if the proper conditions exist.

This directional tendency is so profound and so pervasive that it is difficult to find words to describe this proposition. I have already discussed what Aristotle meant by entelechy, the acorn potentially realizing itself as an oak tree. Erik Erikson's epigenetic principle represents the genetic blueprint deep within the genetic-cellular structure that provides the ground plan for self-actualization of the organism. Organic and psychological needs, however, represent partial facets of this one fundamental need. You might, for example, bring to mind your reading of this book and how it may be satisfying your own need 'to actualize, maintain and enhance' yourself.

V. YOU BEHAVE IN A WAY THAT WILL SATISFY YOUR PRESENT NEED AS YOU PERCEIVE IT IN YOUR WORLD (P. 491)
How we behave at any given moment depends on what needs are operating at the given moment and what we perceive in our environment that can possibly gratify these needs. Remember there are many learned needs subsumed under the one basic motive, 'to actualize, maintain, and enhance the experiencing organism.' This model assumes a here-and-now domination. Behavior is not so much 'caused' by past events, but rather the present ongoing needs are those the individual tends to satisfy. Past experiences certainly give flavor to meanings in present experiences; however, the behavior invariably tends to meet the need in the here and now.

VI. EMOTIONS THAT INVARIABLY ACCOMPANY YOUR BEHAVIOR ARE STRONGEST WHEN YOUR BEHAVIOR INVOLVES YOUR NEED TO MAINTAIN AND ENHANCE YOURSELF AND ARE WEAKER WHEN YOUR NEED TO MAINTAIN AND ENHANCE YOURSELF IS NOT THREATENED (P. 492)

Emotions may appear to fall into two camps: unpleasant and/or excited emotions (the seeking efforts of the organism) and calm and/or gratified emotions (the consummatory experience). For example, terror can give 'wings to our feet' as we jump back from oncoming traffic. The emotion of 'terror' becomes highly intensified because of its life-and-death implication, whereas, your reading this sentence involves a milder level of emotion since it is not as strongly involved with maintenance, actualization or enhancement of our lives as is perceived in the moment of on-coming traffic. The more related to 'life and death' issues, the more intense will the emotions seem.

VII. I CAN BEST UNDERSTAND THE MEANING OF YOUR BEHAVIOR FROM YOUR INTERNAL FRAME OF REFERENCE, BY DEEPLY UNDERSTANDING AND EMPATHIZING WITH YOU, YOUR PERCEPTION OF YOUR WORLD AT THAT MOMENT (P. 494)

When we observe primitive societies we talk of their 'silly behavior,' their awful food and their strange customs, not realizing we make judgments from our frame of reference, not from theirs. An empathic internal frame of reference would be when I try to sense and see your world of experience *as if I were you* (always retaining the 'as if' condition, however). I learn about you only by learning about *your* perceptions of *your* world. Seeing through your eyes and listening through your ears becomes the arena of empathy.

VIII. AS AN INFANT YOUR WORLD (PHENOMENAL FIELD) WAS ONE BIG BABBLING CONFUSION (NOT BAD, NOT GOOD, JUST THERE). AS YOU GREW AND DEVELOPED YOU GRADUALLY BEGAN TO BE AWARE OF YOUR PHYSICAL SELF: TOES, HANDS, BODY, THEN THE 'YOU' THAT DEVELOPED OUT OF INTERACTIONS WITH OTHERS, PARENTS, RELATIVES ETC., UNTIL YOU BEGAN TO HAVE 'YOUR' IDEAS, ATTITUDES, VALUES, ETC. (P. 497)

Our phenomenal self gradually emerges out of our phenomenal field. We soon begin to refer to aspects of our perceptual field as the 'I' or 'me' or the 'mine.' As an infant our world (phenomenal field) appeared as William James would say, 'a bloomin' buzzin' confusion' (not bad, not good, just there). As we grew, we gradually became aware of our physical selves, our belly buttons, our mouth, and fingerprints, then the 'I' or 'me' that developed. The 'self' becomes differentiated out of that bubbling, buzzing world of experience. For example, as infants we focus on our thumb; spending hours looking at it, moving it, sucking it, we bring it into 'figure' out of the 'ground' (background) of our phenomenal field. The more we become *aware* of a sense of *control* the more we find our thumb to be a *part of 'I,' 'me,' 'self.'*

When I sense *awareness* and *control* over a part of me, then that becomes the portion I regard as being part of 'me,' part of my 'self.' Conversely, when a dentist anesthetizes your jaw it drops from 'figure' and into 'ground.' You might recall your leg or arm 'falling asleep.' It was as if your leg were foreign to you because it had fallen back into 'ground' and momentarily was not part of 'you' and your 'self.'

Since IX and X seem to flow together, I will discuss them as one proposition.

IX. THE 'SELF' THAT YOU CALL 'YOU' IS DEVELOPED OUT OF ALL OF YOUR INTERACTIONS WITH YOUR ENVIRONMENT AND THE VALUES ATTACHED TO THE LARGER CULTURE, THE SOCIETY, ITS INSTITUTIONS, AND FAMILY, AND OTHERS (P. 498)

X. THE VALUES THAT YOU ATTACH TO YOUR EXPERIENCES ARE PARTIALLY YOUR OWN AND PARTIALLY TAKEN FROM OTHERS (INTROJECTED) YET PERCEIVED IN A DISTORTED FASHION AS IF THEY WERE YOUR OWN. BY GROWING AND CHANGING YOU WANT TO LEARN TO PICK AND CHOOSE YOUR OWN VALUES AS YOU HEAR THEM FROM OTHERS (P. 498)

As infants you and I explored our phenomenal field by ourselves and we began to attach values to the interactions we had with the environment. Our valuing process was simple, flowing and clear — for the most part it was nonverbal. We learned organismically to 'like' and 'dislike.'

We turned away from sharp noises, from ice cold, from unexpected movement. (Those things perceived as threatening to the maintenance and enhancement of the 'self'; as if, automatically, we sought warmth, love, nourishment and protection.) Above all, we learned to discriminate between those things that threatened and those things that actualized, maintained, and enhanced our 'phenomenal self.' Suddenly and imperceptibly we began to experience being evaluated by others. At first we valued those experiences, which, at the inherent, unconscious levels, somehow were sensed as actualizing and enhancing of our organismic self. Then, like the peeling of an orange, we became aware of verbal and nonverbal systems in our experiencing. Soon parents, siblings, family began to affect us. We found ourselves often struggling to make sense of the contradictory messages that came from without, from others. For example, we sensed an emerging sensation of love, especially feelings of being loved, of feelings of self-worth, of acceptance, which provided powerful motivation toward the need for 'actualization, maintenance, and enhancement of the experiencing self' (how pervasive that IVth proposition is). At the same time, we have experienced positive sensory values which appear as actualizing and enhancing. It is enjoyable and enhancing to have a bladder or bowel movement whenever the physiological tension is experienced. It feels satisfying to grab a stack of papers lying about and fling them in fascinating arcs so that they spill downward all over the floor. Dials and knobs are intriguing objects to be explored, touched, and manipulated. To pull sister's hair and hear her screams can also be enjoyable and exciting. Suddenly, however, we experience a serious threat to our 'selves'; the words and actions of family in regard to these seemingly satisfying behaviors. Now the sounds and actions seem to convey, 'You are naughty, that is bad, we do not love you when you do that.' This places us in a difficult if not untenable position.

First, we may easily deny and make invisible, to awareness, the satisfactions we had originally experienced, 'but I did enjoy pulling sister's hair.' Second, we could easily misinterpret and distort the verbal and nonverbal symbolization. The accurate symbolization might be: 'I sense the folks find my *behavior* unsatisfying to them' and this is probably accurate. However, the distorted message may come out: 'I perceive this behavior as unsatisfying and wrong and therefore *I must be bad.*' In this way parental values become introjected, in a distorted fashion. The very real tragedy here is that we soon begin to question our own organismic functioning and valuing process. The expression of anger, for example, can be experienced as 'bad' even though more accurate symbolization would admit to expression of anger being satisfying and quite natural. Thus, we become separated from our own organismic functioning, i.e., the values which we originally attached to experience were replaced with those attitudes and values held by family and others. We now can easily begin to doubt our own experiencing of events. We move from our internal frame of reference to an external frame.

Unless children can resolve the possible contradiction between their own valuing experience and that of parents and others, they remain conflicted and vulnerable. Note how important parents can be at this juncture. When parents can genuinely understand and accept the feelings of satisfaction the child experiences from unacceptable behavior, they can probably more adequately help the child accept the idea that such behavior is not acceptable to the parents or others. When this occurs the child will not experience any serious conflict, and growth conditions can prevail. Children with these changed perceptions feel little threat to their concept of self as a loved person. They can accept within themselves their thrill at throwing stacks of papers, their fascination with touching and exploring buttons, knobs, and dials, or pulling sister's hair to hear her scream. Even the expression of 'anger' can be modified by children. They can learn to reason that, 'I experience anger as being satisfying at times; however, the expression of my anger may not be acceptable to others and, therefore, not necessarily helpful to me.'

Both propositions IX and X seem involved and lengthy yet they become a foundation for personality development. You might try remembering your childhood and testing some of these hypotheses out. Do you recall any confusing contradictions between your own valuing process and that of parents and/or others?

When I forge values that I discover, I feel whole, together, congruent. However, when I take on others' values as if they were mine, I can feel tense and uncomfortable, especially if I deny that they belong to others. For example, I might enjoy lolling around in the sun; however, others may see this as laziness and as wasteful. Thus, I might deny my enjoyment in the sun, and lose a very special experience to me.

XI. As experiences occur in my life, (1) I become aware of them, symbolize (label, describe) them, give meaning to them because they fit into my sense of 'me,' 'my,' 'self-concept'; (2) I ignore them because I perceive no relationship between them and my needs and self-structure; (3) I distort, misinterpret those experiences which do not seem to fit my view of self (p. 503)

Our perception appears to be highly selective and ever changing. We perceive most clearly those parts of our experience that are compatible with our sense of self and the intensity of our need. For example, if I sense being hungry, isn't it interesting that I suddenly notice restaurants and diners? I can even imagine tastes of different foods as well as suddenly smelling foods, none of which would have risen to my awareness had I not been hungry. However, events that occur that have no meaning in terms of my concept of self or current needs will probably just flow by unnoticed. My need to write this book blocks out the noise of the 40 m.p.h. winds driving curtains of snow outside my window (until I perceive it). This storm does not serve my intellectual need nor does it have anything particular to do with my self-concept, so it goes by ignored (however, how quickly it becomes part of my perceptual field when I have to walk or drive home through it). Sometimes we can deny or distort experiences because they do not seem to fit our concept of self. If I feel worthless, I will distort or deny experiences or events that contradict this. I recall getting an A on a high-school paper and my response 'I was just lucky' demonstrated my acceptance of a self-concept about school which included 'poor writer.'

XII. When I try to meet my needs in the world as I perceive it I will do so in a way that is consistent with my perception of me, my self-structure. I will behave in ways consistent with my view of 'me' (p. 507)

As we strive to attend to our needs in our ever-changing world the ways in which the striving takes must conform to our concept of self. We generally will tend to behave in ways consistent with the view we hold of ourselves. Rationalizations, excuses and blaming others can be a sign of conflict between actual behavior and one's self-concept. For example, I watched a politician's TV interview the other night. He tried to portray his integrity and honesty and I have no doubt he believes himself to be an honest politician. When questioned, however, he began making excuses and blaming the situation as well as others. Interestingly, I noticed how he stopped making eye contact with the interviewer and the TV camera. His behavior became increasingly uncomfortable to watch. It's amazing what lengths we will go in order to maintain some kind of congruence, if we know it to be a fiction at the time. I like the example of the pilot who believes himself to be brave and generally fearless. When assigned to a flight he views as overly dangerous, physiologically he experiences fear and a need to escape. He cannot symbolize these reactions into his consciousness because they would blatantly disagree with his concept of himself. He can, however, perceive his plane as not running properly or that he is sick with the flu. Organically, we can feel the fear yet our conscious behavior takes paths still consistent with our self-concept.

XIII. THERE ARE TIMES WHEN I WILL BEHAVE IN WAYS WHICH ARE INCONSISTENT WITH MY VIEW OF SELF. I WILL NOT BE 'BEING MYSELF' UNDER CERTAIN UNUSUAL OR STRESS CONDITIONS — SOMETIMES THIS INCONSISTENCY MIGHT BE DUE TO NEEDS THAT I HAVE NOT ADMITTED TO MY SELF-STRUCTURE AS HAVING (P. 509)

In unusual emergency situations we may behave in heroic ways but not be aware of it in our conscious symbolization: 'I didn't know what I was doing. I just apparently did it.' Those who snore behave consistently, yet sleeping prevents their owning the behavior. We have probably all heard of situations where individuals have performed incredible deeds and yet have not brought them into conscious symbolization. Recently, the news described a woman who had lifted the front end of a small tractor which had rolled onto her child. After the act she claimed that she didn't know what she was doing. Her self was not involved and her behavior was not regarded as part of herself. How many times have we heard of a brutal act committed by an individual who had no apparent recollection of the act. 'I can't believe I did that! I don't remember anything. I wouldn't ever do such a thing.'

XIV. I MAY FEEL ANXIOUS, CONFUSED, AND TENSE WHEN I DENY TO MY AWARENESS SIGNIFICANT SENSORY AND VISCERAL EXPERIENCES WHICH HAVE NOT BEEN SYMBOLIZED AND ORGANIZED INTO MY SELF-STRUCTURE (P. 510)

When a real discrepancy exists between my own experience and the concept and beliefs I have about myself, I can feel tense, anxious and estranged from my self. We can see this operating in many ways. The young adolescent boy whose self-perception and upbringing have instilled in him a self-concept of purity and lack of any 'evil' sexual thought is astonished when accused of looking through windows at disrobing women. When confronted with this behavior he insisted in his innocence but finally said, 'I was not myself.' There is a real discrepancy between the organic experience as it exists and the concept of the self which has such powerful influences upon behavior.

XV. I MOVE IN THE DIRECTION OF GROWTH AND PSYCHOLOGICAL HEALTH WHEN MY SELF-CONCEPT IS SUCH THAT ALL THE SENSORY AND VISCERAL EXPERIENCES THAT I AM HAVING ARE ASSIMILATED ON A SYMBOLIC LEVEL INTO A CONSISTENT RELATIONSHIP WITH THE CONCEPT I HAVE OF MY SELF (P. 513)

We are said to be integrated or *congruent* when all of our sensory and visceral experiences can be symbolized and organized within the concept we have of ourselves. We feel whole, calm and together; a certain kind of 'happiness.' Put another way, you are said to be integrated or psychologically healthy when all of your sensory and visual experiences are admitted to awareness through accurate symbolization and become internally consistent (congruent) with your sense of self. When the adolescent, previously described, can accept his sexual interests and can accept the reality of the cultural values placed on the suppression of these interests, he will enlarge his self-concept and his inner tension will be considerably lessened. *Awareness becomes the key that unlocks the door to choice.*

XVI. Experiences which are consistent with the organization of structure of my own self-concept I may perceive as threatening and the more of these perceptions there are, the more rigidly my self-structure is organized to maintain myself (p. 515)

We tend to feel threatened when we perceive experiences that appear to be inconsistent with our self-concept. And anxiety can be the emotional reaction to this threat. If a big part of my self-concept is that I believe I'm a poor student and I get a high score, I will muster excuses that fit my concept of being a poor student. If you report that I got a high score on an intelligence test, I might not believe it because of my need to defend my self-concept against this threat of inconsistency. Defensive behavior increases as the number of experiences perceived as threatening to the concept of self increases.

How many people do we know who have certain fixed beliefs about themselves? 'I'm unattractive,' 'nobody likes me,' 'I'm a terrible student,' 'I can't do anything right,' and we begin to bite by arguing with them 'Yes — but' and trying to dispel or contradict their negative self-concept beliefs. The question raised by this proposition is, has it ever worked?

XVII. Under certain conditions (PEGS?) involving primarily the absence of threat to the self-structure, experiences which are inconsistent with it may be perceived and examined and the structure of my self-concept revised to assimilate and include such experiences (p. 517)

The counselor's intervention: when you listen to me, accept me without judgment and you are congruent, I perceive a nonthreatening experience. This allows me to explore ever so gently facets of my self that can be incorporated into my self-concept. Interestingly, for me, you become an 'expander' not a 'shrink.' In Hypnocounseling, for example, with its high PEGS in the relationship, I can gradually be assured that you accept me as I am. It is then that I can begin to explore more readily those experiences that I have denied to symbolization for so long. Once made conscious my concept of self can be 'expanded.'

XVIII. When I perceive and accept into one consistent and integrated system all my sensory and visceral experiences, then I am necessarily more understanding of others as separate individuals to be respected (p. 520)

When we begin to accept all of our sensory and visceral experiences consistent with our self-concept, we become more accepting of self and more accepting of the different uniqueness of others. As we can continue to stretch in this mode, we feel significantly less threatened, less fearful and more open and accepting of the separateness and differences of others.

XIX. As I begin to become aware of and accept these experiences into my self-structure, I find that I am changing my present value system which was primarily based on introjections (others' values that I internalized) (p. 522)

The gradual movement from introjected values to internalized personal values involves, first, an *awareness* of living the values of others and, second, the realization that the individual can begin to construct his/her own organismic valuing process. Each begins to learn to look within to the senses and his/her own physiological equipment rather than look outward toward others. As I begin to become more aware of and accept these experiences into my self-structure, I find that I begin to change my present value system from introjections (others' values) to my own internal locus of control. I become more and more the master and captain of my life. I am more objective and less caught up by the opinions of others. I am who I am.

MILTON H. ERICKSON: TENTATIVE ASSUMPTIONS
(Lankton and Lankton, 1983, pp. 11–27)[1]

As we have already noted, Erickson avoided theory. He believed that theories inevitably evolved into generalizations, and he viewed people as unique, describing twins as having different fingerprints, different personalities, different perceptions. If there are no two people alike, he reasoned, how then could we dare generalize to a theory about all of them?

And now after saying all of that, I believe it is possible to speculate and to make inferences about certain basic assumptions or principles (but not a theory) found in Erickson's contributions. Lankton and Lankton (1983) have done just that. What follows is a set of 11 hypothesized principles which have been extrapolated from his writings, his words and from his behavior. We cannot know how Erickson would react to them, yet you can keep in mind the open-ended structure of each principle:

1. People operate out of their internal maps and not out of sensory experience
We live and exist in our own constructed maps or representation of our perceived world, as Rogers would add, 'of which we are at the center.' Each person constructs a unique frame of reference and the counselor's task becomes one of learning it.

2. People make the best choice for themselves at any given moment
Each choice we make comes from our internal frame of reference and within these limitations each choice represents neither the 'best' nor the 'worst' but rather *in the moment* the choice that seems most appropriate. In Rogers' words the choice represents the attempt to gratify needs as experienced in

---

[1.] Reprinted from Langton, S.R. and Langton C.H. *The Answer Within: A Clinical Framework of Ericksonian Hypnotherapy. (1983)* pp. 11–27. Reprinted with permission. No further reproduction is authorized without written permission from Taylor Francis and Routledge.

the field and as perceived at that very moment. Regrets come from actions that were taken in the past (actions and behaviors that seemed totally appropriate and sensible, then) but, as time goes by, perceptions and needs change and we cannot believe that, 'we did that.' We exist in the *here* and *now* and that's probably why this became the primary focus of Erickson (and Rogers). I have often perceived it, thus, that 'the *past* is our NOW-recollection and the *future* is our NOW-anticipation.'

3. *THE EXPLANATION, THEORY OR METAPHOR USED TO RELATE FACTS ABOUT A PERSON IS NOT THE PERSON*

The explanation or theory represents our 'map,' our frame of reference, *an abstraction*. And that 'abstraction' is not the person and we must be ever so conscious of this. Just as the 'map is not the territory' the theory, the explanation is not the person.

4. *RESPECT ALL MESSAGES FROM THE CLIENT*

Erickson and Rogers emphasized the attitudes of respect and empathy, especially in the many-faceted elements of communication clients bring; verbal, gesture, voice tone, social expressions. We learn to *utilize* all messages (verbal and nonverbal) from the client as a critical part of the utilization and person-centered approaches.

5. *TEACH CHOICE; NEVER ATTEMPT TO TAKE CHOICE AWAY*

The assumption that people can make choices serves as a critical base for both Erickson and Rogers. We don't want to spend time and energy taking away a bad choice; rather, we wish to help our clients learn new associations and choices. Teaching choice involves expanding the client's frame of reference to include additional thoughts, logic, behaviors, and perceptions that expand options. In one of Erickson's suicide cases he suggested to the young woman that she postpone her suicide for at least three months and take a 'last fling.' Why should she die leaving all of that money to those who had treated her so poorly? She agreed. Erickson first suggested she go to the beauty parlor for cosmetics and a new hairdo. She also agreed to seek help in buying an exciting new wardrobe and shopping for a new car. It was suggested she go on a vacation. She chose a cruise ship and on it she joined the dancing classes. Three months later she found herself too busy to consider suicide (perhaps she was enjoying living too much). Many choices were offered and her perceptual field was significantly expanded.

6. *THE RESOURCES THE CLIENT NEEDS LIE WITHIN HIS OWN PERSONAL HISTORY*

This statement about potentialities directs us to look within for solutions, another reason why Erickson and Rogers avoided interpreting and advice-giving. Both believed that clients had within, the resources, the experiences and resolutions they needed to draw upon. These assumptions explain why in Hypnocounseling we invariably go to the client as the source.

7. MEET THE CLIENT AT HER MODEL OF THE WORLD

This becomes the start of building empathy. I try to meet you at your 'map' or model of the world. This rapport (empathy) serves as the initial step toward the goal of teaching choice and change. Erickson and Rogers make it clear that the best vantage point for understanding behavior comes from the internal frame of reference of the person. Erickson utilized the individual's voice tone, rhythm, images, metaphors, behavior, and beliefs — anything that could be considered the person's map of the world.

8. THE PERSON WITH THE MOST FLEXIBILITY WILL BE THE CONTROLLING ELEMENT IN THE SYSTEM

The greater the flexibility, knowledge, and experience of the counselor the more effective she will be at meeting her clients at their model of the world. Flexibility, as opposed to a kind of constant rigidity, provides greater creative outcomes in teaching choice to clients. The uniqueness of each client draws upon the quality and quantity of our flexibility. In addition, flexibility can be viewed as the individual's degree of openness to experiences as well as freedom (the number of options from which the person can choose). This kind of freedom implies that the more options from which I can choose, the greater my freedom. In a world of uncertainty, rather than deny personal freedom by pulling back, clients can learn to draw upon their flexibility and resilience. One way of looking at things can be turned into many ways of looking at things.

9. A PERSON CAN'T NOT COMMUNICATE

Even if I am silent, I still communicate even if it's simply sitting there in front of you. Counselors learn to listen and to observe respectfully and carefully to the most subtle nonverbal cues and behavior: a blink, a movement of the eyes, a grimace or even a twitch. These subtle behavioral responses have come to be called 'ideomotor responses' and each of these can be seen as powerful communication messages from the client.

10. IF IT'S HARD WORK, REDUCE IT DOWN

This principle of therapy and teaching has been described by the Lanktons (1983):
> We frequently promote the idea, humorously, that Custer could have won if the Indians had come over the hill one at a time. In the same way, even complex tasks are manageable if taken one step at a time, in component pieces. (p. 23) [And some forms of reductionism are not all bad.]

Small changes can lead to bigger changes. Learning complex tasks can be 'chunked down' to simpler specific learnings. Some textbooks attempt to start the learner off in simple, progressive stages, one step at a time. This reminds me of a man who stood looking up at a long and arduous staircase *overwhelmed* by its steepness and length and at that moment a woman brushed by him and took the first step and went up.

Recently a college woman came to see me because she was depressed. Shortly, as she talked, she began to realize it wasn't so much depression that she felt, but rather a feeling of being overwhelmed (an important discovery on her part). In that same session, when asked what she had planned to do about it, she excitedly described a strategy to organize her work into separate segments and to do one task at a time. It was exciting for her to become aware of her many choices, of her having goals and the means to carry them out. It took some time, yet I think she learned to be realistic about her plan and her accomplishments. She learned that *one of the most effective antidepressants is accomplishment.*

11. OUTCOMES ARE DETERMINED AT THE PSYCHOLOGICAL LEVEL
It may seem obvious that change and choice occur at the psychological level. By psychological level I mean the mental or thinking level as opposed to behavioral, physical or cellular levels, for example. Hypnosis by itself does not cure, however, the reassociation of the client's experiential life and the search for resources represent a prime 'psychological level.'

Change is a result of rethinking, of previewing outcomes and solutions. Change results from expanding the charts of perception, of changing the point of view. In addition, it is drawing upon one's resources and one's history of experiences to evoke new solutions and new ways of perceiving. Outcome and changes only occur at the psychological level just as it is not things or external events that affect us but rather how we think about them.

A SHORT COURSE IN EPISTEMOLOGIES

The continual thread that runs through this book repeats itself as a caution and as a reminder. As we work with our clients, our assumptions, beliefs, and attitudes have powerful and pervasive impact and one of these assumptions has to do with the nature and origins of knowledge or 'how we know.' When we embark on the study of these concerns we are involved with what the philosopher calls epistemology. Whenever we interact with our clients we draw upon some kind of epistemology (ours and our clients).

The origins and methods by which we come to know things can be sorted out in many ways. I like the three approaches of Thut (1957): knowledge that is *revealed*, knowledge that is *discovered* and knowledge that is *constructed* or created.

1. *Revealed knowledge* — Probably the most easily understood epistemology and the one with the greatest historical roots comes from the religious-spiritual domain. This approach argues that knowledge or truth can only be revealed through rituals, through prayer, by the authority of spiritual figures and/or from the readings of religious literature such as the Bible, the Koran, the Zend-Avesta, the Mahabharata, the Ramayana,

for example.

Knowledge appears as transcendent, i.e., its origins go beyond this world. The source of all true knowledge transcends the reach of human effort. Only from the supernatural and the world beyond can the human hope to gain knowledge. Thus, for you and for me, knowledge exists as absolute, beyond us in the 'realm of ideas,' as Plato described it.

2. *Discovered knowledge* — A second pathway has historical roots that go back to Aristotle and earlier to the pre-Socratics (e.g., Democritus, Thales, Heraclitus) and this route argues that knowledge exists as immanent in this world. Rather than using prayer, religious readings and/or spiritual authority we can use methods of observation and experimentation to *'discover'* truth and knowledge existing in *this* world. Galileo and Sir Isaac Newton serve as good representatives of the route toward discovered truth. From out of their work has come the notion that an absolute objectivity and order exist in the universe, that reality does not exist in some transcendent 'realm of ideas' beyond us, but rather exists in the world out there.

Many western cultures represent the world in terms of reductionism, order, absolute objectivity, linear cause and effect, and determinism. Ian Stewart (1989) describes the Newtonian power of determinism:

> . . . the positions and velocities of every particle of matter in the entire universe, taken at some fixed instant, completely determine its future evolution. The universe follows a unique, predetermined dynamical path. *It can do only one thing.* (p. 10)

At first glance it may seem as if Newton pushed God aside, as if he had tried to nullify the religious pathway. Not at all. Newton meant no disrespect to God in any way, yet it could be suggested that God may have been relegated to the more remote role of *creator and/or first cause.* Later theologians and philosophers began to envision an image of God as the-great-clock-maker.

Nevertheless, sometimes it takes centuries for epistemological shifts to impact on those of us living our everyday lives. The belief that knowledge comes from divine sources is still with us, though perhaps, in different robes. And now, it seems to me, knowledge 'revealed' from transcendent origins seems generally to exist mutually with knowledge 'discovered' through science although the more conservative religious groups within the Christian, Judaic, and Islamic traditions might disagree. For example, 'creationism,' as a movement, shows a clearcut preference for truth divinely revealed in sacred words, symbols and writings.

I think it is safe to suggest that most people in the streets envision something 'out there,' an objective and linear cause-and-effect world and a world that is predictable if we have enough data. In addition, most people not only solve problems by seeking linear causes, but also believe in reductionism, that if we break things down to their irreducible parts we can gain the best understanding. Yet as we move ever closer to objectivity and a linearly caused determinism we learn to view things in dichotomies — black or white, good or bad.

Newton reinforced the traditional idea that we could learn what *really* exists. In philosophical terms we call something *true* only if it corresponds to an independent and objective reality. 'Now, as ever, there reigns the conviction that knowledge is knowledge only if it reflects the world as is' (von Glasersfeld, 1984, p. 20). And surely, Newton's laws convinced us there exists an independent and objective reality out there. You may want to take time to consider those epistemologies you follow. Where do you stand on truths divinely revealed from above and truths discovered out there?

3. *Constructed knowledge* — And yet, certain rumblings were being heard and their implications were not widely recognized. There were sounds that once again a paradigm shift was occurring; that our reality was, perhaps, not so clear, concrete, nor ordered as originally believed. For standing on the shoulders of Newton, such people as Einstein and his relativity theory and Bohr, Heisenberg, Planck *et al.* and their Quantum Mechanics all began to have different inputs on the revealed and discovered way of viewing events.

Toward the end of the nineteenth century, the Gestalt psychologists (Wertheimer, Koffka and Kohler) were providing a holistic model for psychology and were arguing that we cannot view two dissimilar events simultaneously. They described the figure/ground process. As we focus on one thing, event or experience we bring it into *figure* and other events or experiences recede into *ground* (background).

It is fun to test figure/ground by looking away from this page and focusing on something in your field of vision. Notice how this becomes figure and that other visual objects fall back into ground. Now switch. It is easy to see how common this process is in our thinking and our lives in general.

Even more impactful was the Gestaltists' view of the whole. They cautioned against focusing only on irreducible parts arguing and demonstrating that the whole is more than simply the sum of parts.

Because scholars had studied and therefore focused only on linear operations, nonlinear hypotheses which began to emerge challenged the linear cause-and-effect world which begot the LaPlacian determinism of perfect predictability. Questioned was the once strong belief and hope of an absolute objectivity and reality which would ensure predictability and order for all time. Dashed was the mirage of reductionism and the search for those irreducible parts (the atom appeared so real and so basic for a time and then it began to fade as our irreducible building block of the universe). A major shift could be found in the works; more and more shift from objectivity to subjectivity and the nonconscious.

There is increasing evidence that the unconscious influences perception and memory more than was once believed. It is even suggested that people pick up messages of many kinds even when they're unconscious (under anesthesia, for example). Freiberg (1996) suggests that there appears to be evidence that positive suggestions (hypnosis?) under anesthesia affect the amount of pain as perceived by patients after surgery. Also studies are calling into question the once firmly held belief that thinking and behavior are controlled only by the conscious mind. For example, Azar (1996) reported that gender-biased judgments were shown to be made when a series of words were presented to males and females. These words were found to trigger unconscious gender stereotypes. Subjects were asked to judge names on a list which were famous and those which were not. There were an equal number of male/female famous names. Both sexes identified consistently more famous names who were male. Implications of observer objectivity are brought into question. If our conscious perceptions are influenced by the unconscious, how accurate is our objectivity after all?

The third pathway, constructivism, suggests that rather than *discover* an independent reality 'out there' we *construct* or *invent* reality 'in here' (in our minds). For example, the 'discovered' epistemology would suggest that light/color, temperature or sound exist 'out there' independent of us and are picked up through our sensory receptors. On the other hand, the epistemology of constructivism would suggest:

> . . . 'out there' there is no light and no color, there are only electro-magnetic waves; 'out there' there is no sound . . . only periodic variations of the air pressure; 'out there' there is no heat and no cold, there are only moving molecules with more or less mean kinetic energy . . . (von Foerster, 1984, p. 46)

Constructivism might suggest that our brain is such that it internally constructs light and color out of electro-magnetic waves, sound out of variations of air pressure, and heat or cold out of moving molecules with more or less kinetic energy. George Berkeley, an Irish bishop and philosopher, created a construct that has come to be known as *solipsism*. One of the classic puzzles that he loved to play with was the question: does noise exist when the tree falls in the forest and there is no one to hear it? Your answer, interestingly, would depend, to some extent, on which of the epistemologies you hold.

'Constructivism' is not necessarily an easy concept to grasp especially if I am more used to the more conventional ways of knowing. There are many implications for the person in the constructivist's frame of reference.

von Glasersfeld tries to clarify by proposing that 'knowing' is not necessarily searching for a *perfect* mirror-like representation of *reality*, but rather a search *for fitting* or *constructing* approximations. Knowledge then can be seen as something we *invent* in our attempt to make sense or meaning out of that 'amorphous' flow of experiencing by constructing repeatable experiences that can be relatively reliable.

> . . . constructivism itself must not be interpreted as a picture or description of any absolute reality, but as a possible model of 'knowing' and the acquisition of knowledge in cognitive organisms that are

capable of constructing for themselves, on the basis of their own experience, a more or less reliable world. (von Glasersfeld, 1984, p. 39)

While the epistemology of constructivism can be fascinating it can also be disturbing if carried to its logical conclusion. If I 'invent' or 'construct' my reality am I not the 'center of the universe?' For after all, if nothing is real except my inventions where does that leave others? This belief that nothing is real or exists but the self, we can recognize as solipsism (again Bishop Berkeley). However, the minute I meet other humans who invent and construct their own realities my ego-centered claims of reality change.

Interestingly, Cade and O'Hanlon (1993) offer another way through the dilemma of solipsism in their distinction between *things-and-events* and *meanings*. I find this distinction helpful not only in living my life but also in counseling.

At the subatomic level it could be argued that the pencil I hold in my hand exists only as particles of energy moving in a world of probability (matter? no matter). However, for our immediate and practical needs in living and in counseling we can live 'as if' the pen is a *thing* that does exist 'out there' and we can get communal agreement.

The pen and its existence is another pretend-metaphor we live by. There are many pretend-metaphors that we catapult into our reality.

Thus, at the *things-and-events* level we can get at community-group agreement. For those of us who can see we can generally agree that there is daylight, the sun shines in the western sky and it is afternoon. The differences begin to occur, however, as soon as we begin to ascribe (construct) certain *meanings*. One person may quake at the afternoon sun for fear of sunburning. Another man smiles, anticipating a walk on the beach, while a woman dreads the time of day and depresses herself because of the realization that she has not finished a certain task expected to be completed in the afternoon. Another excites herself about the evening meal coming up, while another wrestles with the torture of dieting. An artist pauses and becomes ecstatic as she perceives the unique coloring and shadows of the afternoon sun.

Whether or not there is an objective 'reality' at the *things-and-events* level is really not a concern and Cade and O'Hanlon (1993) humorously describe a city person, a fur trader, an Eskimo hunter and an environmentalist confronting a rather angry polar bear. Does the polar bear *really* exist? Can you imagine any one of these people seriously asking that question? You bet that bear 'exists' out there, and each of these people would agree (at the *things*-and-*events* level) but their constructions at the *meanings* level would differ considerably.

Thus constructivism, it is argued, appears to be the epistemology of choice for Hypnocounseling up to this point (who knows how many new epistemologies will be developed (or constructed) in the future?).

On the topic of determinism we might better back off a bit and re-examine our stand. I do not suggest that eliminating determinism would result in freedom; on the contrary, determinism and free choice are two sides of the same coin. For example, imagine a world totally *without* determinism.

Notice how we have moved away from dichotomizing free choice and determinism. When we find ourselves transcending dichotomies (freedom vs. determinism) particularly those with seemingly apparent contradictions, we are practicing synergy.

Determinism provides us with a sense of predictability. To choose, therefore, invariably seems to imply *choosing* among options of which we can predict probable consequences. And to predict, we must have determinism. So it could be said that we don't so much choose options or alternatives, but rather that we *choose consequences*. Thus, an operational definition of freedom (CIPAR) for Hypnocounseling might include:

1. Clarifying the context or issue in which choice is involved.
2. Identifying options or choices.
3. Predicting or imagining the probable consequence(s) of each option chosen.
4. Acting Responsibly on that choice. Acting responsibly would include other predictions. Would the consequences of my chosen action result in harm or disturbance to world, self or others? If so, a re-examination and reconstruction of other more responsible choices would be repeated.

I should like to call this 'responsible choice,' the heart of Hypnocounseling.

I have covered a lot in a very short space — I hope it is clear that, in a way, this kind of freedom depends upon determinism. Is it not true, that when we choose between A, B or C we choose the one whose probable consequence you can ascertain (determinism)? For example, I can utilize the process of CIPAR in choosing how to go to California. I would start by clarifying (C) the issue or problem. I might list time, pleasure (delight), comfort, and cost as being most important. As I next begin to identify (I) the options I could quickly eliminate walking, skiing, dog sled, glider, horseback etc. since cost might be acceptable the time and comfort factors would rule them out. I would now be choosing among the options of going by rail, car, bus plane, or motorcycle. Since time, comfort, pleasure, and cost were important variables I would now choose to prioritize them. Which would be the most significant variable for me — time, comfort or cost? The airplane would be my choice of options if time were the significant variable. Do you, as a practitioner, believe you could 'teach' clients this process of choosing?

Hypnocounseling holds assumptions contrary to much of the 'discovered' world view. After all, it appears that our assumptions will be the most accurate way to our particular epistemology. For example, notice how the linear cause and effect of absolute determinism negates the concept of *responsible choice*. Notice how reductionism contradicts *eclecticism, holism* and the *phenomenological-field theories* espoused by Hypnocounseling. The vision of some kind of absolute objectivity and reality clearly stands in the way of the concept of the unique human's *constructing* of reality.

How often I recall being told, 'Don't be biased.' How can I not be biased? This is an honest and legitimate question because the real issue is that one becomes fully aware of this bias. I postulate that we must also accept the idea that our realities by and large appear constructed within our internal worlds and that the external world becomes a reflection of our internal projections of our values, beliefs, and assumptions. If you've stayed with all of this, no doubt, you might have become aware of how it challenges the life 'spectacles' with which you and I saw clearly that the real world exists out there not 'in here,' a not-so-obvious illusion. The concept does jar our sensibilities in this case. All my life I have learned that the real world *is* 'out there.' Yes, it is hard to change and if we decide to do so we must be aware of the consequences.

This last portion continually amazes me. It would turn counseling and therapy on its head. For after all, some of you are being asked to view the world, people, and the process of counseling in a different light.

Above all, counselors must learn to 'match' the epistemologies of their clients especially being aware of those from other cultures. Clients who believe primary knowledge comes from divine transcendent sources, for example, will be confused if I try to relate to them from another epistemology. Matching is critical. Note well, 'matching' epistemologies in no way means changing the client's epistemology — this would be unprofessional and unethical. It seems to become wasteful and simply wrong to settle for only revealed, discovered or constructed knowledge. To choose only one path and to strive toward consistency can and does produce a rigidity harmful to self and society. Progress is stunted as human history repeatedly shows.

It is conceivable to me that perhaps we drift in and out of the several epistemologies and this happens as we enter different contexts in our lives. In church, Synagogue, mosque, for example, the assumptions of knowledge as 'revealed' dominate. In problem solving and in linear science and scientific method the 'discovered knowledge' prevails. The famous 'Monkey Trial' of Tennessee forms a marvelous example of the civil war of ideas and assumptions whereby 'creationism'; knowledge 'divinely revealed' from the scriptures battle with the evolutionists who marched to the very different drum of knowledge that is 'discovered.'

Of late, I have come to realize that most all counseling is cross-cultural. For example, certain clients quickly teach me that eye contact is intrusive and threatening and that high PEGS must be delivered differently. My clients can teach me so much if I not only listen to their words but also observe their motions and their nonverbal message. Rogers' admonition to 'listen, listen, listen' and Erickson's exhortation to 'observe, observe, observe' register as excellent reminders for us. In Hypnocounseling the counselor is the learner, the client the teacher. I will remember this unusual relationship. I can learn to be taught by my clients; their views and expectations of counseling, their goals and specific ways of reaching them. When my client is a college male of European descent, as I am, I could start at the *meanings* level by focusing on stereotypes. Stereotypes (the ignominious foundation of racism) are generalizations and also high-level abstractions. Some of those stereotypes might be: 'here's another rich college honky, fraternity redneck, or lazy playboy, spoiled rotten, and drunk most of the time and does as little as he can to get by.' When I meet him at the *meanings* level (stereotypically; racially and ethnically) I can totally miss who this person is. Staying at the stereotypic-*meanings* level I miss out on the fascinating uniqueness of this individual. Stereotyping allows for no individuality and the self-fulfilling prophecy will take over. I will, tragically, perceive in that person what my stereotypes tell me.

Another example: when a black, male client comes to see me it's so easy to treat him as a black male and stay at the *meanings* level (stereotypes). What a shame! I cannot be of help to anyone who I have chained to my fixed stereotypes.

The reader may agree or disagree, yet I am interested in how you perceive the connection between racism and stereotypes. Are there differences between the meanings generated by stereotypes' high levels of abstraction and the events and things as generated by observing and listening to the unique individual?

When I begin at the *things*-and-*events* level I am much freer to observe and listen to my client who happens to be the only person exactly like her/him in the universe. I feel strongly about this. On the one hand our brains and neurological systems are such that we naturally generalize, form stereotypes, and think in ways that are at the *meanings* and *abstraction* levels. We are naturally biased. On the other hand, I try to become *aware* of these biases, in the form of generalized stereotypes so that I can *choose* (choice so clearly demands awareness) to move them aside as I interact with the individual in front of me. I have a metaphor; I view my biases as filters or screens that limit or hide the individuality of the person. As I become aware of these biases only then can I move the screens aside and 'tabula rasa-like' quietly meet the person at his/her map of the universe. This is hard work yet I've made it into a beginning ritual with each new client.

Constructivism and phenomenology supply a certain explanatory backdrop for Hypnocounseling, as does the nonlinear theory of Chaos or Complexity and Quantum Mechanics. Both Rogers and Erickson repeatedly emphasize the *uniqueness* of each individual, a major building block for their approaches as well as for Hypnocounseling.

I don't recall seeing the hyphenated label phenomenological-constructivism anywhere in the literature, however, it does seem a fitting label to describe not only the person-centered approach of Rogers, the utilization approach of Erickson, as well as the soon to be discussed concept, Hypnocounseling.

Looking back at Rogers' Proposition XI (pp. 58–72), it is interesting to see how many reflect the concept of phenomenological-constructivism.

As I have been suggesting, psychology, counseling, and psychotherapy have been based on a physical world view that we have come to call classical or Newtonian physics. The assumption has been that the human organism exists in this world and is a part of it. Therefore this assumed condition reflects a simplistic reductionism, a linear cause-effect determinism, a predisposition to dichotomous thinking, and the idea of an absolute and predictable objectivity 'out there.' Hypnocounseling as well as similar approaches in counseling assume a profoundly different set of assumptions regarding the physical world and the human condition, assumptions significantly different than found in the classical-Newtonian world view. At the least, humans are not assumed to be locked into the chains of cause-and-effect determinism. The human is assumed to be 'holistic' and not enshrouded in reductionism. Humans are not neatly nor precisely predictable. They have a certain spontaneity. They are dynamic, complex, emerging systems that move them beyond a mechanical-robot existence.

My contention is that as humans we are a part of nature and the physical world, yet theories of complexity and quantum mechanics hold within them assumptions of that physical world considerably more compatible with Hypnocounseling than with classical Newtonian physics.

In the next section we shall examine chaos, chaos-complexity, and quantum theory and what each has to say to humanistic psychology as well as Hypnocounseling, in particular.

Chapter 3
Mysteries from Physics

In books of this nature, authors should claim writing space in order to offer challenging ideas that seem unreasonable, far out or even daft. Chapter 3 is an attempt to do just that.

This has been a most difficult chapter to write. Not only have I had to explore areas of the newer physics in which I had no background, but also I had to struggle with assumptions so puzzling and mysterious that I felt like the Alice in Gilmore's (1995) *Alice in Quantumland.* I found myself wondering if you, the reader, would find it helpful or would you choose to skip past it on the grounds that it is irrelevant, superficial, boring or simply not helpful. I have taken special care with this chapter because of its importance for me. I especially appreciate Robert Oppenheimer's quote that follows (but ultimately you shall choose how to treat this chapter).

> ... it seems to me that the worst of all possible misunderstandings would be that psychology be influenced to model itself after a physics which is not there anymore, which has been quite outdated.
> (Oppenheimer, 1965, p. 213)

Historically, psychology found itself in the embrace of philosophy and had to rid itself of philisophy's dominance. Finding itself a young science and needing to prove itself, psychology turned to assumptions of Newtonian physics as a model to emulate. At least a cursory examination of recent developments in physics would seem in order based on the assumption that physics has had such a profound influence on the evolution of psychology (Berenda, 1957; Heisenberg, 1958; May, 1961; Oppenheimer, 1965; Severin, 1965; VanKaam, 1958).

As one way to justify itself as a legitimate science, psychology attempted to adopt the rigor and absolute objectivity that classical physics provided in its mission to study human beings, even though it saw running the risk of copying assumptions and procedures not appropriate to its own unique field of study. The study of human behavior turned out to be very different from the study of the internal and external worlds of the other sciences. Does it not present a problem for the brain that begot the scientific method, to now turn itself on to studying itself? Could there not be some problems with this kind of convoluted argument? Newtonian physics appeared as statements, principles and laws that seemed immutable and eternal; some argued that if we could collect enough data, we could predict perfectly.

A NEW OXYMORON: ORDERED CHAOS-COMPLEXITY ON THE EDGE OF CHAOS — THE STORY OF NONLINEAR EMERGING SYSTEMS

> ... *twentieth-century science will be remembered for just three things: relativity, quantum mechanics and chaos. Chaos ... has become the century's third great revolution in the physical sciences ... Of the three, the revolution on chaos applies to the universe we see and touch, to objects at human scale.*
> Gleick, 1987, p. 6

> *In all chaos time is a cosmos, in all disorder a secret order,*
> Carl Jung

> *Confusion is a word we have invented for an order which is not understood.*
> Henry Miller

Furthermore, Gleick (1987) contends that chaos can serve as a lens to our experiences of the world; that theoretical physics had strayed too far from the human experience. Chaos speaks to a nonlinear universe made up of dynamic holistic systems. We should note, however, an interesting fact that chaos is still part of classical physics and is not found in quantum mechanics.

At one time the *linearity* and *reductionism* of Newton's classical physics were used as the standard from which observations were made. In the linear system the whole was precisely equal to its parts and linear, as an equation, when plotted on graph paper, became a straight line.

Chaos reversed this process by standing our linear assumptions upside down. Chaos-complexity changed our frame of reference. Goerner (1994) refers to chaos and complexity as 'pop labels.' She 'describes' 'nonlinear dynamics' as being a more accurate description than the term 'chaos' or 'complexity'. Lorenz (1993) suggested that 'the term *complexity* has almost as many definitions as *chaos*' (p. 163).

Another basic problem with the labels is their implications. For example, complexity deals with complex interdependency like that found in the weather, economics, the brain, human beings and all life systems, among other things. However, complexity can be misleading in that what at first appears complex may actually be very simple. Field and Golubitsky

(1992) suggest that chaos and complexity are systems that show simplicity hidden in complexity and order hidden in chaos.

Thus, new buzzwords creep up all over. An international conference sponsored by the Royal Society of London in 1986, struggled to come up with a definition of chaos. Waldrop (1992) expresses his perplexity saying, 'the science of "complexity" is so new that no one really knows its boundaries or can agree on a definition' (p. 12).

Roger Lewin (1992) discusses the current difficulty of trying to define the difference between chaos and complexity. He likened it to the metaphor of the snakes chasing their tails trying to find out if they (chaos and complexity) are indeed the same or different. I agree that chaos-complexity has been more usefully described in the following terms used by many researchers. These terms imply such attributes as holism, movement, continual changes, seamless interconnectedness, systemic organization, and growth or health dynamic — an actualization hypothesis:

'nonlinear dynamics'
'emergent systems'
'complex adaptive systems'
'dynamic-holistic systems'
'self-organizing systems'

In a more descriptive sense I prefer these terms over complexity and/or chaos because they seem to describe more accurately the processes, behaviors, and functions of the human organism. I have settled on 'dynamic, holistic and emerging systems' since this label most clearly describes the human condition to me. Hypnocounseling assumes that we as humans are dynamic, emerging, and holistic systems rather than closed and predetermined.

One of the problems in science is the observation that unexpected, uncontrollable influences appear ubiquitous. The experimental method is a process trying to control, compensate, and isolate those outside influences. While social sciences were not considered 'scientific' within the classical science rubric, they easily fell within the nonlinear dynamic systems of chaos. The advent of chaos (nonlinearity) allows us to study human behavior individually and in groups because the mathematics have changed — social science may borrow from principles of mathematical statistics in order to filter out from chaotic motion the underlying order. 'Statistics is a method for panning precious order from the sands of complexity' (Stewart, 1989, p. 53) and how I love that quote. As Pickover (1994) suggests, 'Although chaos often seems totally random and unpredictable, it actually obeys strict mathematical rules that derive from equations that can be formulated and studied' (p. 29).

Briggs and Peat (1989) point out that Henri Poincaré has been described as the 'father of modern chaos theory.' When rethinking some of Newton's laws regarding the celestial bodies, Poincaré stumbled onto the 'Palace Secret.' His equations worked splendidly with the closed system of two bodies, for example the earth's movements around the sun. Yet when a third body was added Newton's equations proved unsolvable. Calculus had been the temporary mathematical attempt at breaking down planetary motion by simpler curvilinear mathematics. Poincaré pointed out another way by coming at the problem from the opposite direction.

> He proved the three body problem could not be solved by such approximation methods . . . calculus won't work on the world at large, classical physics' fundamental approach cannot even handle the interactions of three or more bodies. (Goerner, 1994, p. 53)

Poincaré noticed that chaos seemed to be at the heart of nonlinear systems. The slightest gravitational pull of a third body could cause instability in the orbits of orbiting particles. Alarming as these discoveries were, physics left chaos and began walking a parallel path away from Newton's laws: toward relativity, quantum theory, and the principles of uncertainty and complementarity; the thinking of Einstein, Planck, Heisenberg, and Bohr.

While Poincaré was challenging the Newtonian world view, the paradigm change had to wait until the advent of the computer. As with the development of the microscope, the computer promoted research, design, and understandings that were not possible before. The new approaches being devised by mathematicians required vast and repetitive calculation that only the computer could handle. The world of chaos emerged.

In a fascinating way, chaos could have been discovered long ago. As Milton Erickson was wont to say, theories can blind us. Vast systems such as Newton's acted for years as blinders. There are strong ego involvements in the construction of models and systems. The individual who dares to question or look at something differently becomes either a fool or a martyr rather than a unique and creative person. Poincaré startled the scientific community by stating that reductionism might be an illusion. His work slowly began to erode the grand Newtonian paradigm. Poincaré's discoveries were temporarily interrupted as Quantum Mechanics swept across physics.

A most successful theory in the history of science, Quantum Mechanics made accurate predictions about a host of molecular, atomic, optical and solid state phenomena. But with it came troubling paradoxes.

> Physicists learned, for example, that an elementary unit of light can behave schizophrenically like a wave or like a particle, depending on what the experimenter chooses to measure. (Briggs and Peat, 1989, p. 28)

As Ian Stewart (1989) suggests, our earliest ancestors lived in a world of capriciousness; a world of unpredictability inhabited by demons; creatures beyond the pale, deities of every description. Chaos ruled in every corner. These same ancestors spent most of their lives not only procuring shelter and sustenance but also placating these terrifying beings and creating rituals to bring as much predictability to their lives as possible.

Interestingly, Abraham Maslow (1970, 1971) in his hierarchy of human needs described the need for safety (predictability) as being only slightly less basic than physiological needs (food, water, oxygen, shelter, etc.). Maslow knew the importance of safety needs (for structure, predictability, limits, freedom from fear). Safety loomed as a powerful and omnipresent need. We need to know that food, water, oxygen, shelter (the physiological needs) are there on a *predictable* basis. Out of this need for safety came a perceptual reconstructing of our world into predictability and need for order. And so we constructed order even if there were none. By the eighteenth century (and remember Newton lived in the seventeenth and eighteenth centuries) science had created such order that it seemed as if there were little more to be known.

And so, chaos for years lay there like a seed, quietly germinating before emerging and blossoming. In the early 1960s a mathematician turned meteorologist, Edward Lorenz, stumbled upon something that would become another viewpoint in science. Using a very primitive computer Lorenz programmed it to reduce weather patterns down to their basic parts (reductionism again). Over and over again he could reproduce weather in recognizably earthly patterns; air pressure rising and falling, temperature and precipitation changes, air streams swinging first in one direction and then another. 'But the repetitions were never quite exact. There was pattern with disturbance. An orderly disorder' (Gleick, 1987, p. 15).

One winter day in 1961, Lorenz was examining one sequence at greater length and instead of repeating the whole computer-run over again; he started part way through. A memorable coffee break changed Lorenz's way of looking at the weather and at his world. After returning from his 'break' he had expected the run to identically repeat itself, since the program had not been changed. The new printout showed an entirely different weather pattern. Lorenz was shocked. However, he noticed that before his coffee break he had been typing in six decimal places .506127 and then to shorten his work he rounded off to three decimal places .506 — an inconsequential change, or so he thought. This seemingly inconsequential rounding off had a profound impact; he found that a small puff of air was like a single numerical error and inconsequentiality was no longer inconsequential. On that winter day Lorenz realized that accurate long-range forecasting of the weather was doomed and the 'Butterfly Effect' became a new aphorism to describe chaos:

> Tiny differences in input could quickly become overwhelming differences in output — a phenomenon given the name 'sensitive dependence on initial conditions.' In weather, for example, this translates into what is half-jokingly known as the Butterfly Effect — the notion that a butterfly stirring the air today in Peking (or Brazil or Hong Kong) can transform storm systems next month in New York. (Gleick, 1987, p. 8)

Barbara Tuchman (1978), a favorite historian of mine, writes of events that can change history as the flap of butterfly wings can change weather.

> An attack of gout suffered by Bajazet [Turkish Sultan] which supposedly prevented him from advancing, evoked from Gibbon the proposition that, 'An acrimonious humor falling on a single fibre of one man may prevent or suspend the misery of nations.' (p. 564)

Chaos even finds its way into the childhood proverb stressing the importance of one nail as well as determinism:

> For want of a nail
> the shoe was lost.
> For want of a shoe
> the horse was lost.
> For want of a horse
> the rider was lost.
> For want of a rider
> the battle was lost.
> For want of a battle
> the kingdom was lost.
> And all for want
> of a horseshoe-nail.

So many times I have experienced awe and bewilderment while looking at the night sky. How small and irrelevant I have felt. Have you shared a similar feeling? Briggs and Peat (1989) claim that chaos theory may give us the sense that, 'inconsequential things can have a huge effect in a nonlinear universe' (p. 75). They point out that if conditions had varied at the point of the big bang by one quantum of energy (the smallest known thing we can measure) our universe, our planet would be a vastly different place.

> ... there remains the widespread phenomenon of chaos, in which the outcome of a dynamic process is so sensitive to initial conditions that a minuscule change in the situation at the beginning of the process results in a large difference at the end. (Gell-Mann, 1994, p. 25)

All of this excites me. It so clearly explains how one small pattern interruption in counseling can have a great impact. Simply asking a client to get out of bed differently or 'stopping thinking' or getting up and exercising; any of these interruptions might have a major impact. As clients relax, for example, they can interrupt the flow of unwanted negative thinking or feeling. They can choose to interrupt and control themselves.

Chaos is still on the leading edge and is just now becoming a part of the common language. There are constructs and systems such as financial markets, population, traffic problems, and weather inextricably tied to chaos theory, and let us not forget to include the human organism, the brain as well as the concept of mind!

I have long admired the presentations and readings of Ernest L. Rossi and his theories and explanations have greatly influenced me. He suggests that

> ... the new mathematics of complex adaptive systems may be the means by which we can understand the complete interaction of psycho-biological dynamics. This would propel us forward to avoid the prediction-control model of stimulus-response, black-box behaviorism. (Rossi, 1993, p. 71)

In addition, Lloyd and Rossi (1992) have used an approach (similar to chaos theory) to describe the integration of physiology and its interconnection in mind-body healing. Many recent investigations in mind/body connections seem partially to involve chaos-complexity theory. Because what is being studied is so complex and at the edge of chaos, the classical science of linear processes no longer fit and have run out of answers.

Fascinating, to me, are the changing views of astronomers as they wrestle with two of the great enduring questions: What is our place in the universe? Are we alone? And chaos-complexity may provide another model to aid us in these questions.

> The real voyage of discovery
> consists not in seeking new landscapes,
> but in having new eyes. (Marcel Proust)

If we look at the universe through mental telescopes constructed on the premises of classical science, as we have discussed, then we must view life elsewhere in the universe as being impossible. This view would maintain that life is purely an aberration and has occurred totally by chance. This all is a very highly debatable point, nevertheless intriguing. Darwinian biology is blind and evolution is a kind of random process that simply happened by chance. These telescopes also reflect the assumption that the universe is increasing in entropy.

If our telescopes should become ones of chaos-complexity (dynamical-emergent systems), we view a different universe, one that is evolving toward higher more harmonious and developed systems (syntropy). It was, after all, Szent-Gyoergyi (1974) who stressed the difference between the animate and inanimate world.

> You know well that if you use your car too much and your legs too little, your car gets worn out while your legs atrophy, just fade away. This is one of the most characteristic differences between the living and non-living. The non-living is worn out by use, while the living is improved, developed by it. Life keeps life going, building up and improving itself, while inactivity makes it go to pieces. (p. 17)

Each path becomes a major mental construct and which path or combination you choose will make a profound difference.

In the 1950s and 1960s the now classic debates between C. R. Rogers and B.F. Skinner (1948) took place. Unbeknownst to many of us in graduate school in those days perhaps we were actually witnessing an historical event, the debates between the nonlinear actualization view of Rogers vs. the linear and classical behaviorism of Skinner.

It is interesting to notice how psychology has been slowly moving toward chaos-complexity and quantum theories. No longer do we, necessarily, view the human condition in terms of linear cause and effect best understood by the reduction to the reflex arc. Chaos-complexity portrays a backdrop against which each individual can be viewed as unique, where each individual can be said to be a *complex adaptive system tending toward self-actualization,* '... we are, after all, complex adaptive systems ourselves' (Gell-Mann, 1994, p. 89). The theory helps explain the surprise, the unpredictability, and the spontaneity that so often occur in counseling and human behavior. The essential uniqueness of the human being, a critical assumption of Hypnocounseling, becomes clearer when viewed through the lens of chaos theory: an interesting parallel.

Chaos exists more as an oxymoron than a paradox. For between ordered determinism, on the one hand, and randomness on the other, lies a space of complexity where our world plays itself out. Thus, complexity allows for expression of utter uniqueness, yet orderly enough to make choices in which consequences inhere (Dupré, 1993; Stewart and Golubitsky, 1992).

QUANTUM CHAOS: A FOOTNOTE

A footnote here suggests that a few physicists today talk of a concept they label, quantum chaos. Others agree that the concept is almost impossible to define and may not even exist. Joseph Ford (Pool, 1989), physicist at Georgia Tech, however, claims that quantum chaos challenges our beliefs as to how the world works and senses a paradigm revolution in the works: 'If chaos does exist on the quantum level, it raises confusing questions about the meaning of quantum mechanics; if it does not the result could be even more profound' (p. 893).

Researchers are presently exploring the border between Newtonian physics and quantum physics. This border country is where Newtonian mechanics meets the fuzziness of the quantum world. It had been assumed that chaos emerged from classical physics and could not be a part of quantum mechanics (Brown, 1996; Pool, 1989).

> Chaos in classical physics is often represented by systems of weather, population, and yet the standard example seems to be the orbit of Pluto. Orbits in our solar system are generally regular and predictable, Pluto's orbit is complicated and impossible to predict because it is gravitationally kicked by other planets as it circles the sun. This results in an orbit so sensitive to deviations that a change in just ten feet in its position could completely change its location

in the next several thousand years. (Pool, 1989)

It appears that as chaos moves closer to the quantum world, quantum mechanics and Heisenberg's uncertainty principle work somehow together to superimpose their own order on chaos — so many mysteries so many questions. Because of this, a growing number of physicists are still uncomfortable with quantum mechanics. Freedman (1991) quotes Georgia Tech physicist Joseph Ford as saying, 'It's clear to me and a growing number of physicists that something is wrong with quantum mechanics, but coming out and attacking it directly puts you on the lunatic fringe' (p. 626).

I include all of this because it seems to be evidence for a kind of synergy at work and also demonstrates the continual questioning and experimenting with every aspect of science and not taking it as fixed truth until all criteria have been met — the process of science exhibits the process of change.

QUANTUM MECHANICS
AKA QM; AKA QUANTUM THEORY; AKA THE COPENHAGEN INTERPRETATION; AKA THE NEWER PHYSICS

> *... I am not unlike some of the more advanced thinkers in physics and chemistry. As they push their theories further, picturing a 'reality' which has no solidarity, which is no more than oscillations of energy, they too begin to talk in terms of the transcendent, the indescribable, the unexpected — the sort of phenomena we have absorbed in the person-centered approach.*
> Carl Rogers

> *Anyone who is not shocked by quantum theory has not understood it.*
> Niels Bohr

At the turn of the century classical physics or classical mechanics (Newtonian physics) had begun to be poked and tickled by scientists who dared to question the basic concept. In 1905, a patent clerk in Zurich named Einstein published a new theory of space and time — the special theory of relativity and followed by 'the general theory of relativity, an intellectual achievement which surpassed by far the special theory of relativity' (Stapp, 1993, p. 16). Only relative motion could be of interest to science since there was no way of observing *absolute* motion in space. The repercussions were shocking. For the rest of us, including scientists, the idea of questioning absolute objectivity in measurement was heresy. By the time Einstein's next two papers were published, there was no stopping an emerging 'newer' physics (Gribbin, 1984; Herbert, 1987; Zukav, 1979).

Physicists began to sense that the heart and soul of science was changing. The erosion of linear continuity and precise predictability caused a wide chasm. The exact laws of classical physics were suddenly being challenged and replaced by a gathering of statistical laws of probability. The classical explanation of particles as materials being pushed and pulled in predictable ways in space and time changed with quantum theory — now particles behaved in sudden and unpredictable jumps. This appeared to violate the laws of causality. It seemed as if nature moved in a new and confusing capriciousness.

We are living in a world which screams out at us, 'nothing is real unless it is observed.' Here with the advent of new possibilities in statistics, probability serves as our guide. We speak in terms of probable realities. In the meantime while the Copenhagen theorists in Quantum Mechanics (Bohr and Heisenberg) were postulating 'no underlying reality' to the world, Einstein and many of his colleagues emphatically disagreed.

Bohr and Heinsenberg's 'no underlying reality' shocked physicists, and consternation still exists in many forms. Even Einstein, whose mathematical and scientific genius helped develop many of the foundations of quantum mechanics, still could not believe its implications: 'God does not play dice' (Hawking, 1993). Einstein could not agree with the 'quantum purists' (Bohr, Heisenberg, *et al.*) who believed in a world of outcomes as a result of random 'choices' of possibilities at the quantum level. Quantum mechanics makes it difficult for you and me to make sense of 'physical reality' or lack of it, which quantum theory seems to impose on our world (Capra, 1975; Chachere, 1969; Gilmore, 1995; Kuhn, 1970; Martin, 1981; Penrose, 1989, 1994; Stapp, 1993).

As we would expect with science, when fundamental new discoveries and constructions are made, constructions as profound as quantum mechanics, constructions that tear at the very core of a cherished theory, there begins a tug-of-war between the upstarts and the older generation. This natural process Kuhn called a 'crisis.' Crisis is a term used to describe the times and events that follow an emerging paradigm shift — a 'crisis' in perception within a community: '. . . though the world does not change with a change of paradigm, the scientist works in a different world' (Kuhn, 1970, p. 121). As Kuhn describes a world that 'does not change with a change of paradigms,' he inserts his belief right into the middle of the Bohr-Einstein debate. Kuhn assumes there is a deep reality 'out there' as did Einstein.

No one set out to prove or discover quantum mechanics. It developed as a natural outcome of more sophisticated mathematics, inventions of new and extraordinary measuring, recording, and laboratory systems and equipment. Yet the birth of quantum mechanics was due primarily to the creative geniuses who learned how to experiment, revise, and create a very different questioning process. As Heisenberg (1958) put it, 'What we observe is not nature itself, but nature exposed to our method of questioning' (p. 58). I find this summary quote from Wheeler (1994) clear and impelling:

> In broader terms, we find that nature at the quantum level is not a machine that goes its inexorable way. Instead, what answer we get depends on the question we ask, the experiment we arrange, the registering device we choose. We are inescapably involved in bringing about that which appears to be happening. (p. 120)

Wheeler saw the involvement of the observer as a major issue in quantum theory. Capra (1975) commented on Wheeler's use of the word 'participator,' recommending that we use this term rather than 'observer.' We are continually 'participating' in a participatory quantum world of which we are at the center (p. 141).

Martin (1981) tries to assure us that quantum mechanics is not complicated, that our problem is its being so unfamiliar. Quantum mechanics simply does not fit our everyday experience of the world. Yet, even today physicists still squirm when they fully realize the exponential implications of quantum physics:

> The science behind atoms, photons, electrons, and other subatomic particles — particles that jump from point to point, occupy several positions at once and, on top of all this, seem to communicate faster than the speed of light. (Yam, 1997, p. 124)

The word 'quantum' is derived from the Latin 'quantus' which means quantity (or bits and pieces of energy, for example) and mechanics means motion. Simply put, quantum mechanics translates into the study of the motion of quantities (Zukav, 1979).

Sometimes our dichotomous thinking (from classical physics — right/wrong; either/or) can get in the way by assuming that quantum mechanics does away with Newton's classical mechanics. If quantum theory is correct then classical physics must be wrong. However, this is incorrect. Quantum mechanics does not replace Newtonian physics, but rather includes it (both-and). Bohr and others learned that as classical physics served well the macroscopic world it 'ran out of steam' in the atomic and subatomic world. At each level of nature a 'different' physics prevailed.

Alfred Romer (1960), Emeritus Professor of Physics at St. Lawrence University, reminds us that classical physics is not dead. In his own words he reminded me that the 'laws of classical physics got the astronauts to the moon and brought them back, even the Apollo 13 crew who lost their main power on the way out.' It may seem too easy to dichotomize, however, it's crucial to remember that classical physics and quantum physics lie on a continuum (not either/or) as a way of thinking about the macro-micro world.

Werner Heisenberg was struck by certain insights which were to become crucial in the development of quantum mechanics. He rushed to Niels Bohr in Copenhagen, Denmark. Bohr became fascinated and in intense and lengthy discussions they formulated what most physicists describe today as the 'Copenhagen interpretation' of quantum theory. As a result of their thinking and discussions each began to formulate two principles which had risen to the top like cream: Bohr's principle of complementarity and Heisenberg's uncertainty principle (Cline, 1965; Gribbin, 1984; Herbert, 1987; Jeans, 1945).

The Copenhagen interpretation held steady for a number of years, yet theoretical physicists of many stripes, began to pick at it (Buckley and Peat, 1996). Stapp (1993) pointed out major criticisms of QM. He argued that there are many published articles each differently attempting to define the Copenhagen interpretation. 'The striking thing about these articles is the *diversity* they reveal in prevailing conceptions of the Copenhagen interpretation itself' (p. 49). Because of lingering technical and philosophical issues many physicists today are attempting clarifications and inventions and adding other interpretations. Lest we forget, the equations and predictions of Quantum Mechanics are not being challenged, only the way we talk about them and deliberate upon their meanings. As is the unstated rule of science, nothing is fixed in stone.

THE PRINCIPLE OF COMPLEMENTARITY

Perhaps no two concepts can have had more of a potential metaphorical impact on counseling, therapy, and psychology in general than Bohr's complementarity principle and Heisenberg's indeterminacy or uncertainty principle.

A caution deserves notice here. When we borrow a specific process or construct from one field (physics) and try to affix it to another (psychology) we can and do run the risk of inaccurate and illogical results. We shall see an attempt to borrow from Bohr (complementarity) and Heisenberg (indeterminacy) using their principles tentatively to explain certain conditions of human behavior and perception, only this time the results seem to be heuristic rather than illogical or inaccurate.

It was Einstein's position as early as 1909 that physics must begin to construct a theory of light which would fuse wave and emission theories. Interestingly, at that point, Einstein was already hinting at the puzzle of 'complementarity' so crucial to Bohr and quantum theory yet, at the time, he (Einstein) was unaware of the implications of his suggestion (Gribbin, 1984).

Complementarity as a principle originally was an attempt to solve the problems of wave-particle duality which had bothered the quantum theorists in the mid-twenties (Murdoch, 1987). It still seems to hold as the better explanation. Waves and particles are mutually exclusive and complementary aspects of light. In observing waves we destroy the particle nature and vice versa, both are necessary to understand light. Bohr answered the question, 'What are electrons?' by suggesting that they were neither particles nor waves; the parts of atoms cannot be described completely as being either particle-like or wave-like, but rather sometimes appearing as particles and at other times experienced as wave-like (Capra, 1975; Hawking, 1993; Teller, 1969; Zukav, 1979).

> The difference between waves and particles are profound. A particle is *local*, it is a little *lump* which moves bodily from one place to another. A wave is spread out in space. It is formed by back and forth motions across some *medium* like air or water. The wave moves when this back-and-forthing shifts, but the medium itself stays in the same place. In quantum mechanics, the energy of a particle depends on the frequency of its wave, and the wave length of a wave depends on the momentum of its particle... In the wave particle duality of photons and electrons it is not a question of *either/or* but rather of *both-and*. (Alfred Romer, Professor Emeritus of Physics, St. Lawrence University, personal correspondence)

Teller (1969) describes Niels Bohr as having an almost obsessive fascination with puzzles particularly contradictions and paradoxes.

> The idea of complementarity is that in order to describe a situation you have to use (at least on certain occasions) two mutually exclusive approaches. If you omit either, the description is incomplete. (p. 83)

The principle of complementarity fascinates me because it breaks the back of dichotomous and 'one right way' thinking. I hold the principle of complementarity to be at the heart of the *eclectic* stance in Hypnocounseling:

> Complementarity says that nature is too subtle to be described from any *single point of view*. To obtain an adequate description, you have to look at things from several points of view, even though the different viewpoints are incompatible and cannot be viewed simultaneously. Statements that are true when seen from one point of view may be false when seen from another. There is no logical contradiction here, because the behavior of the object you are observing changes as you change your point of view. (Dyson, 1992, p. 188)

I think *complementarity* can serve as an excellent metaphor.

A metaphor provides an open-ended opportunity to stretch resolutions and answers, especially when we are confronted with an unfamiliar, perplexing problem, a problem never encountered before. Complementarity as metaphor assists us not only in the physical world, but also in the theological, philosophical and psychotherapeutic worlds, as well as in our everyday lives.

The idea of complementarity is neither new, nor that unusual. For example to say that I am an organism (matter) that follows the physical laws of nature is incomplete; for I am more than just matter I am (both-and) my introspective, subjective self as well as feelings, thoughts, intuition, intentions, etc.

> Bohr's very natural statement would be that the description of a person will be incomplete — ridiculously incomplete — unless he is described as both the thing he appears to be from the outside, which is subject to laws of physics, and as the entity he appears to be from the inside, which might conceivably be subject to laws of psychology, if any. (Teller, 1969, p. 84)

Bohr believed complementarity was not confined to the atomic microscopic world, but also could be applied to the mind/body dichotomy. Complementarity could also be found in biological and psychological synergy. Yet, Bohr found something even more important. He discovered that going beyond linear and dichotomous thinking and founding one's thoughts on mutually exclusive concepts has turned out to be grounded in a mathematical base.

> We need not regard the simultaneous consideration of two mutually exclusive concepts as mysticism because at least in one case, that of the theory of atoms, complementarity and mathematical rigor coexist. (Teller, 1969, p. 93)

Bohr perceived classical and quantum physics as coming together. He called this the correspondence principle. He believed that one day there would be a new physics broad enough to contain the old within its scope. Classical physics certainly would continue to hold where it had been in the past; the future would reveal it as part of a larger theory.

Bohr was knighted by the Danish government in appreciation of his monumental accomplishments. In creating his coat of arms (a requirement for knighthood) he chose as the central motif the Chinese symbol of opposites — *yin* and *yang*. Bohr was well aware of the connection of complementarity with Chinese thought, having visited China and studied Eastern culture. Bohr in choosing the Latin inscription, '*"Contraria sunt complementa"* (opposites are complementary) . . . acknowledged the profound harmony between ancient Eastern wisdom and modern Western science' (Capra, 1975, p. 160).

THE UNCERTAINTY PRINCIPLE

Conventional observation which is so much a part of classical physics becomes increasingly impossible as we approach the quantum world. The electron within the atom cannot be directly observed. The early Wilson cloud chamber allowed us to 'see' indirectly an electron only by the trail that it left as it passed through the molecules of gas much as we see a jet's condensation trails high in the sky, but we don't see the jet itself (Jeans, 1945). Nevertheless, this counts as an observation.

Perception and observation became a major focus in quantum mechanics. In classical physics we assume the universe can be divided into distinct parts: a perceiving subject and a perceived object. Einstein's theory of relativity first began the breakdown of this division when it appeared that an observer constructs a picture of the world that appears *local*, that is, perceivable by any other observer, but in the exact same spot. From any other spot, however, there are infinite other perceptions. It was Bohr who pointed out that in classical physics we imagine a system of interacting particles to function perfectly whether or not the system is observed. In quantum mechanics the observer interacts with the system in such a way that the 'observed' system cannot be thought of as having an independent existence (Gribbin, 1984; Herbert, 1987).

Werner Heisenberg (1971) often talked with fondness of the walks and cross-country ski trips he took with Niels Bohr. On one such excursion they discussed the phenomena of observation; its uncertainty and subjectivity (thus the birth of the uncertainty principle). This very same stroll took them to Kronborg Castle. Bohr went on to comment how as scientists they viewed the architecture, the stones and green patina of the roof, as well as the wood carvings and beauty found in the chapel and yet how strange that as soon as they learned that Shakespeare's Hamlet lived there:

> Suddenly the walls and the ramparts speak a quite different language. The courtyard becomes an entire world, a dark corner reminds us of the darkness in the human soul, we hear Hamlet's 'to be or not to be.' Yet all we know about Hamlet is that his name appears in a thirteenth-century chronicle. No one can prove that he really lived, let alone that he lived here. But everyone knows the questions Shakespeare had him ask, the human despair he was made to reveal, and so, he, too, had to be found a place on earth, here in Kronborg. And once we know that, Kronborg becomes quite a different castle for us. (p. 51)

Classical science convinced us of the potential for accuracy of measurement involved in absolute objectivity and because of the invasion of quantum theories we slowly have had to shift away from this premise.

Heisenberg (1971) wrote of how he stumbled upon the insight that would lead him to the uncertainty principle. He recalled a statement by Einstein in conversation, 'It is the theory which decides what we can observe' (p. 77). This statement jarred his thinking to the point that he began to realize they were all seeking something that their theories told them was there — but what if they weren't? Subsequently, he began to design mathematically experimental situations. Again, changing the question made an immense difference:

> The right question should therefore be: Can quantum mechanics represent the fact that an electron finds itself *approximately* in a given place and that it moves *approximately* with a given velocity, and can we make these *approximations* so close that they do not cause experimental difficulties? [Italics added] (p. 78)

Not only was the realization that changing the question made all the difference important, but also the tightening up and more careful use of language was critical.

We rely on language for our primary means of communication. Language evolved through our interactions with ourselves and society as well as in our descriptive language of the natural world we live in. Bohr reminds us that our language is effectively and efficiently matched with our large-scale world and that pitfalls and errors must abound as we try to fit that descriptive language to the microworld of quantum particles (Buckley and Peat, 1996, p. 192). For example, when we begin to ask questions we run into traps, 'Does the *electron really* have a *path* when we are *observing* it? What do we mean by *electron, really, path, observing*?'

The end point of the measuring process ultimately stops in the consciousness and the language of the observer and science is the interaction between the world 'out there' and ourselves.

Probably the physicist could or would agree however, to the psychologist, this seems to be an appropriate premise and a stepping stone from one science to another.

Heisenberg's struggle with the uncertainty principle came through his wrestling with the *momentum* and *position* of particles. When observing a particle he found he could not measure both momentum and position simultaneously with any accuracy (Capra, 1975; Cline, 1965; Hawking, 1993).

> . . . it is not possible to measure both the position and the momentum of a particle accurately at the same time . . . If the position were measured to *infinite* precision, then the momentum would become *completely* uncertain; on the other hand, if the momentum is measured exactly, then the particle's location becomes completely uncertain. (Penrose, 1989, p. 248)

As Cassidy (1992) acknowledged, 'and this reciprocal relationship between uncertainties in measurement also holds for other conjugate pairs of variables, such as energy and time. This, in a few words, is Heisenberg's uncertainty principle' (p. 228).

In the uncertainty principle, Heisenberg had to accept a rough and imprecise measure of both quantities. This uncertainty was not due to the observer or to the apparatus but rather the inherent limitation found in the subatomic world. In addition, quantum physicists were quick to learn that they could no longer play the role of the objective, detached observers, but rather had to become involved in the phenomena observed and, thus, could not help affect the observed objects. Objectivity and absolutes faded.

Interestingly, the physicist Wheeler recommended using the word 'participator' rather than the word, 'observer.' We are continually 'participating' in the quantum world in which we are at the center (Capra, 1975). Here we can see the emphasis placed on 'phenomenology' by Hypnocounseling.

Bohr and Einstein had their differences over the interpretation and the implications of quantum mechanics and each represented a position that has carried down to the present time.

Einstein turned to quantum mechanics after he had finished his masterful work on the General Theory of Relativity. He aided the exploration of quanta by devising 'devil's-advocacy' questions which helped Bohr, Heisenberg, and their associates sharpen and clarify quantum theory. However, Einstein became more and more despairing because he felt quantum mechanics was incomplete. As the realist he was (and remember realists believe that there is a 'real' world), Einstein argued that a theory must correspond to the phenomena that exist. All of this showed Einstein's deep belief in a 'deep reality' in nature. It was as if we could eventually find true reality if we could develop the appropriate theory. In many ways Einstein still felt closer to classical physics than to this newer physics (his General Theory of Relativity is still a part of classical physics in that it does not challenge determinism).

Bohr, an experimentalist or pragmatist, believed that physical theory must be based on experiments and measurable quantities. Ehrenfest, a friend of Einstein, believed that Einstein ignored his own rule, 'physics must be built on measurable relationships and not on preconceived notions' (Cline, 1965, p. 238). Still, Einstein held to determinism and a deep reality out there to be discovered. His search through physics was for something outside and independent of himself, 'an underlying pattern in the universe, a pattern he called "God"' (Cline, 1965, p. 141).

On the other hand, Stapp (1993) describes an interaction Heisenberg had with Einstein. 'Heisenberg... pointed out that he was merely following the philosophy that Einstein himself had used. To this Einstein replied: "Perhaps I did use such a philosophy earlier, and even wrote it, but it is nonsense all the same"'.

Heisenberg was 'astonished': Einstein had reversed himself on the idea with which he had revolutionized physics!' (p. 15).

The questions still remain. Will the new ideas and explanations eliminate quanta and describe the thing in itself (deep reality) as Einstein believed? Not likely, since these hidden variable theories, especially of Einstein, have been challenged by experiment and Bell's theorem. Or will the new theory leave indeterminacy and the uncertainty and complementarity principles essentially unchanged (Cline, 1965)? Or, more likely, will there be a synergizing (complementary) effect among the different positions?

Whenever crises in science occur, usually there appears to be a serious correction and challenge of the old order (Kuhn, 1970). In quantum mechanics and theory this certainly is true. In fact, while most physicists today acknowledge quantum theory in one form or another there still exists a multiplicity of interpretations which, however, all give the same results experimentally. As in counseling and psychotherapy there are a myriad of approaches each with their own adherents.

Realists, such as Einstein and Hawking among others, believe there is a real world out there independent of our observation. From these assumptions and differences, physicists take off in many directions. The acceptance of these differences naturally leads to greater increase in knowledge and the continued pursuit of truth — the goal of science.

> Some physicists would prefer to come back to the idea of an objective real world whose smallest parts exist objectively in the same sense as stones or trees exist independently of whether we observe them. This, however, is impossible. (Werner Heisenberg)

As we have noted, when psychology moved toward becoming a science, breaking away from philosophy, it borrowed heavily from classical physics with its assumptions of reductionism and determinism. Hypnocounseling and other holistic-humanistic psychologies were found to be strange bedfellows in classical psychology.

For example, classical psychology mirrored the reductionism of classical physics by reducing human functioning to a basic part, the stimulus response arc. Hypnocounseling views the human, not as a collection of stimulus-response arcs, but rather as an holistic and integrated organism.

Quantum mechanics teaches us again and again that matter and the basic phenomena pertaining to it are all interrelated and interconnected: a physical Gestalt of subatomic particles cannot be understood by *reduction* to isolated entities — it only can be understood as integrated parts of the whole.

> Quantum theory forces us to see the universe not as a collection of physical objects but rather as a complicated web of relations between the various parts of a unified whole. (Capra, 1975, p. 138)

> The world thus appears as a complicated tissue of events, in which connections of various kinds alternate or overlap or combine and thereby determine the textures of the whole. (Heisenberg, 1958, p. 107)

Rigor and exactitude in language have always been a proper and realistic concern for physicists and other scientists. Richard Feynman, one of the best and best known teachers of quantum mechanics, argued that he abhorred the fuzzy buzzword, *holistic*, yet he felt there was no word more appropriate to describe the quantum world. 'It is *holistic*; the parts are in some sense in touch with the whole' (Gribbin, 1984, p. 172).

To me, there are several critical assumptions in quantum theory which speak to Hypnocounseling and other similar approaches; yet few are more crucial than the concept of *holistic* when referring to the human organism.

CHOICE — FREE WILL

Another cherished assumption of Hypnocounseling is that the human has choice. So rooted in determinism is Newton's classical physics that the door to human choice is permanently double locked. The newer quantum physics, while not supporting choice directly, at least throws out a hope that the door might be unlocked if we could find the door knob (Jeans, 1945).

In *The Emperor's New Mind*, Roger Penrose (1989) states that the questions of free will or choice 'hovers at the background, throughout this book — though for most of what I shall have to say, it will remain only in the background' (p. 169). In both of his books Penrose (1989, 1994) struggled with the issue of consciousness and its place in quantum mechanics since it is a meaningless term in classical physics. For Penrose (1994), consciousness involves the implications of 'intelligence,' that presumes 'understanding' and 'understanding' that requires 'awareness.' 'Awareness I take to be one aspect of the phenomenon of consciousness. Consciousness has an active aspect also, namely the feeling of *free will*' (p. 39). Awareness, then, seems to be a prerequisite for choice.

The concept of consciousness appears invaluable here as we try to find some place for existence of choice or free will. Consciousness appears to be the most important feature of mental phenomena and that my writing these words and your reading them are prime examples of our consciousness at work (Searle, 1984). When Searle writes, 'consciousness, for example, is a real property of the brain that can cause things to happen' (p. 26), he implies a choosing or acting component in consciousness.

In addition, the pursuit of the concept and definition of consciousness elicits the age-old (Cartesian) mind/body problem (a problem to which 'complementarity' can bring closure).

Penrose (1994) unequivocally writes that 'a scientific world-view which does not profoundly come to terms with the problem of conscious minds can have no serious pretensions of completeness' (p. 8). Consciousness is part of our universe. Any physical theory of nature that does not include it is not providing an honest description of the world (Penrose, 1994). It follows, then, if consciousness is part of the natural world then it must be part of a quantum theory that up to this time is yet unknown to physics. This physics is the missing theory that plays in that zone that straddles the quantum and classical levels.

According to Freedman (1994), Penrose proposes that consciousness is created by a mysterious new quantum mechanical phenomenon that takes place in a newly discovered cellular structure called a microtubule which makes an exceptionally good conductor of physical vibrations (sound waves). These bundles of microtubules serve as complex organizers of cell behavior and also serve as highly efficient communication networks, marvelously efficient at carrying signals. For example, an electron microscopic photograph of a microelectronic switch of a computer chip was found to be amazingly similar to a microtubule. Complex and powerful, microtubules exist as networks in a single brain cell and may be a plausible site for the roots of consciousness at the quantum level.

Still there exists no evidence for free will or choice although some physicists argue that if it's to be found it will be found in a newer quantum physics modeled upon a new conception of mind (Freedman, 1994; Gilmore, 1995; Jeans, 1945; Penrose, 1989, 1994).

Remember that Hypnocounseling views freedom/choice in at least two ways. First we act 'as if' we had choice. In a sense, this is what Jeans (1945) called *unconscious determinism*, '. . . we so act that we are not conscious of being determined to a particular action by any external force' (p. 214). Second, we can view freedom/choice and determinism in a complementary fashion. Here, we use our consciousness to gain understanding of the issue as well as the awareness of determinism. By awareness of determinism I mean that we can be aware of causes and their effects (consequences); that is, we can predict the probable consequences of the options (causes) we choose. Interestingly, from all of this, we could operationally define freedom/choice. Individuals become 'free' to the extent that they can identify options (potential causes), choose among those options and then act on them (consequences or effects). If we can more accurately predict consequences, we have used determinism in a complementary way to enhance our freedom (see discussion of freedom and choice, Chapter 2). And we have applied the pragmatic test to the best option or choice.

Stephen Hawking (1993), fellow physicist, writing-collaborator, and colleague of Roger Penrose, follows upon some of Penrose's thoughts on consciousness. In a finely tuned essay, 'Is Everything Determined?', Hawking makes some interesting arguments that indirectly challenge determinism and suggest the possibility of free choice.

If everything we do is determined by some Grand Unified Theory (GUT) — Hawking (1993) believes this may be achieved in the next 20 years — then this raises major difficulties. The GUT presumably is simple, elegant, and special about the theory of everything. Yet, how can the certain number of equations in the grand and unified theory account for the complexity and mass of trivia we see in our everyday lives? Can this grand theory predict the moment in which I got up this morning, the moment and place I swatted a kitchen fly or even the moment Stephen Hawking contracted motor neurone disease (Lou Gehrig's disease)?

> A second problem with the idea that everything is determined by a grand unified theory is that anything we say is also determined by the theory. But why should it be determined to be correct? Isn't it more likely to be wrong, because there are many possible incorrect statements for every true one? . . . Yet presumably the grand unified theory has determined that we are correct. (Hawking, 1993, p. 129)

Hawking attributes a lot of his uncertainty to Heisenberg's Uncertainty

Principle of Quantum Mechanics and so his 'determinism' seems weaker and more remote leaving lots of room for chance (or could it be human choice?).

Hawking (1993) believes in the 'necessity' for choice:
> The ultimate objective test of free will would seem to be: Can we predict the behavior of the organism? If one can, then it clearly doesn't have free will but is predetermined. On the other hand, if one cannot predict the behavior, one could take that as an operational definition that the organism has free will. (pp. 132–3)

In our case, we cannot use any unified theory to predict what we will do. First, we cannot solve the equations for the massive number of particles involved. Second, and even if we could arrive at solutions, making a prediction would disturb the system and could lead to different outcomes.

To add to the difficulty of the problem Hawking (1993) reminds us that the human brain is also affected by the uncertainty principle accounting for the randomness and unpredictability associated with quantum mechanics in human behavior. 'The real reason we cannot predict human behavior is that it is just too difficult . . . The human brain contains about 10^{26} or a hundred million billion billion particles' (p. 133). We cannot base our conduct on the idea that everything is determined because we do not know what has been determined. 'Instead, one has to adopt the effective theory that one has free will and that one is responsible for one's actions' (p. 134). In addition we can turn to Darwinian thinking to bolster our belief in free will. Societies in which individuals feel that they have free choice and are responsible for the consequences of their actions are more likely to work together and survive to change and spread their values. Even though ants live and work successfully in static societies they cannot respond to unfamiliar challenges or create new opportunities and change.

> So as we cannot predict human behavior, we may as well adopt the effective theory that humans are free agents who can choose what to do. It seems that there are definite survival advantages to believing in free will and responsibility for one's actions. That means this belief should be reinforced by natural selection. (Hawking, 1993, p. 138)

To me, it seems critical to conclude this section with a summary of the work and directions taken by another leading quantum physicist, Henry Stapp.

I had written this chapter several times, and yet just prior to submitting it to my publisher, Henry Stapp's (1993) *Mind, Matter, and Quantum Mechanics* arrived in my library. It was quickly apparent that here was the set of combinations for which I had been looking. To me, Stapp's ideas fleshed out my original hunches in exciting and heuristic ways. Stapp draws upon a synergy or a coupling of Heisenberg's quantum mechanics with William James's psychology, a psychology that strongly refuted the behaviorism of the time and a way of thinking that included the basic assumption that later became identified as humanistic psychology. Stapp (1993) suggested that the model of physics 'proposed by Heisenberg is, in my opinion, the best. Coupled to James's conception of mind (the H/J model) produces a model of the mind-matter universe that realizes, within contemporary physical theory, the idea that brain processes are causally influenced by subjective conscious experience' (p. 4).

Many scientists and philosophers have suggested a link between consciousness and quantum theory. Henry Stapp for example, has made, in my view, a direct attempt to link the Copenhagen interpretation (especially W. Heisenberg's view) with the phenomenological-humanistic themes of the nineteenth century philosopher-psychologist, William James. Stapp (1993) asks the tough question, 'How are one's conscious processes related to brain processes? (p. vii)' And using the Heisenberg/James (H/J) model Stapp points out the parallel and complementary relationship between the two scientists' approaches.

James apparently foresaw the difficulties of the mind/brain problem when viewed only from the standpoint of classical physics. He explained that we must:

> understand how great is the darkness in which we grope, and never forget that the natural science assumptions with which we started are provisional and reversible things. (James, 1893, p. 468)

The compatibility of James with Heisenberg's quantum theory is made clearer when we know more about James's psychology. James' conception of mind 'is the science of mental life including such things as "feelings, desires, cognitions, reasonings, decisions" and the like' (Stapp, 1993, p. 9). It is a psychology built on phenomenology, choice, and holism (ingredients of Humanistic psychology and Hypnocounseling in particular). James clearly built his conception of mind and consciousness on a *phenomenological* approach in which '. . . consciousness is at all times a *selecting agency*' (Stapp, 1993, p. 11). This 'selecting agency' is present when *choices* must be made and this . . . 'is understandable if consciousness plays a role in making, or actualizing, these *selections*' (Stapp, 1993, p. 11). Thus the *selecting agency* is inextricably joined with choice and free will.

The following statement could be read as a total repudiation by William James of B. F. Skinner's famous declaration that 'free will is an illusion.'

> Man's free will is no illusion. It constitutes his essence. And it rests upon the law of necessity. Any play of chance would falsify the idea that I, from the ground of my essential nature, make a true choice. (Stapp, 1993, p. 91)

James continued with his assumptions when he described 'holism' as the principal claim at the fundamental level of consciousness. Stapp argues that in his *Principles of Psychology*, James declares his central thesis:

that each conscious thought is essentially a complex whole: each thought has components which can be examined by subsequent analysis, but, *as given* is a unified whole that cannot be reduced to a collection of parts without destroying its essence. (Stapp, 1993, p. 178)

Some have called William James the father of modern psychology and humanistic psychology, and, for our purposes, Hypnocounseling.

James noticed the absence of choice, the rampant determinism, the closed system, the avoidance of constructs such as holism, conscious thoughts and the importance of personal experience. All of which were represented by the classical physics of his day. Above all, arguing against these assumptions of Newton's world view, James was first and foremost a pragmatist. Ideas came to be called 'true' if they corresponded with the original source. A picture was said to be real (true) to the degree it fit the subject.

James argued that this seemed backward. An idea is true when the consequences predicted are verified in experience. The importance of experience and consciousness are equally as crucial in quantum theory. James described putting ideas to work as the pragmatic test. Instead of looking for first causes, principles, categories he looked for results, consequences, the end product, facts. An idea was said to be true, in other words, when the consequences were those the idea led us to expect. Quantum theory has often been described as pragmatic, as well.

The H/J model provides a set of crucial assumptions about the nature of the world, the nature of science, and the nature of the human mind. Let us tease out some of these assumptions of the H/J formula:

1. The concept of choice/free will might be a part of the new physics ('holism').
2. The realization that there is no place for pure objectivity, that the person necessary for observing affects that which is being measured (complementarity and indeterminacy).
3. We create our solutions which do not lie out there, but rather create them in our brain/mind (phenomenology/constructionism).
4. We can view truth now as being that which 'works' and has consequences (pragmatism).
5. We live in a world of indeterminacy and conscious experience (tentativeness of science).
6. Our parts are holistic. We are Gestalt-like where the whole is greater than its parts.

On the first page of this Chapter 3, I quoted from Oppenheimer (1965):
> It seems to me that the worst of all possible misunderstanding would be that psychology be influenced to model itself after a physics which is not there anymore, which has been quite outdated. (p. 213)

We have explored this declaration from many points of view yet the more important questions should be what are the misunderstandings and what is an outdated physics? When psychology continues to follow the nature of mind and brain with the understanding that free choice is possible then we will add much to our lives.

And now the major caveat. These pages on the stories of physics were written to help you see the continual paths science takes in its inexorable search for 'truth.' All has been written not as 'truth,' but rather as the study of the speculation regarding the process of science. Science has been built upon hard work and continual change in development. As it has become a more open system, vagueness has had to enter. There is no truth in my scribbling only statements of possibilities. And you must be the judge of their accuracy. I hope you will read the metaphorical quote by Martin Seligman:

> Science in my view is an endless series of first downs, incomplete passes and off sides penalties. There are no touchdowns; and at best only halting progress.

Chapter 4
Hypnosis and Hypnocounseling

The fault, dear Brutus, is not in our stars, But in ourselves . . .
                                                William Shakespeare

When the psychiatrist approves of a person's actions, he judges that person to have acted with 'free choice'; when he disapproves, he judges him to have acted without 'free choice.' It is small wonder that people find 'free choice' a confusing idea: 'free choice' appears to refer to what the person being judged (often called the patient) DOES, whereas it is actually what the person making the judgement (often a psychiatrist or other mental health worker) THINKS.
                                                Thomas Szasz

HYPNOSIS

The history of hypnosis could be traced back into the mists of time to our earliest ancestors. We could find traces of hypnosis in the prehistoric rituals of healing and spirituality. Rather than pursue that early history (and I do find it fascinating), I choose to begin with Freud because of his adamant rejection of hypnosis.

Freud first bumped into hypnosis through his friend Joseph Breuer. Freud was, apparently, excited about the possibilities of hypnosis which were further stimulated by his studies with Charcot, Bernheim, and others. However, when Freud began to experiment with hypnosis he discovered he could hypnotize only a small percentage of patients. And he almost immediately terminated his interest in hypnosis. Cheek (1995) quotes Freud as saying, 'But I soon came to dislike hypnosis for it was a temperamental and, one might say, a mystical ally' (p. 213). And so this 'temperamental' and 'mystical ally' was quickly discarded. Freud summarizes his view of hypnosis in an autocratic and absolute sense: 'Hypnosis conceals the resistance and renders a certain area of the mind accessible but, as against this, it builds up resistance at the frontiers of this area into a wall that makes everything beyond inaccessible' (Cheek, 1995, p. 213).

This quote of Freud's 'reification' of hypnosis making it into a 'wall' leaves us wondering. What are the 'frontiers'? What 'wall'? What does he mean? We must remember the powerful, if not authoritarian, influence that Freud had on colleagues, protégés and the whole artistic-intellectual community. Furthermore, it is Cheek's (1995) belief that had Freud not renounced hypnosis, Adler, Jung, Ferenczi *et al.* would have been using hypnosis extensively and effectively. As it was, hypnosis lay fallow until people such as Cheek, Hilgard, Hull, Erickson, and others began reviewing the literature, designing research and experimenting with it. One of the leading people in this modern-day retrieval has been Milton Erickson.

There are countless myths regarding hypnosis such as the 'whammy eye,' 'devil magic,' myths such as loss of control, and the frightening dangers of hypnosis, as well as the belief that hypnosis is a magical force, or a healing sleep, etc. Some people still hold beliefs that seem to indicate hypnosis can cause harm because we can be made to behave in ways contrary to our overall values. However, as Erickson (1980c) stated:

> ... the hypnotic state is essentially a psychological phenomenon, unrelated to physiological sleep, and dependent entirely upon full cooperation between hypnotist and subject; neither is it injurious or detrimental to the subject in any way, nor can it be used for antisocial or criminal purposes. Each of these statements is based upon extensive, carefully controlled experimental investigations too numerous to cite ... (p. 14)

Invariably, some would question this by citing research studies that seemed to indicate that hypnotized subjects in a contrived experiment could be induced to perform harmful acts. Interestingly, Elizabeth M. Erickson (1962), wife of Milton H. Erickson, wrote a balanced and thoughtful rejoinder that put these findings in doubt. Too, Erickson (1980b) had a deep and profound respect for each person and the unconscious and emphatically stated:

> ... Any attempt to force upon hypnotic subjects, however deep the trance, suggestions unacceptable to their total personalities leads to a transformation of them so that they can then be satisfied by pretense behavior. (p. 146)

Some may object to the use of Ericksonian hypnosis and Hypnocounseling because they could be perceived as overly manipulative. With the many myths and misunderstandings surrounding the phenomenon of hypnosis, this conclusion may seem warranted. Erickson (1980i), however, through experimental procedures, struggled to demystify and clarify the process of hypnosis:

> Today there are still those who think of hypnosis as a healing sleep, a magical force, a kind of demoniacal power, as has been thought

for thousands of years. But what is hypnosis as we understand it scientifically today? It is not some special power of magic, nor is it some barbaric force arising from evil sources. It is, in simple terms, nothing more than a special state of conscious awareness . . . encountered when attention and the thinking processes are directed to the body of experiential learning acquired from, or achieved in, the experiences of living . . . Hypnosis cannot create new abilities within a person, but it can assist in a greater and better utilization of abilities already possessed. (p. 54)

It should be repeated that the myth of the hypnotist-hypnocounselor being in control of the client is just that, a myth (Erickson, 1980a). Erickson (1980j) in summarizing a number of experiments points out:

Instead of blind, submissive, automatic, unthinking obedience and acquiescence to the hypnotist . . . subjects demonstrated a full capacity and ability for self-protection [self-control] ready and complete understanding . . . In addition many demonstrated a full capacity to take over control of the hypnotic situation . . . (p. 529).

What is more, Erickson was well aware that a hypnotist's personality problems could stimulate hysterical behavior in the clients with whom he or she worked. In these cases ill effects were traceable to the personality of the hypnotist and not the hypnosis. (Lankton and Lankton, 1983, p. 132)

Hypnosis and Hypnocounseling are no more manipulative or damaging than any other form of counseling-therapy or 'normal' communication. Manipulation does not necessarily have to mean deviousness. In their preferred definition, Stein (1984) argues that most dictionaries allude to 'manipulation' as, '1. *skillful* or *artful* management' (p. 813). Even Rogers (1977) moved away from the term 'nondirective' as he became aware of the influential power inherent in the process of working with others.

It was Fritz Renick, one of my first mentors, who pointed out and then showed me that many suggestive and naturalistic hypnotic patterns of Erickson exist unrecognized in person-centered interchanges. Empathic responses, for example, have within them powerful hypnotic elements (Gunnison and Renick, 1985b).

Notice, if you will, this counselor's response, 'You must feel furious — sort of betrayed — because he said he'd be there for you and yet never showed up.' This response contains not only directive (manipulative?) but also highly suggestive aspects. It directs the person's consciousness on a portion of his/her emotional and cognitive experiences and then suggests what he/she might feel. The whole process of conveying PEGS (the elements of a therapeutic relationship) becomes one of indirect focusing and of suggestive elements which I must remember. My language with clients can be powerful and I must continually walk in their shoes, their experiencing, and the meanings they make. Consider this admonition from Erickson:

> So, I warn all of you, don't ever, when you are listening to a patient, think you understand the patient, because you're listening with *your* ears and thinking with *your* vocabulary. [Italics added] (Zeig, 1980, p. 58)

I wonder what you think about Erickson's quote, above? What does it mean to you? I wish I had written that — so simple yet so far reaching in its implications.

I speculate that, even in the most careful work of counselors and therapists, clients are directly or indirectly influenced in ways that may not be present in the conscious awareness of either party. Thus, it seems appropriate that we strive toward increasing awareness of indirect suggestion and hypnotic patterns and language that can lead us toward more effective and judicious utilization of the primary approaches with which we strongly identify. Lankton and Lankton (1983) explain:

> *We speculate that all effective therapies, hypnotic or otherwise, involve the same elements of indirect suggestion and hypnotic trance phenomena.* This psychological level of communication directs the framework of trance phenomena and ultimately the understanding and experiences conveyed. We expect that this situation is true with all or nearly all 'normal' communications. (p. 241)

More specifically, Wolberg (1955) states, '*Suggestion* plays a part in every psychotherapeutic relationship' (p. 21). The use of suggestion, a core of Hypnocounseling, seems to be prevalent in all counseling (Lankton, 1982). Suggestion also plays a part in the definition of hypnosis by the American Psychological Association's Division of Psychological Hypnosis (1993), which views hypnosis as a procedure wherein changes in sensations, perceptions, thoughts, feelings, or behavior are *suggested.*

Even empathy genuinely expressed in the relationship has within it powerful hypnotic elements of suggestion. Often, as the counselor and client sit in silence, indirect hypnotic elements may occur. How often have counselors observed clients silently changing with plans of action, decisions, and active insights? And in the same way, how many times have I intruded by interrupting that precious working silence only to lose a fragile connection with my client? How do we develop our patience? How do I expand my trust of the client so as to avoid these many-faceted interruptions?

Lankton and Lankton (1983) use an Ericksonian analysis of Rogers' work with the client Gloria in the now classic film *Three Approaches to Psychotherapy*. They argue that 'client-centered counseling' (technique), at first glance, seems to be almost the antithesis of hypnosis, yet the Lanktons make an intriguing case for many hidden hypnotic patterns. 'Client-centered therapy is generally thought to involve the therapist empathically reflecting the client's experience and demonstrating unconditional positive regard with congruence and genuineness' (Lankton and Lankton, 1983, p. 237). They contend that indirect hypnotic suggestion occurs when empathy and genuineness exist. Gloria demonstrated age regression, an hypnotic phenomenon, when she found herself talking to Rogers in ways she wished she could have talked to her father. Her comment, 'Gee, I'd like you for my father' elicited a genuine response from Rogers, 'You look to me like a pretty nice daughter' (Lankton and Lankton, 1983, p. 238). This congruent and empathic exchange (altered state) indirectly gave her permission to explore her feelings further. Gloria demonstrated an even deeper age regression when she switched from past tense to the present tense: 'But do you know what I *think I want* him to say?' (Lankton and Lankton, 1983, p. 239, italics added). If, in fact, hypnotic language and patterns inhere in counseling, then it behooves us to become aware of these phenomena and learn how best to utilize them. In fact, Atkinson (1983) and Ross (1981) have gone so far as to suggest that the phenomenon of hypnosis is such a critical aspect of interpersonal communication that it should be included in the formal training of counselors and therapists.

I believe that Hypnocounseling naturally exists whenever relaxation or fantasy-imagery is being utilized to augment a particular therapeutic strategy as in Systematic Desensitization (Wolpe, 1961), Fantasy Relaxation and Fantasy Door Approaches (Gunnison, 1976b, 1982), Rational Emotive Imagery (Ellis, 1979) as well as in decision-making procedures using fantasy and imagery (Gunnison, Shapiro and Bradley, 1982).

Notice the interesting form of Hypnocounseling that Cerio (1983) employed in using the Fantasy Relaxation Technique (Gunnison, 1976b). A student named Mike presented himself two weeks before finals. He was unable to take final exams, 'blocking out,' and showing debilitating anxiety and panic. 'Since panic seemed to be the primary block to better performance, Fantasy Relaxation Technique [FRT] seemed to be indicated as an appropriate treatment [the primary strategy]' (Cerio, 1983, p. 436). Because time was of the essence, Cerio chose to use Hypnocounseling 'to hasten the process and still get good results' (p. 436). Mike, it appeared, was extremely suggestible and so, through use of implication and presupposition, Cerio suggested:

> that whenever Mike used the countdown to relax himself, he could also touch his fingers to his forehead. When he did . . . his thoughts would be clear and his ability to concentrate would be strong. Later in the session when the imagery component was used, Mike was spontan-eously touching his forehead and clearing his thoughts. (p. 436)

Cerio was employing Hypnocounseling's eclecticism because he was using relaxation, imagery, hypno-suggestive language, and anchoring (Grinder and Bandler, 1981) in conjunction with the primary strategy of FRT, a form of behavioral counseling.

Hypnosis can be most compatible with counseling, particularly when we conceptualize counseling as helping clients re-examine, clarify, and understand specific issues. Rarely is anything totally new taking place. 'Counseling does not attempt to restructure personality, but to develop what already exists' (Hansen, Stevic Warner, 1982, p. 14). Similarly:

> Erickson refused to accept that the abilities demonstrated by hypnotized subjects are unique to the hypnotic condition. On the contrary, he vehemently insisted that all hypnotic alterations in behavior or experience are merely the intensified manifestations of ordinary behavior. Hypnosis itself neither *adds to nor detracts from* the subject's capacities and personality; the person remains the same individual. Hypnosis merely provides an opportunity for that individual to *utilize* normal learnings and capacities in a more directed manner. (Havens, 1985, p. 236, italics added)

This can be perceived as a person-centered approach of Hypnocounseling because the underlying belief is that change, growth, and solutions reside within the client rather than in an outside authority (Gunnison, 1985a, 1985b).

At any rate what does all of this mean for counselors? When the therapeutic conditions of positive regard, empathy, genuineness, and specificity of expression (PEGS) are operating, then hypnosis or Ericksonian patterns of Hypnocounseling can be helpful, and at the least, not harmful.

DEFINITIONS — HYPNOSIS

> 'Hypnotism' and 'hypnosis' are the terms applied to a unique, complex form of unusual behavior which can probably be induced [*elicited*] in every normal person under suitable conditions and also in persons suffering from many types of abnormality. It is primarily a special psychological state with certain physiological attributes, resembling sleep only superficially, and characterized by a functioning of the individual at a level of awareness other than the ordinary state . . . (Erickson, 1980e, p. 21)

Even though I prize this description of Erickson's, I felt compelled to add the word *elicited* for he believed *elicitation* was a more accurate way of putting it (Erickson, 1980a; Erickson and Rossi, 1979; Erickson, Rossi and Rossi, 1976). I cannot induce 'trance' (another word for hypnosis); however, my words and actions can *elicit* trance. When I invite you to go into trance, you can instantly be aware that you have control and choice. There appears to be little truth to the notion that the hypnotist has taken control of the subject.

When a hypnotist tries to elicit a trance in me, I can choose to 'go under' or not. When I trust the hypnotist and perceive a high trust (high PEGS) climate, I feel a mental and visceral shift in my body, as if I mentally tell myself, 'It's ok, just let go.' Oh yes, another thing, the phrases 'to go into trance,' 'to go under,' can be misleading. I often tell clients they may be let down when they realize that, for the most part, nothing terribly magical happens. In trance we become very aware, we lose neither consciousness nor control; we may notice a peaceful deep relaxation, however. When I experience hypnosis, I sense a narrowing of my attention, a kind of tunnel vision, a deeply focused concentration.

Erickson believed hypnosis has existed for as long as there has been a human history and that hypnosis is a natural, common everyday occurrence. Hypnosis probably takes place when I become deeply engaged in a book, listen to music, or watch a TV show; when driving and reaching my destination but not recalling how I got there. I find it fascinating that while driving in an 'automatic state' I become instantly alert and focused if anything in the car or on the road goes awry. How amazing this organism of ours, as if our unconscious continually guards us. I became so engrossed in writing this last paragraph that I wasn't aware of my dog, Tugs, until he barked and interrupted my pattern.

The reader might wish to take a few moments to access those 'hypnotic times' they have experienced. Are the examples I have used recognizable?

HYPNOTIC PHENOMENA

Scientific research and clinical observation have resulted in a clearer understanding and consensus among theorists as to what phenomena can be associated with hypnosis. For example, Kirsch and Lynn (1975, pp. 846–58) summarize the findings from recent research and clinical observation:

(a) *The ability to experience hypnosis does not mean gullibility or weakness* (p. 846). It was once believed, erroneously, that subjects who could be hypnotized had weak egos, low self-concepts or were naively gullible.

(b) *Hypnosis is not related to sleep* (p. 846). Although the word 'hypnosis' comes from the Greek word 'hypnos' meaning sleep, there is no direct link physiological or otherwise.

(c) *Hypnotic responsiveness depends more on the efforts and abilities of the person hypnotized than on the skill of the hypnotist* (p. 846). This fits the values/beliefs of Hypnocounseling which hold the client as the source and center of the whole process (person-centered).

(d) *Participants retain the ability to control their behavior during hypnosis, and they are aware of their surroundings and can monitor events outside of the framework of suggestions during hypnosis* (p. 846). I can choose to go 'under' and 'let go' or get up and leave. I can attend to outside or inside sensations because I am in control. I 'hypnotize' myself.

(e) *Spontaneous posthypnotic amnesia is relatively rare* (pp. 846, 847). I could respond to a posthypnotic amnesia, if suggested, however, rarely would it happen without suggestion.

(f) *Suggestions can be responded to with or without hypnosis and the function of an hypnotic induction is merely to increase suggestibility to a minor degree* (p. 847). Hypnocounseling rarely results in hypnotic induction (or elicitation); rather, it depends on hypno-suggestive language as will be demonstrated. There is growing evidence that suggestion can be useful even without hypnotic induction.

(g) *Hypnosis is not a dangerous procedure when practised by qualified clinicians and researchers* (p. 847). When the hypnotist conveys positive regard and respect, deep empathy and genuineness (PEGS) to the client, hypnosis is not likely to do any harm.

(h) *Most hypnotized persons are neither faking nor merely complying with suggestions* (p. 847). However, one technique I find is 'pretending.' For example, I might ask you to *pretend* what it would *be like* to be hypnotized in helpful and therapeutic ways, but *don't go into hypnosis*. So when I request 'faking' a suggestion, the faking becomes a real choice on your part.

(i) *Hypnosis does not increase the accuracy of memory* (p. 847). Hypnosis may help us to remember (increased accuracy is difficult to measure).

(j) *Hypnosis does not foster a literal re-experiencing of childhood memories* (p. 847). Hypnosis may help me to remember childhood memories, but not a literal re-experiencing of them.

At one point there existed an ongoing debate in hypnosis between the state theorists and non-state theorists (Erickson and Rogers can be considered state theorists). State theorists argued that there is such a process as a trance state, an altered state, whereas the non-state proponents argued that we don't need a construct such as hypnosis and that it is best described simply as a social phenomenon of compliance. Furthermore, they argued, hypnosis does not exist as a *thing* (or state), but rather it is only a construct we create to describe a certain phenomenon. Instead of two warring camps, the dichotomy has turned into a continuum of positions. Currently, most hypnosis researchers describe the effects of hypnosis as being due to the interpersonal process, social influence and personal abilities, not a trance-like state of altered consciousness (Kirsch and Lynn, 1975).

Interestingly, I can see both sides. One end of the continuum takes the stand that, 'Yes, hypnosis is a very special altered state, a state of sharply focused and fixed attention.' The other, as emphatically, claims hypnosis is *not* a *thing* but rather an internal process, the effects of which come from the social interactions and personal abilities of the individual being hypnotized. Interestingly, this could be interpreted as Bohr's 'complementarity.' Each explanation complements the other. It may be that both descriptions are helpful, indeed necessary, to more completely understand the phenomenon of hypnosis.

Now, after I have set you up for all of that, I should continue by saying, 'there's no such thing as hypnosis; however, it makes it much easier to examine it as if it were a thing.' What we can do is describe what hypnosis does, what it feels like and how it is experienced.

Meditation can be shown to exist because we can demonstrate its very special and unique brain waves. Hypnosis has no special brain waves. The state theorists must prove there is such a state as hypnosis, but as yet they haven't. O'Hanlon playfully examines the split.

> Actually I agree with both points of view . . . I think that trance isn't a thing at all . . . It's just like they haven't been able to measure love, but you know when you're in it, but they haven't measured it physiologically . . . so the bad news is there is no such thing as trance state and the good news is it doesn't seem to matter. (O'Hanlon and Martin, 1992, pp. 20, 21)

For our purposes I will choose to discuss hypnosis 'as if' it were a powerful metaphor; 'as if' it were a thing, a special kind of trance state, an altered state.

In many ways Erickson caused a not so quiet revolution in hypnosis as did Rogers in psychotherapy. The traditional and conventional hypnotherapists were viewed as experts who tended to be responsible for their 'patients' and were most directive. Generally they repeated their suggestions which came through as orders, 'You will close your eyes! Relax!'

Until recently there was a strong belief that many people simply could not be hypnotized. Hypnotherapists, influenced by Erickson, on the other hand, believe most people *can be* hypnotized and they 'utilize' whatever the person brings in to the sessions including anger, depression, helplessness and hopelessness, resistance, confusion. They go with their clients. Ericksonian counselors and therapists generally behave in person-centered ways, believing in their clients' freedom to choose, believing that clients have within themselves the resources and solutions to their problems. Ericksonian therapists invariably use language that appears respectful, tentative, permissive, open-ended, and allows for choice. The Ericksonian roots of Hypnocounseling certainly become quite clear.

DEFINITIONS — HYPNOCOUNSELING

Whatever technique I use, from whatever theory, it must serve a person-centered function. It must be respectful of the integrity of the person, must keep open the avenues of options and personal choices, and directly or indirectly must be relevant to what the individual wants.

Might there be needs or goals of clients in which a particular therapist, you or I, for example, would choose not to participate? What might those conditions be? How would you clarify this with your client? Is not this a form of your own genuineness and a test of your own integrity?

The approach used, above all, must respect the internal locus of control of the client and to respect my need to honor the client. It is this that led me to Hypnocounseling.

Hypnocounseling, as presented here, is an eclectic model based on the merging of Rogers' person-centered approach and Erickson's utilization approach. The critical importance of building the therapeutic relationship between counselor and client is central to these approaches.

In Hypnocounseling, Ericksonian hypno-suggestive language is used from the very start. While the therapeutic relationship (PEGS) serves as the foundation, hypno-suggestive language serves as the medium through which the primary strategy (whether it be Adlerian, the behavior therapies, brief therapies, Gestalt, Rational Emotive, and/or Reality Therapies, etc.) evolves. Presently, the example of the primary strategy used in this book is Brief Solution-Focused Therapy (BST); however, Hypnocounseling acts as a catalyst and an adjunct, improving effectiveness and efficiency of any of the major therapeutic approaches.

Hypnocounseling does not have as a goal the elicitation of trance, although trance may occur and, if so, would certainly be utilized. Hypnocounseling introduces the hypno-suggestive language of hypnosis without the necessity of the counselor having to be concerned about trance and levels of trance. If the client seems to be in a trance, that can be utilized, as well. The goal of Hypnocounseling is not a formal trance, however. Watzlawick (1985), in a sense, spoke for Hypnocounseling when he described, '... linguistic structures ... that have a virtually hypnotic effect although no formal trance induction precedes them' (p. 6). The use of counseling based upon an Ericksonian context of hypnosis serves to suggest, directly or indirectly, changes in perception, thinking, behavior, and/or feelings elicited from within the client's locus of control. Thus, Hypnocounseling refers to the interspersing of Ericksonian hypnotic language patterns within the person-centered therapeutic climate (PEGS) as an adjunct, catalyst and support of the counselor's primary *modus operandi*.

Hypnocounseling is not dissimilar to T. X. Barber's (1985) 'hypno-suggestive' approaches that he argues can be used effectively with most psychotherapies. In a similar vein, Scroggs (1986) writes, 'Ericksonian communications approaches are useful within many fields of therapy: family, Adlerian, Jungian, Gestalt and behavioral, as well as other models of therapy' (p. 506).

IMPLIED DIRECTIVE LANGUAGE (IDL): THE CORE OF HYPNOCOUNSELING

At the heart of the utilization and person-centered approaches lies the goal of personal empowerment of clients and control of their own lives. Implied Directive Language (IDL) contains the structure, indirect suggestion and language patterns that bring this about.

Lankton and Lankton (1983) discuss the importance of IDL which sets the tone for reclaiming personal power, sense of tentativeness and implied permission. Instead of saying, 'sit back in the chair and relax, while you listen to my voice,' by using 'implied directive language' the word 'can' and 'might' change the interpretation dramatically: 'You *can* sit back in the chair and you *might* even relax and listen to my voice.' The word 'can' suggests that you have the ability to sit back in your chair and also sets up an implied choice, that 'you can *choose* to sit back in the chair, if you want to — *or not*.' 'The result of this "packaging", if done well, is a reduction in the client's resistance, doubt and skepticism' (Lankton and Lankton, 1983, p. 136). The use of such words as 'can,' 'might,' 'could,' 'possibly,' etc., makes for communication that is tentative and highly respectful of the client's world and wishes, and also indirectly implies client choice and power. 'Implied directives which use words about consciousness such as "wonder," "surprise," "curious," "know," "doubt," and "hope" for example, will affect clients in another noticeable manner' (Lankton and Lankton, 1983, p. 136).

Cl: Sometimes I feel so depressed, like I'm all alone.
C: Yes, and you feel so down and so cut off from everyone and everything that it overwhelms, is that it? [FOCUSED EMPATHY]
Cl: Yeah, right!
C: And you even begin to 'wonder' *how* you will be changing and growing and *when* you will be changing and growing — maybe immediately, maybe right after our session, maybe down the road. I *don't know*, but *you do*. [IDL LANGUAGE HERE IN ITALICS. NOTICE THE PRESUPPOSITION THAT YOU *WILL* BE CHANGING]

The Hypnocounseling here illustrates a high level of empathy followed by a suggestion of movement forward and taking responsibility. The counselor's last remarks represent a seeding of possibilities that the client may not pick up now but will remain as a suggestion that can be refocused upon, later (Erickson, 1980f). There is no command, no order, no telling the client how to respond. The power and choice are left with the client — only a suggestion is offered.

You no doubt will notice how thoroughly IDL pervades the hypnotic language patterns of Hypnocounseling that follow.

HYPNO-SUGGESTIVE LANGUAGE PATTERNS OF HYPNOCOUNSELING (IDL)

Depending upon who is doing the analysis of Erickson's work there are literally hundreds of his patterns that various authors have discovered.[1] I have arbitrarily selected only a few. There will be no special order in which I have presented the hypnotic language patterns, with one exception. I start with *Interspersals-Analogue Marking* only because I have already used them previously (in italics and/or capitals) without any explanation. In addition, I have selected those patterns which I think are easily learned and whose use will be readily apparent to most counselors and therapists.

INTERSPERSALS — ANALOGUE MARKING
(ERICKSON, 1980F, 1980G; ERICKSON AND ROSSI, 1975, 1979, 1980, 1981; ERICKSON, ROSSI AND ROSSI, 1976; GRINDER AND BANDLER, 1981; O'HANLON AND MARTIN, 1992)

Erickson 'has described the *Interspersal* approach along with *Nonrepetition* as his most important contributions to the practice of suggestion. The interspersal approach ... is a suitable means of presenting suggestions in a manner that enables the patient's [client's] own unconscious to utilize them in its own unique way' (Erickson and Rossi, 1979, pp. 19, 20). The Interspersal technique first involves talking about highly relevant and meaningful material to the conscious mind of the client and, second, interspersing words, phrases, or sentences that 'seed' and elicit indirect suggestions for potentiality, possibilities, resolutions, 'person-centered' outcomes. 'You can now CURIOUSLY take this time to WONDER about different ways to CHANGE. Isn't it exciting to realize that you have the POWER to CHOOSE different ways of being.'

The capitalized words translate as *interspersals* (CURIOUSLY, WONDER, CHANGE, POWER, CHOOSE) that are emphasized when set apart from the rest of the sentence. Interspersals seem difficult to read, yet their effectiveness becomes most potent when heard by lowering or raising the voice, changing voice tone, or even signaling nonverbally with hands, fingers, or other body movements.

By *nonrepetition*, Erickson meant the boring repeating of direct suggestions over and over, a habit quite common in the more conventional hypnotherapies.

'You will relax ... You will relax, now ... Relax, Relax.'

As well as there being repetition, we can detect a sense of commanding or ordering and many people will resist by doing just the opposite of the command.

---

1. I especially appreciate the writings of Stephen and Carol Lankton (1983), which have served as excellent models for my description of hypno-suggestive language.

PACING — MATCHING
(BANDLER AND GRINDER, 1975; GRINDER AND BANDLER, 1981; LANKTON, 1980)

Empathy is at the heart of Hypnocounseling. Empathy in its verbal form helps the counselor 'connect' with the client. Pacing or Matching is another powerful means of 'connecting.'

Almost immediately, I find myself automatically matching or pacing the breathing and voice rhythm-tone of the client. While pacing and matching is not a language pattern as in the case of IDL, it equates to being one of the foundations of the hypno-suggestive language and permeates the entire process of my counseling.

This is a powerful technique to help build rapport and empathy with a client. Pacing 'involves meeting the client at his model of the world and establishing a conscious and, more importantly, unconscious affinity with him' (Lankton, 1980, p. 59). Probably 'pacing,' or as Lankton (1980) called it, 'matching,' is best described when you make contact with the client by matching breathing tempo, tone and tempo of voice. Talking to a client in the same rhythm and tempo of his or her breathing is a potent and useful example of pacing. Pacing is contacting and once achieved can result in 'leading' the client in other directions. I make contact with the anxious person by breathing and talking in tempo (pacing), then I can 'lead' the individual to greater calmness by gradually slowing my breathing, and talking more softly and slowly. Empathic counselor responses can involve 'pacing-matching' and 'leading' as well. In the example, 'Is it that you feel SAD and EMPTY because your dog died last night? It's as if it's a LOSS of a special member of the family?' pacing-matching occurs when the counselor attempts to connect with the client at his/her 'feeling map' of sadness, emptiness and loss. Note also the *Interspersals* as well. The 'leading' component of the reflective statement might take place when the counselor 'leads' the client into considering plausible and natural reasons for the sadness '. . . your dog died last night' and '. . . loss of a special member of the family.'

ACCESSING REPRESENTATIONAL SYSTEMS
(BANDLER AND GRINDER, 1975, 1979; LANKTON, 1980)

Hypnocounseling draws heavily from the field of Neuro-Linguistic Programming (NLP). Neuro (of NLP) refers to the brain and nervous system while Linguistic refers to language. NLP was devised by Richard Bandler a mathematician, therapist and computer wizard and John Grinder, who I remember as a brilliant linguist and an exceptional teacher-therapist. The NLP founders developed their system of interactions by modeling the works and behaviors of four masters: Milton Erickson, Virginia Satir (family therapist extraordinaire), Gregory Bateson (creative revolutionary in anthropology), and Fritz Perls (founder of Gestalt therapy). Bandler and Grinder (1975, 1979, 1982) devised a system that systematically explores our language (verbal and nonverbal) and how it interacts with our nervous system. Furthermore, in an elegant and efficient way they describe interactions and how we can program our brains.

In addition to the 'matching' of physiology, Bandler and Grinder devoted time and study to how each of us represents or perceives our world. How do the brain and perceptual portions of our nervous system take in the world? The acronym 'VAKOG' provides our tentative answer. Basically you and I represent our worlds in a **V**isual, **A**uditory, **K**inesthetic, **O**lfactory (smell) or **G**ustatory (taste) sense.

As we access our representational systems (how we represent our world) we can see another subset of empathy. If you and I converse in the same system, whether visual, auditory, or kinesthetic, we 'connect.' Breakdowns in communication often occur because those conversing are operating in different systems.

People tend to prefer one of the representational systems, Visual, Auditory or Kinesthetic. In other words, those of us who primarily create scenes in our 'mind's eye' represent our worlds Visually. We even begin to talk about our visual experience by using visual words and predicates. I can't *see* how you do it. It's a relief to *see* the light at the end of the tunnel. Your position is *unclear*. Do you get a *clear picture* of what I mean? I can't *picture* your wearing that costume.

Visualizers tend to speak in a rapid, high-pitched voice. They breath more rapidly and higher in the diaphragm. They tend to use hand signals and point a lot. Visualizers often have hunched and tense shoulders, all of which are cues we can learn to notice.

As you might expect, Auditory folks tend to have clear and pleasant-sounding voices as if they are more aware of the *sound* of their voices. Their breathing is slower and deeper in the diaphragm area of the chest. When they appear to be crossing their arms or holding their hands they are 'listening' to their auditory accession. In their speech they tend to use phrases, words and predicates that imply auditory representations.

'That idea *sounds* good.'
'I *hear* your idea.'
'Does that *ring a bell* with you?'
'Are you *loud* and *clear* on this?'

The kinesthetic accessors generally seem to have speech patterns that are deeper and slower, with long pauses. They show a lot of body language and movement which accompanies their kinesthetic accessing; often they show us upturned hands with bent arms — a characteristic of kinesthetic people. Their words and predicates give away their kinesthetic accessing.

'So how does that *feel* to you?'
'My depression *feels* so *heavy* to me.'
'He's just *out of touch* with everything.'
'It's as if I *carry* a huge *weight* around.'

It is interesting to reflect upon our own processing and discover with which of the primary accessing routes we each identify, Visual, Auditory, Kinesthetic?

Here is an example of a counselor (C) and client (Cl) dialogue that illustrates a mismatch in representational systems:

C: What brings you here? What do you hope to get from counseling?

Cl: I really don't know — it's a pretty *bleak* world I *face* and I just don't *see any hope*. (Rapid and high-pitched voice tone, sitting formally no slouch, breathing rapidly.) [CLIENT SEEMS TO BE ACCESSING HIS WORLD VISUALLY, YET NOTICE MY RESPONSE.]

C: (talking in a slow voice, matching his posture and breathing rhythm) So things seem *vague* and your world *weighs heavily* on you now, is that it? [WHILE HE IS VISUAL, I RESPOND VISUALLY BUT MORE STRONGLY IN A KINESTHETIC SENSE.]

It's hard to imagine how he would respond to me. He would probably be confused, 'turned off' because of my primary Kinesthetic response to his visual accessing. We would be like two ships passing in the night. Now as I begin to become aware of his accessing route I can better respond to him.

C: So from your *vantage point*, everything *appears dark* and there doesn't seem to be any *light* at the end of the tunnel, is that how things *look* to you?

Although exaggerated, this response 'matches' his representational system more accurately.

Empathy, as discussed by Rogers, has many dimensions, more than just the verbal. We also demonstrate empathy not only through 'pacing and matching' and 'accessing representational systems,' but also by our nonverbal (physiological) communication.

Although research evidence seems inconclusive, Bandler and Grinder (1979) assert that individuals communicate by their eye movements. For example, tell someone to think about a close friend by imagining they can *see* them. Notice how their eyes momentarily look up and to the left or right or remain fixed staring off straight ahead. Looking right or left may signify that individuals are accessing their world through an *auditory* representation. In a like manner, those looking down to their right or left probably are Kinesthetically orienting. I have found that in most forms of fantasy-imagery or action-resolution work, I invariably have clients not only see (V), but also hear (A), feel (K) and even sometimes smell (O) or taste (G). This produces a much richer and wider view, more apt to be retained and learned.

If you are not already familiar with this, you might try testing this by observing people's eye movements and listening to their language.

TRUISMS — YES-SETS
(ERICKSON, 1980E; ERICKSON AND ROSSI, 1979; ERICKSON, ROSSI AND ROSSI, 1976; LANKTON AND LANKTON, 1983)

A truism is a statement of truth or fact. It sets up agreement or acceptance of the suggestion that follows; for example, 'Most people feel very comfortable when they relax (that's a generally acceptable truth or fact) and you may want to feel comfortably relaxed yourself, now.' The truism is a basic statement of fact that no one can deny. 'Truisms are indirect hypnotic forms in so far as they initiate a *yes* or *acceptance set* for whatever other suggestion the therapist may choose to add to the situation' (Erickson, 1980f, p. 483). Thus, by providing the client with a series of statements that are obviously true, the individual begins to get used to nodding in agreement and thus be more likely to accept a question or statement that slightly changes the direction. Notice how the counselor sets up these 'yes-sets' in the following:

C. As you can now notice how your breathing has changed — from shallow to deeper, more rhythmical. You can be aware of your arms resting at your side and your hands clasped in your lap, your feet planted comfortably on the floor, you might even be aware of a thought or an idea forming in your mind that can be helpful to us.

This may seem simple, obvious and I suppose it is; however, I regularly use this language pattern because it seems so universally effective. *Caution*: its effectiveness only comes when the suggested direction parallels or is compatible with the client's needs and goals.

IMPLICATION — PRESUPPOSITION
(ERICKSON, 1980D; ERICKSON AND ROSSI, 1979; ERICKSON, ROSSI AND ROSSI, 1976; GRINDER AND BANDLER, 1981; LANKTON AND LANKTON, 1983; O'HANLON AND MARTIN, 1992)

Implication and presupposition exemplify language patterns which most clearly show Erickson's indirect approach. In implication, we provide a presupposition stimulus which the listener picks up on and internalizes in his/her own mental processes. We imply that something will happen. Notice, too, how Implied Directive Language (IDL) contains so much of presupposition and implication. For example, 'As you *change* your breathing you *can relax* more deeply.' (Here the assumption is that you will change your breathing and will relax.)

Presupposing has words for time (as, before, when, after). Presuppositions can be used often because of their 'seeding' ('seeding' of suggestions) power. These indirect suggestions are forward moving and therefore imply change in thinking and, thus, *change* in the direction of perception and can be used with most primary strategies counselors regularly utilize.

As a child I often forgot (or as Erickson might describe it, 'remembered to forget') to take the garbage out each evening. It clearly startled me one day when my father said, 'I wonder WHEN you will take the garbage out — BEFORE supper or AFTER supper?' (or something like that). The question presupposed that I would take out the garbage and then the interspersals implied at least the 'illusion of choice.'

REFRAMING
(BANDLER AND GRINDER, 1982; BEAHRS, 1982; CADE AND O'HANLON, 1993; LANKTON, 1980; LANKTON AND LANKTON, 1983)

Reframing is the technique of helping the individual transform problems into assets or 'turning . . . client's negative behavior, thoughts or feelings into resources' (Lankton, 1980, p. 114). Specifically, reframing '. . . refers to the process of helping the client to identify a different perception or framework for understanding and responding to a problem' (Lankton and Lankton, 1983, p. 336). How a picture of daffodils is amazingly transformed when it is framed in a glossy *black* or *white* or *pink* frame!

> The classic case is Tom Sawyer, forced to spend a tedious day whitewashing the fence and fearing an even worse calamity, ridicule by the other boys. The perfect redefining question [reframing] of *'How often does a boy get the opportunity* to whitewash a fence?' turns the ridicule of others to envy and soon he is being *paid* by the other children for the 'opportunity' to do his work for him. (Beahrs, 1982, p. 72, italics added)

Another example might be: 'You know I can hear your sadness and loss and at the same time I sense a very deep courage inside of you that you can draw upon. Isn't it interesting that some people can discover strengths they didn't realize they had during times of travail and pain?' Stating a truism that, 'some people can discover strengths they didn't realize they had,' distances the suggestion, and the client probably would accept it more readily than if I had said 'you should discover' which is definitely more condescending, 'preachy' and off-putting. In such cases I often use the first person. It seems generally more acceptable, if when reframing with the client, I use the first person, So, *'I* feel sad', *'I* have to get through it' and 'Is that your sense of it?'

Cl: (Tears) I feel so bad about losing my dog. He was so good.
C: Yeah, a best friend who has died and you're so sad. And those tears are sort of like a cleansing?
Cl: Yeah, I guess so. *I* just don't know what to do. *I* am so depressed.
C: It is so damned difficult right now, *I'm* feeling so helplessly sad and *I* wonder how *I'm* going to get through all of this? Is that part of it?

Somehow switching to the first person has a strange, but powerful effect. Perhaps it is because clients feel even more accurately listened to when the counselor responds in the first person (I). It's as if clients can listen to themselves differently in a more unguarded sense. Any reframing or suggestion of change is likely to be listened to and thus heard differently.

Cl: Well, it just seems impossible. It hurts so much.
C: Yes, is it that right NOW I'm so hurt, so sad because of Rover's death [I FIND THAT EUPHEMISMS, SUCH AS 'PASSED AWAY' OR 'WENT DOWN THE TRAIL,' ARE NOT NECESSARILY SO IMPORTANT IF I SAY THEM IN THE FIRST PERSON] that *I* just want to grieve, really face it and then *I* want to move on carrying his memory in a different way. Is that part of what you feel? [INSTEAD OF SAYING *YOU* SHOULD, MUST, HAVE TO MOVE ON, I SAY IT IN THE FIRST PERSON AND THE CLIENT SEEMS TO HEAR IT DIFFERENTLY NOT AS ADULT ADVICE, BUT RATHER AS AN OPTION THAT THE COUNSELOR OFFERS AS IF HE/SHE WERE GOING THROUGH THE WHOLE EXPERIENCE HIM/HERSELF.]
Cl: Yeah, maybe... (silence).
C: (Silence — then breathing in very slowly) *I* hurt so much from this loss and yet another part of me knows that *I'm* being tested and *I* hope to dip into *my* courage, NOW. Know what *I* mean? [A FIRST PERSON (I) SUGGESTION AND REFRAME.]

I appreciate reframing in counseling and in life. For example, for far too many years I dichotomized emotions as positive or negative instead of putting them on a flexible continuum. Now I tend to view emotions as does Remen (1996). An emotion becomes negative to the degree that it becomes blocked, stuck or frozen within. Anger, for example, is only negative if it is continually with us. On the other hand, we can use the energy of anger to help us reframe so as to let go and move on. As Remen (1996) puts it:

> ... anger is a demand for change and a mobilization of the individual. It often represents an engagement with life... It is far healthier than apathy, helpless-hopelessness and resignation. (p. 25)

Would you not agree in the power of this kind of reframing? We can utilize most any emotion and reframe it. The process of getting into an emotion; deeply experiencing it, being ready to let go and move on is at the heart of reframing. With clients I also like to access their visual representation. For example, as I talk to a client about the process of letting go, I will stop and I might lift my hand, palm open toward my face. I press my thumb (the emotion) into my palm and wrap my four fingers around it. I hold this thumbless fist toward them and then thrust my arm downward at the same time opening my fist as if throwing something away. Clients sometimes look at me as if I were crazy and remark that my actions so surprised them that at first they didn't know what I was doing and then it hit them with quite an impact. I believe that when I was talking (Audio) to them on the conscious level things were fine. But when I lifted my hand, made a strange fist and threw it as if to put it by, I believe I was connecting with the unconscious mind. I was now accessing at the visual level (Visual).

Reframing teaches a lesson clients can indirectly learn; that they have choice as to how they want to perceive a situation. Clients can learn to reframe for themselves which can empower them in meaningful ways.

METAPHORICAL LANGUAGE: STORIES, JOKES, PUNS, ANALOGIES
(ERICKSON, ROSSI AND ROSSI, 1976; GORDON AND MEYERS-ANDERSON, 1981; HALEY, 1973; O'HANLON AND WEINER-DAVIS, 1989; OVERHOLSER, 1985; ROSEN, 1982; WALLAS, 1985)

As in the case with many of the hypnotic language patterns, we are communicating on two levels: the conscious and the unconscious (Gordon and Meyers-Anderson, 1981; Rosen, 1982; Wallas, 1985). The conscious mind can be attracted by metaphors, analogies and stories and yet deeper meanings and suggestions bypass the conscious and are stored in the unconscious. These metaphorical languages may even confuse the conscious mind while the unconscious mind picks up the underlying patterns and messages and creates a suggestion that there are 'different ways of looking at things' (Overholser, 1985, p. 282). Relevant and appropriate analogies and stories 'appeal to the conscious mind because of their inherent interest while mobilizing the resources of the unconscious by many processes of association' (Erickson, Rossi and Rossi, 1976, p. 225).

Client resistance often arises when the counselor makes a direct suggestion or gives direct advice; Rogers and Erickson avoided this. Often, through the use of a story, clients get the point; yet, because of the safe distance between themselves and 'a story,' they can change their perception and eventually their behavior. A student who lacks perseverance in studying, for example, if told directly might react very differently than if told the story of the little Dutch boy who stuck his finger in the dike and through this act of persevering and enduring saved property and lives.

I recall telling classes, 'That reminds me of a story.' I watch the effects; pens and pencils are put aside, eyes defocus, breathing rhythms of the class begin to merge (match), and bodily positions shift. Once again, this is a fascinating pattern interruption. And when I can insert a lesson into this story, unusual and amazing learning can take place. Here is another study for someone, the use of Hypnocounseling in teaching.

I have a very close friend, Dr. C., who is a professor of history. He is a most popular yet rigorous teacher and one day years ago I went to his class in Russian History to talk to him. While waiting for the time break, I looked in on his class. It became obvious to me that not only was he in an hypnotic state, but his class was as well. Their eyes were fixed and focused with a faraway look, accompanied by a flattening of their facial muscles. The students and Dr. C.'s breathing were slow, rhythmical, diaphragmatic, and in unison. The class was fixed on the words of their professor which seemed slower than usual and different in tone. I was awed. While talking with him after class, he was unaware of anything that was going on beyond the usual. It was from this experience that I have learned to use Hypnocounseling in classes. I have often thought that an article should be written about the use of hypno-suggestive language and the therapeutic-learning climate (in the manner of Hypnocounseling) in the education of teachers.

> C: [TO THE CLIENT WHO WANTS TO LET GO AND MOVE ON — YET TELLING HER DIRECTLY MIGHT BE TOO INTRUSIVE OR WOULDN'T BE HEARD.] Someone told me or I read a story about a certain tribe in the S.W. Pacific who trapped a CERTAIN kind of small monkey that was perceived as most SUCCULENT to the natives. A log was hollowed out with a hole just big enough for the monkey's fist. Inside, the trapper placed a prized bait. This special day the hunters of the tribe set out their 'trap' and waited at a reasonable distance. The head of the monkey clan came upon the hollowed-out log and proceeded to put his/her [USE GENDER OF CLIENT] fist in, she anticipated the sumptuous bait but heard the trapper-warriors coming down the path. At that point, she realized she could not pull out her paw filled with food unless she LET GO of the bait so that she could MOVE ON and LIVE another day. And I wonder what that story means to you?

As the story verbally (Audio) describes the process of 'letting go' and 'moving on' I can reinforce this by simultaneously (Visual) using my hand to form a fist holding the 'bait' in a log. 'Letting go' can be illustrated when I relax my fist letting go of the bait and pulling my hand from the log. I find that the more representations I can use, the more effective is my interaction. In this case both Audio and Visual have a greater impact than either strategy done separately. Most of us do this normally when talking with others — i.e., using nonverbal gestures (metaphors).

Metaphors can be compelling figures of speech and frequently, even though indirect, can be one of the most effective ways of suggestion. While some have a series of stories or metaphors already in mind, with some practice, I have found that many people can surprise themselves by 'ad-libbing' stories that indirectly relate to self or others' issues and/or predicaments.

ILLUSIONS OF CHOICE — BINDS OF COMPARABLE ALTERNATIVES
(ERICKSON AND ROSSI, 1975; GRINDER AND BANDLER, 1981; LANKTON AND LANKTON, 1983)

Here the client is faced with several alternatives, whichever he or she chooses will be in the desired direction. 'Do you want to study NOW or LATER?' 'Do you wish to CHANGE TODAY or TOMORROW?' 'You might

LEARN from all of this NOW or you might USE what you've learned LATER.' In each case, a bind, there is the indirect suggestion (presupposition) that underlies the choice; the presupposition that you will 'study,' 'change,' or 'learn' or 'use.' 'I'm not sure when you'll understand this, NOW as you read it or LATER as you practice it.' How many times did our parents delight in giving us their illusions of choice? 'When will you start your homework or feed the dog), BEFORE you go out to play or AFTER?' I hope it's clear how illusions of choice, like so many other IDL phrases, include presupposition.

ANCHORING
(BANDLER AND GRINDER, 1975, 1979; GRINDER AND BANDLER, 1981; LANKTON, 1980)

'Stated simply, an anchor is any stimulus that evokes a consistent response pattern from a person' (Lankton, 1980, p. 55). Anchoring can be accomplished in each of the representational systems (VAKOG). The word 'rose' (Auditory anchor) can be anchored to the smell and sight (O and V) of the flower.

I use (Kinesthetic) anchoring with college hockey players (Gunnison, 1985b) with whom I work. As they recall moments of excellent physical and mental play, I have them VAKOG those memories. They 'see' themselves, the arena, others (V). They 'hear' the sounds of skates, sticks, the puck, the arena (A). They 'feel' their balance, their wholeness and the wind on their faces (K). I ask them if there are any tastes (G) or smells (O). At that moment when they see, hear, feel, smell or taste their remembrance of excellence in hockey, I touch their knee (K). They then surprise themselves as to how they can anchor that whole image themselves by touching the identical area and pressure on their knee — a Kinesthetic anchor.

SPLITTING OR DISSOCIATION
(LANKTON AND LANKTON, 1983; GILLIGAN, 1982; O'HANLON AND MARTIN, 1992)

Splitting occurs when separating two concepts; for example, conscious vs. unconscious, front of the mind vs. back of the mind. As O'Hanlon and Martin (1992) describe it, 'Splitting is distinguishing between two things that haven't been distinguished before, or separating into parts something that was seen as a unified thing' (p. 31). Remember, we are splitting constructs or abstractions, not things. I cannot weigh a 'conscious' or 'unconscious' nor could I hold either in my hand. I dissociate when I ride my bike or drive my car, whenever I'm performing a complex task that I have mastered. I drive to the next town, Potsdam, and, upon arriving, I wonder how I got there, a common natural hypnotic experience.

Fortunately, I was able to dissociate and split when passing a kidney stone some years ago. I was not correctly medicated and the pain was intense. I remember drifting and noticing that the pain seemed to be removed and located some 10–12 inches from my right side. I also recall noticing the pain had taken on strange characteristics. Not only was it removed from my body, but also it had certain physical attributes of its own. It was as large as a grapefruit or softball and seemed to look like a ball of writhing worms or pasta. It was exceptionally hot. I had split or dissociated using Visual and Kinesthetic representations (I do not recall any Audio, Olfactory or Gustatory sensations). Was I not in trance?

What 'splitting' seems to do is suggest another perspective; we tend to look at things a little differently and the ability to see things from several points of view gives us a certain flexibility that can help us more in the direction of change, *when we provide choice.*

C: How, will you know when our counseling has worked for you? [A BRIEF THERAPY QUESTION.]
Cl: I guess when I can make choices . . .
C: So in the recent past you have been stuck, frozen, unable to choose.
Cl: Yeah!
C: Is it as if a part of you, the *choosing part* has almost vanished and recently the *stuck and frozen part* has taken over. [HERE WE USE 'SPLITTING' TO SET OFF THE APPARENT OPPOSITES AND THIS PROMPTS US TO ASK THE OBVIOUS QUESTIONS (FROM BRIEF THERAPY) — TO BE DISCUSSED IN FUTURE CHAPTERS.] When was it? What were you doing when you were *choosing?* Now you might want to *pretend* a scene of how and what you might *choose* in the present situation? ['PRETEND' IS AN EXCEPTIONAL PATTERN INTERRUPTION.]

When I review my own counseling I am struck by the frequency with which I use splitting. To the depressed person there is a part of him that is not depressed. To the hopeless individual I can suggest she also focus on her hopeful part and how, what, where and when that hopeful part emerges.

PARADOXICAL INTERVENTIONS
(CADE AND O'HANLON, 1993; ERICKSON, 1980A; ERICKSON AND ROSSI, 1981; FRANKL, 1965, 1970; LANKTON AND LANKTON, 1983; O'HANLON, 1987)

C: Right now you're just not sure of how anxious you are, is that it?
Cl: Yeah.
C: I wonder if you can increase your anxiety now? Take your time and let me know when you notice it increase, even if only slightly . . . (long pause).
Cl: OK it's increased . . .
C: Isn't it a wonder that you can choose to increase your anxiety? [USING A METAPHOR.] It's fun to realize that when you climb up a mountain you have also begun to learn how to climb down the mountain [ALSO A TRUISM HERE]. I also wonder HOW you increased your anxiety. What did you do?

Cl:	I just started to think of how I was ever going to finish my final paper that was due yesterday.
C:	Did you see the situation? Did you hear any self-talk or talk from others? Or were you aware of any unusual feelings? [THIS LATTER CAN BE AN ATTEMPT TO VAKOG THE SITUATIONAL ANXIETY.]
Cl:	Yeah my teacher's voice and expression on his face.
C:	Isn't it INTERESTING that you made it worse and, in so doing, you MIGHT use the same process to LESSEN your anxiety, could you not?

In Hypnocounseling, we do not try to teach something from outside; rather, we try to elicit learning and inner experiencing. Rather than tell clients the solution, we invariably try to evoke the solution through helping them tap into their own inner resources. Many times we can evoke change responses when we ask clients to exaggerate the symptom (requesting they do something voluntarily that originally they claimed to be involuntary). Paradoxical Interventions help to expand awareness and choice, elicit a different perspective, and tend to interrupt the habitual ways of thinking, thus increasing personal empowerment.

Paradoxical Interventions represent a pattern interruption whereby the client follows a suggestion to increase or exaggerate the symptom. By encouraging me to increase the level of my depression, for example, I indirectly learn I have choice and, therefore, if I choose to increase the symptom, I can lessen it. I can be more in control.

PATTERN INTERRUPTION AS A CONFUSION TECHNIQUE
(GILLIGAN, 1982; HALEY, 1973; O'HANLON AND MARTIN, 1992; ROSSI, 1980)

I am perplexed as to why I chose to leave pattern interruption to the last. I would like to believe that it was done because pattern interruption can serve as a summary and, interestingly, seems to permeate almost all of the other hypno-suggestive language patterns. When clients share their misery with you and you ask for them to increase it (paradoxical pattern interruption) you have also broken their pattern of focusing and momentarily they have altered their states, as it were. As you review the hypno-suggestive language patterns you may want to notice how many contain forms of pattern interruptions.

Having clients break patterns of their behavior often changes outcomes. For example, having clients get out of bed differently in the morning can start their day differently, or having them get up and change chairs can also have interesting results. Interrupting their thinking, having them consider something else, having them look out a window and describe what pleasant sights they see — all can change perception.

I interrupted a client struggling and going round and round in circles about her depression. I happened to share a favorite quote from Shakespeare, 'Nothing is either good or bad, but thinking makes it so.' She stopped and looked at me with eyes defocused, as if she were in trance. Exciting to notice how one *small* quote led to larger changes in her perceptions, behavior and outlook. Out of the tiniest, smallest changes can come major changes. Pattern interruption does, in fact, promote confusion, an interruption during which the client is distracted and has the time to respond to suggestions that may not have been available before. The experience of a Paradoxical Intervention to 'depress myself even more' confuses me to the point where I snap out of the compulsive way I have been using my depression. In addition, the invitation, 'to depress myself,' further interrupts and confuses me, because it evokes within me the idea that I depress myself, that I am responsible; a very powerful suggestion indeed!

CONCLUSION

As you re-examine this list of Implied Directive Language you may note the overlaps, and interconnections among the IDL components. For example, notice how Presupposition and/or Pattern Interruption can be found in many of the IDL patterns. Together with the high trust, high PEGS relationship, the Ericksonian language and hypnotic behavior serve as the foundation of Hypnocounseling. You might begin by reviewing them and then choosing those language patterns with which you feel most comfortable.

Chapter 5
Eclecticism

Every truth is so true that any truth must be false.
Francis Herbert Bradley

The quest for certainty blocks the search for meaning. Uncertainty is the very condition to impel man to unfold his powers.
Erich Fromm

There is no such source of error as the pursuit of absolute truth.
Samuel Butler

Human beings are perhaps never more frightening then when they are convinced beyond doubt that they are right.
Laurens van der Post

DEFINITIONS AND DISCUSSIONS

It started a long time ago. I recall interactions I had with Sunday School teachers, priests and ministers who tried to teach me the absolute ways of their religious views; I recall the excitement and even enjoyment in challenging and questioning their beliefs. I recognized what I came later to call, 'One-Right-Wayisms.' It seemed the person acted as an authority for the only way for everyone else. When asked why there were so many other religious belief systems, I ran into awkward silences, outright denials of other ways or, most often, the response that theirs was the only True and Divinely Revealed way. Ever since, I have been suspicious of this kind of absolutism. It's as if most of us on the planet are wrong and the one-true-believer has the inside track.

Ten to fifteen years ago I watched the politically correct movement develop in the colleges. It seemed necessary, important, and humane. The movement attempted to correct attitudes and language that worked unfairly against minorities and gender. At first there was 'friendly' correction smilingly administered. You become quickly aware that there was a way of speaking and that political correctness was not just a passing fancy. It became the only way to speak. The one right way. It is as if political correctness has become the creed of the millennium.

The lesson here is that there is a real incompatibility between 'one right way' creed and liberty. A perfect belief or creed by definition cannot tolerate any form of questioning or opposition. Freedom has absolutely no meaning when the right to differ is denied. Eclecticism may very well be a major bulwark against the encroachment of these forms of extremism.

We all have Right-Wayisms in our lives (radio and TV are filled with them). They exist in almost every facet of our lives — in politics, economics, school, organized religion. There are possible parallels between Right-Wayisms and the absolutes, dichotomies, and linear systems of the Newtonian Classical science. It is interesting to speculate how religion, politics, education, economics would look through the other set of spectacles: chaos-complexity (emergent-dynamic systems theory) or quantum mechanics.

Each of us drags with us certain scripts, admonitions, and internally voiced 'shoulds,' that are gathered up along the way throughout our lives. More often than not, they tend to be messages (often indirect and possibly misunderstood) from parents, relatives, friends, church, the school — 'Children should be seen and not heard,' 'Be consistent,' 'Don't ever brag,' 'Always be sure of yourself,' 'Don't ever fail,' 'Be happy,' 'Be tolerant' are examples that come quickly to mind, though the list is endless.

Throughout the book, the emphasis has been placed on the importance of counselor attitudes, beliefs, and values. They become critical because they determine to a great extent what we perceive, what we experience and what we do. Above all, as counselors, they determine how we relate to and what we do with our clients.

These internal scripts, which I experienced in myriad forms as I grew up, became woven into the general fabric of my beliefs, attitudes, and value systems. These act as my eyes and ears. My attitudes, beliefs and values act as the filters that *determine* what I perceive.

I remember a teacher in high school who treated us as if we were ignorant, incapable and unworthy. We disliked him and noticed how differently he behaved as compared to an English teacher who assumed we were worthwhile, teachable and capable of learning. Their varying beliefs and attitudes about us made all the difference (the self-fulfilling prophesy).

Mr. Oxenford, a high school chemistry teacher I once had, queried us, 'Why do you continue to think that there must be only one explanation, that one is right therefore the other wrong? Could it be that each is partially right and wrong and that several hypotheses give us a richer and wider view of the phenomenon?' (Was this my first introduction to Bohr's complementarity principle?) Ever since, I have become aware of a certain wariness in me regarding the one right way, the only explanation, the only one right answer. As I listen to clients who appear so right, who have tried everything, I perk up my ears and start to listen to their deletions, generalizations, and unchecked assumptions.

My journey through graduate school, I assume, was typical. I became involved in the routine of classes, the research and readings. For a time, I couldn't get enough; it was as if I sponged up as much information as I could. Eventually, however, I became full and almost dizzy with so many new concepts. My confusion grew as I confronted the dichotomies of philosophical assumptions, values and beliefs within each of the theories (schools) that we studied. In addition, each approach generated its own different assumptions regarding the human condition. I responded with excitement at the not so subtle differences that each theory produced and with amazement that the whole process was open-ended — the process was infinite.

The following questions occurred to me (it is not an exhaustive list):
1. Does this theory represent a closed or an open system or does it fall on a continuum somewhere between the extremes?
2. Where do you fall on the continuum from choice to determinism?
3. Where do you stand on client *history*; client's *present* world?
4. What is the nature and/or meaning of such constructs as: motivation, responsibility, growth, pathology, diagnosis, reaction vs. proaction?
5. Where do you place humankind on the continuum of good or evil?

As a graduate student studying the various 'schools' of counseling and therapy, I began to try each one on my clients in my most consistent way. As I studied Freud and the neo-Freudians, I analyzed each person. When discovering Skinner and his operant conditioning, I became so excited that I tried to operantly condition each client. The discovery of Gestalt, of RET, and Reality Therapy seemed so sensible and acceptable that I 'Gestalted them,' 'RET'd them,' 'Reality Therapied them,' hoping for success. In my drive for 'consistency' I focused on the techniques and roles, ignoring the person's needs and perceptions. Embarrassingly, I found myself acting as if I were the authority for my clients' world views, realities, thoughts, and feelings. My 'One-Right-Wayisms' determined how I should perceive and behave toward my clients.

Many have asked me how, when and where I changed. I cannot be specific; however, I know I began to feel unsettled and uncomfortable when first introduced to the writings of Rogers. And possibly this was due to the way he perceived each human being. Major differences crept up. Rogers focused on the internal frame of reference of the person, movement away from an absolute, objective truth and toward a unique, more subjective view of truth as perceived and constructed by the individual. In addition, I believe that changes began when I first realized I had not listened at all to my clients, focusing and listening only to what I was going to say next.

My need to be consistent was challenged; it meant a rearranging of the furniture in the room of my mind. That furniture consisted of my assumptions, values and beliefs regarding not only counseling but the human condition as well. I reminded myself of Emmerson's observation that 'a foolish consistency is the hobgoblin of little minds.' Soon I began to perceive each of the major theorists and their approaches quite differently. I noticed that each spoke as if his or her system represented the right way. Rogers and Erickson seemed to be less rigidly dogmatic, allowing for other possible views and ways. As I began to learn and experiment with Rogers' person-centered approach, I became aware of how I differed from so many of my colleagues. This became clearer to me as I studied with Rogers at conferences, workshops, seminars and group meetings. The message that I found so encouraging, echoed a fundamental appreciation of differences: not just accepting or tolerating them, but rather amounted to a strong prizing of differences. At one meeting of adherents of a person-centered approach I presented a paper on 'Hypnocounseling: The Merging of Rogers and Erickson.' What followed confused me. Attacked and scolded by one of the inner circle, I realized that, even in this company, one must follow the party line: 'One-Right-Wayism' had raised its tiresome head even after I had shown the group an article Rogers (1985) had written in support of Hypnocounseling. There was no prizing of differences there! I had learned to be deeply skeptical of diversity (whose diversity?). My disillusionment emerged out of the realization that even in this seemingly open, tolerant, and accepting approach it had followers who could be judgmental and self-righteous in their beliefs.

For many of these reasons, I began to explore eclecticism. One of my strongly held beliefs in counseling has been a faith in my clients to have within themselves a tendency toward growth and a belief that they can be the ultimate source for resolutions and answers to their dilemmas, problems or issues. I do not sit with 'sick' people as much as I sit with individuals temporarily blocked or 'stuck' in their growth and development. Eclecticism seemed the path for me to follow and certainly served to 'unblock' me in my search for a counseling approach which was not undergoing re-examination and change.

Eclecticism has brought about lively discussion, with many varied and opposing viewpoints. Rather than be sidetracked by repeating these, I simply will state the development of my 'eclecticism' and what it currently means to me and how this description has served as one of the critical stepping stones for this work.

The first thing that struck me was that all approaches emerged as a result of one person's theorizing. Freud's Psychoanalysis, Skinner's Operant Conditioning, Perls' Gestalt Therapy, Ellis' Rational Emotive Therapy, M. H. Erickson's utilization approach, Glasser's Reality Therapy, Rogers' person-centered approach all represent examples of this tendency. On the other hand the same could be said for eclecticism. Is not eclecticism just another One-Wayism in sheep's clothes? Possibly, but eclecticism, for me, was not spawned by anyone person and it has the important advantage of being more accepting of many views. Since, as Rogers and Erickson do,

I try to focus on the person in all contexts, I first accept the uniqueness of each client, and I observe and listen closely to how the individual presents herself. As I listen, I begin to hear issues and/or client perceptions that may 'fit' any one of many models or theories. This client sounds as if he would be comfortable with Ellis' RET. Or some kind of behavioral modification seems the preferred approach with this person; while another expresses things in such a way that a psychodynamic emphasis seems appropriate. After examining the section on Hypnocounseling, I should like to come back to this use of many models with examples of how Hypnocounseling can serve as an adjunct and catalyst to our primary strategy that we have been given indirectly from our clients. Clients rarely tell us, 'Gestalt me,' 'RET me' or 'RT me,' yet their disclosures can give us various clues. I remember my confusion when I first became aware of these thoughts; my need for consistency ran amuck and it was then that I moved more and more in the direction of eclecticism.

My first attempt to be eclectic resulted in my borrowing from any approach and mixing and matching without any apparent base. Soon it became clear that the results, generally, were not helpful, but even more than that, this way of doing business bordered on the unprofessional and the unethical. Thus, eclecticism changed for me: it was *not* flying by the seat of my pants and trying any approach that came to mind or conjuring up the approach which I had just been studying — a form of syncretism.

Patterson (1985) quotes English and English on the critical difference between *eclecticism* and *syncretism*,

> In theoretical system building, the selection and orderly combination of compatible features from diverse sources . . .
> Eclecticism is to be distinguished from an unsystematic and uncritical combination for which the name is syncretism. (p. v)

By 'flying by the seat of my pants,' I indulged in 'syncretism' and by borrowing haphazardly and unsystematically I had been repeating a tendency, I fear, too frequently and incorrectly labeled, 'eclectic.' In addition, I continue to be amazed at how eclecticism can become a front for ignorance.

I once asked a colleague what approach he used, and he told me his approach was eclectic. As we talked further, I got the impression that by eclectic he meant he had knowledge about a lot of approaches but didn't really know any of them very well. To me, it becomes essential that students be well grounded in the major systems in counseling and psychotherapy. Then they can choose their approach more wisely or can become eclectic in sound, theoretical, and therapeutic ways.

According to Norcross (1987), systematic eclecticism comprises those approaches that have a solid theoretical foundation with compatible interventions based on clinical experience and/or research findings. My approach, Hypnocounseling, is a form of systematic eclecticism called 'technical eclecticism' which contains a variety of techniques compatible within a preferred theory (Rogers and Erickson).

What has become clear is that the eclecticism to which I aspire should be thoroughly grounded in a theoretical-philosophical base. Thus, a major task in this book becomes one of identifying and constructing a theoretical-philosophical foundation upon which I build my eclecticism for counseling and therapy.

That's quite a bit to swallow and rather than let it fly away like the bird, we might ask ourselves: Where do I stand? Do I lean toward building my own eclecticism as it emerges from my client or does it fit better for me to stay with one approach with my clients? For me, there appears no right answer.

R. R. CARKHUFF, ET AL.

In Chapter 1 we focused on the theoretical-philosophical marriage of the works of M. H. Erickson and C. R. Rogers to build our eclectic foundation. However, my brand of eclecticism also includes the research findings of R. R. Carkhuff and his associates. From the results of their studies I borrow two significant elements which become apparent if my counseling elicits constructive change: first, the core conditions (Rogers's facilitative conditions) and, second, the three-phase process of counseling. As Rogers (1961) put it in relation to the facilitative, or core conditions:

> I can state the overall hypothesis in one sentence, as follows. If I can provide a certain type of relationship, the other person will discover within himself the capacity to use that relationship for growth, and change and personal development will occur. (p. 33)

THE CORE CONDITIONS (A CERTAIN TYPE OF RELATIONSHIP)

While Rogers repeatedly emphasized the importance of research, of putting his approach to the empirical test, Carkhuff and his associates provided corroboration and extension of Rogers' discoveries. In addition to the three phase-process of counseling, Carkhuff became involved in analyzing levels of the therapeutic relationship, the heart of the process of counseling.

Since our verbal interventions can be both helpful and unhelpful (and even downright destructive), it behooves us to understand and acknowledge the dynamics of helpful and therapeutic communication. But what comprises therapeutic communication? What makes up the therapeutic relationship, that Rogers called the necessary and sufficient conditions? Rogers (1951) begins his response to these questions:

> As our experience has moved us forward, it has become increasingly evident that the probability of therapeutic movements in a particular case depends primarily not upon the counselor's

> personality, nor upon his techniques, nor even upon his attitudes, but upon the way all of these are experienced by the client in the relationship. (p. 65)

From his earliest studies, Rogers increasingly wanted to know what was going on, and especially what was happening within the human when personality change began to occur. Consistently, Rogers and his students found that when clients perceived their counselors as respecting them without judging, empathizing sensitively, and as being congruent and genuine, then constructive change was much more likely to take place.

In his classic paper entitled, 'The Necessary and Sufficient Conditions of Therapeutic Personality Change,' Rogers (1957) caused quite a stir in the conventional halls of counseling and psychotherapy. My experience tells me that while I believe the core conditions are essential and necessary, they may not be 'sufficient,' especially if time parameters exist. Yes, frequently I have experienced clients who 'steep' in the core conditions as tea bags steep in warm water and at their own rate and in their own way the therapeutic climate appears 'sufficient.' However, more often than not, the core conditions (Carkhuff, *et al.*) set the foundation for what this book is about.

No matter how we label it, this *'definable climate of facilitative psychological attitudes'* (the 'core conditions' of Carkhuff's work) bears repeating and reviewing. Without this therapeutic climate our counseling approaches dramatically suffer.

POSITIVE REGARD

Positive regard represents a condition of acceptance and care. Rogers (1961) put it this way:
> By acceptance I mean a warm regard for him as a person of unconditional self-worth — of value no matter what his condition, his behavior or his feelings. It means a respect and liking for him as a separate person, a willingness for him to possess his own feelings in his own way. (p. 34)

This rare kind of acceptance can be experienced by the client as a 'relationship of warmth and safety, and the safety of being liked and prized as a person' (p. 34).

If my respect, my positive regard seem lacking, for whatever reasons, I must consciously work at separating the *person* from the unwanted, disliked *behavior*. If I still cannot let go of my judgmental feeling and referral seems unlikely then I do not know how successful our time together will be, so critical is positive regard to the therapeutic relationship. In fact, Patterson and Hidore (1997) mention Schofield's (1964) *Psychotherapy: The Purchase of Friendship* and argue that their own book might have been titled *Psychotherapy: The Purchase of love*. 'Love — brotherly love, or agape

— would be a good description of psychotherapy' (Patterson and Hidore, 1997, p. xv).

EMPATHY

Empathy could be viewed as a very special kind of understanding, the client consistently experiencing being understood. For example, if I feel empathy from you, I have the courage to push the limits because of the confidence the empathy instills. What a magical sensation it is to sense you listening to me and accepting and prizing my frame of reference, while at the same time allowing differences to exist (whether you are my counselor or friend). Dafler (1996), focusing on psychobiology and psychoneuroimmunology, still comes back to the criticalness of empathy in the human interaction:

> . . . empathic and compassionate attunement is the *essence* of process-oriented therapy, which *activates* and *utilizes* emotions and other psychological capacities in the service of increasing biopsychosocial flexibility, social connectedness, and *possibly physical healing*. (p. 43, italics added)

GENUINENESS

Genuineness, also described as congruence or realness, exists when the client experiences and appreciates the humanness of the counselor. As Rogers (1961) mentioned, being genuine, transparent or authentic

> . . . involves the willingness to be and to express, in my own words and my behavior, the various feelings and attitudes which exist in me . . . It is only by providing the genuine reality which is in me, that the other person can successfully seek for the reality in him . . . It seems extremely important to be real. (p. 33)

Carkhuff and Berenson (1977) state it pithily, 'If there can be no authenticity in therapy, then there can be no authenticity in life' (p. 12).

SPECIFICITY OF EXPRESSION

Specificity of expression, or *concreteness*, refers to the language of the counselor and was described by Carkhuff and his associates as a fourth critical condition. As you, the counselor, talk with me, eliminating vagueness, abstractions and generalities in your wording and phraseology, I feel more comfortable and my thinking and verbalizing clarifies. I feel much closer to you. Carkhuff and Berenson (1977) summarize:

> Concreteness or specificity of expression, a variable that is largely under the therapist's direct control, involves the fluent, direct and complete expression of specific feelings and experiences, regardless of their emotional content. (p. 13)

Specificity of expression seems most valuable in establishing connections with clients particularly in the earlier exploration phases of counseling. There will be times, however, when Hypnocounseling language will appear to be just the opposite. Vague and confusing language (confusion techniques) can be utilized to encourage clients to construct their own experiences and solutions. This hypno-suggestive language has been explored in the previous chapter on Hypnosis and Hypnocounseling.

LEVELS OF COMMUNICATION — A SCALE

Carkhuff and his colleagues (Carkhuff, 1969; Carkhuff and Berenson, 1977) began lengthy and intensive analysis of what makes for helpful and constructive levels of communication. They created a *five-point scale* to describe the various levels of counselor-helper functioning in each of the core dimensions: positive regard, empathy, genuineness and specificity of expression (PEGS). For brevity and clarity I will be discussing the five point scales yet using examples for empathy only.

Levels 1 and 2 represent different degrees of a lack in communication. On the street we have what I call 'social-lubrication-rituals' and these usually are at levels 1 or 2.

'How are ya?'
'Fine — how are you?'
'Fine.'

These represent acknowledgment of the other, but little more. These rituals are so automatic that when changed in any way they disrupt social lubrication.

'How are ya?'
'Lousy' (oops!)

Now the original greeter has to make a decision: to take time to acknowledge and listen to the meaning of 'lousy' (level 3 or above) or, 'that's too bad' and move on (level 2). However, because the automatic exchange becomes such a ritual, greeters may not even hear 'Lousy' and respond with 'fine' and move on anyway (level 1 or -1). These examples remind me of the painful 'dog-dying' episode from my past.

In my stint in the service I taught in the Hospital Corpsman School. I taught Materia Medica, Anatomy and Physiology, and Sanitation and Hygiene, and in college I was an English major. It seems obvious to me, now, that my career choice was formed there in the Groton, Connecticut training schools, although the subject matter was different, the process was the same.

One of my first jobs after leaving the service came about serendipitously. The wife of a friend of mine had become pregnant and wondered if I wanted her job, teaching English in a small centralized school, grades 8–12. (And what an honor. I even had a title, Chair of the

English department. Of course it must be known that I was the *only* English teacher.) I jumped at this opportunity and while I had majored in English literature, I had no formal training in teaching of any kind. All I had was the 'personal experience' of being taught. I taught the way I was taught. I became known for being a strict, no-nonsense teacher and one who distanced himself from the students. These behaviors, which were very 'professional' by the way, made me much appreciated by the administration, the board, teachers, some parents, and very few students.

Every Wednesday became known as Spelling Test Day. There was consistency along with no excuses; everyone knew this test was more important than anything else in the school, of course. (What audacity I had in those early days!)

On a cold February morning following the Wednesday test day, a young woman remained after class. Perhaps you would recognize the type: she was from the country, grade nine age level, and perhaps a little overweight. She wore a clean cotton dress with a torn hem, sneakers a little worn in the toes (hand-me-downs?), maybe a little too much lipstick and sat in the same seat at the back of the room and rarely spoke. Each day she came unnoticed to school and left just as anonymously. She was one of the countless, nameless, faceless students who come and go without being noticed in any way. However, she will not remain faceless or countless although I cannot remember her name.

She stood in front of my desk with her hands writhing in front of her and with dark downcast eyes that still haunt me. But I believed in trying to uphold a role and I was trying to be sincere. (I recall a mentor saying, 'Be wary of sincere people.') And then began an exchange I will long remember:

'You missed THE test yesterday,' I said.

(no answer)

'Why weren't you in class?'

'Yesterday my dog died,' she responded, wiping away the tears.

(I continued) 'Well, that's too bad, but you know how important these tests are, oh, and turn off the waterworks. They'll not help you in the real world.'

She left that day and spent the rest of the year with eyes averted, quietly sitting in the same seat, rarely saying anything.

I wonder what level of response do you believe I gave? What feelings or reactions did you have to my response? Putting yourself in the young woman's place, what do you think she felt about school, teachers? What, I wonder, does she tell her children and grandchildren about her school days? I think I know, though I often wish I didn't.

I didn't know what happened. Too busily rationalizing my purpose, my needs, my trying to be sincere and remain 'consistent' with my role (or at least the role I thought I was expected to play), I ignored her feelings, her perceptions. I denied and distorted that scene because, I realize, my own visceral-emotional experience did not fit my self-concept of being a 'good teacher.' That young woman, so many years ago, changed me in ways she could never imagine.

When I share this experience with colleagues, students and workshop participants, it invariably elicits astonishment in the form of groans and mumblings. Yes, it may be an excellent lesson; however, the human cost becomes too exorbitant. I ask someone in the audience to time the response I wish I had made to that young woman. My response takes only 6–10 seconds.

'How sad you must feel; it's as if a member of the family has gone.'

Just that attempt to acknowledge her feelings makes all the difference. And I have gone through my 'if onlys,' which don't help. What does help seems to be my recollection of our words and the scene. I have learned at her expense, tragically. Perhaps that lost experience so long ago became the impetus, the motivation to begin graduate training in counseling and therapy. At least I'd like to think so.

Using our example, 'Yesterday my dog died,' we can illustrate the various levels. You might take a few moments to become that person who shares this news with me and carefully sense your reactions to each of my levels of responding.

> *You share:* 'Yesterday my dog died.'
> *My response:* 'That's good. I never liked him anyway.' [LEVEL 1 SHOWS NO UNDERSTANDING OR ATTENDING TO WHAT YOU HAVE SHARED AND ACTUALLY BECOMES HURTFUL. NOTICE HOW IN LEVELS 1 AND 2 YOU CAN SENSE AN INTERRUPTION, AN INTERNAL FELT SHIFT, AS IF YOU COULDN'T QUITE BELIEVE YOUR EARS?]
>
> or
>
> 'How old was he?' [NOTE YOUR INTERNAL DISTRACTING SHIFT NOW YOU HAVE TO INTERRUPT YOUR FOCUS TO RECALL HOW OLD HE WAS — AT THIS POINT IT SEEMS IRRELEVANT TO YOU AND YOUR FEELINGS — LEVEL 2.]

Level 3 responses appear as minimally helpful and, at best, become attempts to respond to your communication and can be considered *interchangeable responses*, because they minimally correspond with your level of affect and meaning.

> *You:* 'Yesterday my dog died.'
> *My response:* 'You must feel sad.'
> or
> 'It must really hurt.'

We must remain open and flexible in our responding. For example, some years ago a friend reported the death of his dog. I had known this beautiful animal ever since she was a puppy. When I tried to imagine how I would have felt (for this is the origin of empathy) I responded with a level 3; 'You must have felt so sad. What a loss.' I was startled when he said, 'Well, not really. It was a relief since she had become blind, lost the use of her rear legs as well as loss of control of her bladder.' I had to jump shift quickly. 'Yes, now I see, the relief was feeling a sense of peace for her now — you just couldn't stand having her suffer anymore. Is that it?' I often find it helpful to tack on that question. It provides a tentativeness and an invitation to come back into the conversation. I was struck with how the British people in everyday conversation tack on the conversational question, 'Lovely day, *isn't it?*' or 'A smashing play, *wasn't it?*' It may be an attempt to smooth over disagreement or conflict yet it still serves to elicit a response. Tentativeness becomes a crucial issue, such expressions as, 'could it be that?', 'possibly' or 'maybe what you're sensing or feeling . . .'

The level 4 response includes the level 3, yet reflects an *additive response*, that of understanding or insight.

> 'Yesterday my dog died.'
> 'You must feel so sad [LEVEL 3] because she was a part of the family [LEVEL 4], is that it?'

The level 4 response then attempts to help you explore your feelings, and then understand the how and why of your feelings.

While the level 5 includes levels 3 and 4, its importance lies in the *forward movement* it implies, a directional suggestion, actions:

> 'You feel sad [LEVEL 3] because your dog was like a member of the family [LEVEL 4] and you want to get through the grieving process [LEVEL 5] — is that part of it?'

This level 5 statement includes level 3, the interchangeable response of sadness, the level 4 response suggesting an understanding of the event and affect, and the level 5 purports to suggest or imply movement forward toward action and resolution.

Notice how enticing it is to become involved with levels of response and yet how technically artificial our exchanges become. Rogers warned of the consequences of the emphasis on technique alone. 'Levels' are training steps only where we, hopefully, learn to internalize and truly own these techniques so that they transform themselves into genuine interactions.

The first of the two basic assumptions of person-centered counseling asserts that each individual has an inherent, actualizing, growth potential. The second belief holds that a definable climate of facilitative psychological attitudes (PEGS) must exist for growth to be realized. Hypnocounseling makes it clear that genuineness, congruence or personal honesty become the crucial foundation for the therapeutic relationship (perhaps to be more accurate PEGS should have been rewritten as GEPS with *Genuineness* as the psychological attitude of priority; however, this would have made for a more awkward acronym).

You probably would wonder how much you could trust counselors if you sensed they were pretending to respect and care for you as if these were merely attitudes learned by role. In fact, any form of pretense would probably put you on guard. Thus, genuineness (or honesty) becomes the foundation of high trust and the facilitative climate. As counselors create this climate, a problem arises, however. Rogers talked about some of the misinterpretations of the facilitative climate, that these conditions could evolve as a kind of rigid set of conforming standards or techniques. It became apparent that some people, in their attempts to create the growth climate, actually created monsters. These attempts result in a series of 'shoulds,' and what was originally a therapeutic climate becomes a toxic climate. The more counselors tried to force their respect and empathy, the more rigid and gimmicky they became. This is because the value of the facilitative climate equates with it being spontaneous and natural. A reminder of the importance, once again, of our *genuineness*. The core conditions (PEGS) only facilitated and were helpful to the degree that they were perceived by the *client* as genuine, empathic, respectful and specific. For example, the attitudes of counselors was critical, not that he/she could listen and respond accurately, but rather had a deep desire to understand the client. This authentic and genuine deep desire to understand the other lies at the heart, not only of empathy but also of positive regard, each of which can be directly and indirectly conveyed.

We must continually go back to clients' perceptions as our map of their reality. If clients do not perceive our therapeutic climate as helpful, then it is not, no matter how technically correct you and I might judge it. I recall an incident where a client nailed me to the wall. Her perception was accurate.

Cl: You don't understand a thing I've said!

First, I was taken aback and then I realized she was correct; I had not been listening to her. Second, I felt good in that she felt free and strong enough to challenge me.

C: You're right. I wasn't listening to you and I feel badly about that. I wish I had an excuse, I don't. My only hope NOW is that you'll choose to give me another chance.
Cl: (She shrugged ... pause.)
C: It really has to hurt when you've been risking and sharing and I haven't even heard it.
Cl: Yeah ...

In our highly technological world there is constant pressure to have highly technological strategies, interventions and diagnostic tools in counseling. Perhaps this is why so many counseling students and fellow professionals shrug off my emphasis on the importance of the therapeutic climate. This nourishing interpersonal climate becomes far more difficult to establish than does a set of slick and technical strategies. The therapeutic climate requires far more from the 'person' of the counselor — a process too often ignored in our training. An aside here; it seems crucial to stress that in

Erickson's tapes and scripts as well as in personal learning with Carol and Stephen Lankton, Bill O'Hanlon, Ernest Rossi, Jeffrey Zeig, and others I have been touched by the respectful PEGS I witnessed and I am equally impressed with their therapeutic strategies. Maybe because counselors and therapists view themselves as masters of therapeutic strategies, it seems disheartening to think that those years of graduate professional training may be no more important than being a sensitive and caring human, an upsetting notion at best. And to add insult to injury, there appears to be little relationship between grade point average and effectiveness in counseling (Pierce, 1966).

Creating a therapeutic, nourishing climate asks a great deal of us. I must risk with the client-person, opening myself to respect and care, free of judgment. How can I be free of judgment? We often hear of the 'nonjudgmental' stance, and Rogers certainly emphasizes this view. I am sure that I cannot be 'nonjudgmental'; however, what I can do is to learn how to be more aware of my biases, my judging, and then in this awareness be able to put it aside to let the client in. Being human is to judge; I am biased, as well. And in choosing to be aware I can make expedient changes in my technique without losing my genuineness.

As a counselor, I must genuinely convey to you my deep respect and acceptance of you as a unique human being with unique attributes, experiences, and hopes. I focus on you as a one-of-a-kind, worthwhile person with your own almost limitless potentials. While I am with you, I try to exist there as fully as I can. This, too, conveys my respect and acceptance of you (positive regard). I must tune myself in — altering my state so as to listen at unusually clear levels, removing my spectacles so there is the least interference from my thoughts, values, ideas, staying with and feeding back to you what, I believe, I hear (empathy). I must risk being as authentic as I can, not hiding behind roles or masks, even the role and mask of a counselor (genuineness). And finally, I must carefully choose language that is concrete, operational and descriptive, not talk that may be filled with clichés or highly abstract labels (specificity of expression).

How can I teach these facilitative conditions? I have wrestled with this for years, although the evidence (Carkhuff, 1969; Carkhuff and Berenson, 1977) seems to be clear that humans can train others to become more empathic, caring, and authentic. Once again, I doubt that I can teach you anything of any significance but I can 'learn' you much if you choose to learn.

The critical factor, however, for the learning would really begin when you initiate, involve and personally experience these facilitative conditions first-hand. This would be best achieved in role-playing and practice in everyday situations. Here, moving abstract constructs from the idea to the action, experimenting levels (from the meaning to the things-and-events levels) would result in what I call the process of experiential learning. I believe that all of the theory and knowledge about counseling does not help you or me become a better counselor until we have personally experienced the process, therefore, I recommend that each of us choose to find a colleague-counselor with whom we could work.

Let us examine how PEGS (the therapeutic climate) might work. What do unconditional positive regard, caring, and respect mean to you? How do you know when someone conveys this form of respect? As you dwell on these questions you might even access scenes, word sounds, feelings, maybe even smells or tastes (VAKOG — Visual, Auditory, Kinesthetic, Olfactory and Gustatory) from some person in your life who communicated this special kind of love? I wonder if there are any common threads regarding this unconditional positive regard with which we both might agree? What verbal and/or nonverbal cues does that caring person display? How exciting that we might agree that part of this sense of regard and respect from another seems most clearly present when it appears as unconditional. I feel loved, respected, cared about when the other accepts me as I exist at that moment. There appears to be no apparent message, 'I will love you if you ___ or when you ___.' The respect is sensed as unconditional. My sense of self becomes filled when I am respected by you without judgment or constant evaluation.

Cl: Yeah, I suppose my mother loves me. They're supposed to, you know. But I get the feeling that she only loves me when I'm behaving exactly the way she wants.

C: Is it kind of disappointing, sort of that you wish she would just love you for being you, not for being what she wants you to be?

Cl: Yeah, exactly (pause) now dad's a different story. I know he loves me for who I am. Oh, he can get on my case a lot and we have our arguments and differ, but I know he cares about me.

The client demonstrates an understanding of unconditional positive regard in his discussion of the mother's and father's love. In addition, he probably senses the empathy in his counselor's response (he really heard me) as well as the positive regard indirectly conveyed.

When you focus and listen (empathy) to me, I can't help but feel respected, prized and special. You took the time and energy to be with me in those special ways (positive regard). If your words were clear, relevant and concrete (specificity of expression) and I sensed your honesty and realness (genuineness) I would have directly and indirectly experienced the core conditions and you would become a very special person to me.

'For me,' could be the prestatement of everything I say because my perceptions, observations and beliefs come ultimately 'from me' and 'for me.' The assumption in this, for me, seems to be that each of us continually constructs our perceptions of self and the world via the internal processing within our organisms. For me, when someone cares or respects me they genuinely move closer to me. They look me directly in the eyes. Probably at the preconscious level I pick up bodily cues from them that convey trust and comfortableness. I feel less suspicious, less on guard. If I take time to become aware of my internal processes, my thoughts are calmer, my feelings are soothing, probably my breathing becomes more rhythmical and slowed, my pulse rate and even blood pressure lowers. In general, my entire body seems more relaxed and this might even show in the visible parts such as face and hands. Readers might want to test this out for themselves — the next time you are with someone you know who cares, observe her, seeing and sensing what it is she does to convey this caring for you.

I have learned over the years that positive regard and genuineness (or realness) probably depend as much on nonverbal components of interaction. Yes, our words do give us clues as to one's genuineness and respect and care for us, yet probably the nonverbal cues stand out significantly as powerful messages, as well (research agrees, e.g., Watzlawick, Beavin and Jackson, 1967).

I have begun to formulate and extend a further facet of positive regard. While the unconditional and nonjudgmental stance that the counselor conveys tends to be generally helpful, another subtle part involves *trust*. The trust I speak of arises out of my unconditional respect and acceptance of you. It translates into a sense that you can do; that you can work through your own morass; you can choose, you can create your own reality; in short, you can be trusted. The regard and respect to which I refer does not mean a condescending 'smother' love, but rather a challenging love, a belief that you can be capable of becoming a fully functioning human being who can take responsibility for his/her own life. In other words I can trust you! How difficult it seems to transform this belief into practice. What really becomes the implied good seems to be a faith in you, that you can face your fear, your depression, your confusion, your pain and that only *you* can take it away. The counselor's belief and faith in the client comes through. I cannot fix you up. I cannot take your fears away from you. I cannot live and direct your life for you, but I can have the faith and belief that you can go into the depths of self to explore and accept your pain and fear and move out and on. Let's examine an actual situation:

Cl: But how can I deal with this; so horrible, so painful?

C: Yeah, you wonder how much more you can take and right now you're just not sure.

Cl: That's it. It hurts so damned much. I wish you could take all of this away, NOW. [HERE, THE COUNSELOR LISTENS TO THE HURT AND EXPRESSES THAT TO THE CLIENT. THE CLIENT CORROBORATES THE COUNSELOR'S UNDERSTANDING.]

C: Yeah, part of me wishes I could take the pain away yet the stronger part tells me that even if I could, I'd take something even more crucial, your self-respect.

Cl: Well, I don't know. I can't go on much longer like this.

Now the counselor has reached that critical existential impasse so prevalent and so much a part of counseling. The belief, although positive, is that we exist primarily alone and are continually in the process of carving out and creating our essence. It further translates into the belief that emotions such as despair, hurt and loneliness are real and not to be manipulated into solely logical or illogical compartments. The problem with treating the hurt by attempting to relieve it deals with only half the issue. The hurt may be relieved, but it will inevitably cycle back to be denied, distorted and relieved again with little or no resolution of the curative aspects of the total acceptance of the hurt. To plummet to the depths so to speak, to go deep inside and to become totally immersed in it, to cry and sob until tears no longer exist takes what Paul Tillich once described as 'the courage to be.'

Cl: I feel so desolate and lonely I want to cry (bursts into tears).
C: (In a caring voice) I know it feels awful, but tears will only make it worse. Can we try to think of ways you can get over your loneliness?

I believe this counselor cares, yet not in the way we've described. There may be an indirect message of 'I'm uncomfortable with your tears and hurt and I want to take them away from you because I don't think you can.' Once again, it's nearly impossible to be nondirective. We continually communicate something. What does the next counselor communicate differently?

Cl: I feel so desolate and lonely I want to cry (bursts into tears).
C: Yes, the hurt — so devastating.
Cl: Yeah (nodding her head up and down in agreement, hands closely holding head).
C: (Tentatively) So damned lonely; those tears have new meanings and I wonder if your hands aren't trying to hold and console you — saying it's ok, just to go with it?
Cl: (Long pause ... with crying and hands shifting, slowly caressing face and head.)
C: So lonely, yet so warming to realize that you can comfort yourself — is that part of it?
Cl: (Nodding her head affirmatively, sobbing more slowly now.)

This counselor in trying to stay closer to the experiences and feelings of the client surely conveys empathy; however, notice the more subtle empathy projected onto the nonverbal communication — the meanings of tears and the movement of hands. Counseling emerges as more than the parroting of the client's words (and repeating, 'unh, uh').

In summary, the therapeutic benefits of positive regard exist in a nonjudgmental climate where the person's potential is *trusted* far more than the person herself could imagine and where the lines begin to dim. For surely we have begun to realize that positive regard can be conveyed indirectly through other core foundations: realness, empathy and specificity of expression.

For the most part, each of us wants to be with those similar to us. 'We like those who are like us.' Opposites attract only slightly; over the long haul, however, those with common values, interests and experiences are those who come together. Generally it seems people feel more comfortably connected around those people with whom they feel a certain affinity or commonality (which makes for community).

Affinity or commonality can be conveyed through high PEGS and language, particularly via the highly empathic language we have discussed. When you listen to me in what I perceive as a highly empathic level (3–5), I feel an affinity and connection. You understand me at a deeper level. But what I'm 'hearing' is deeper than your sounds. Your physiology or body language communicates even more powerfully. Breathing tempo, voice tones, facial expressions, gestures and the varied quality of your bodily movements provide me with much more than words alone and much of this I pick up at the preconscious level, i.e., I'm hardly even aware of it. Can you recall a parent's voice tone or facial expression that represents much more than words? How different would be the voice tone and facial characteristics of your mother conveying love and acceptance vs. disapproval or criticalness?

Erickson's use of 'matching-pacing,' as discussed in the earlier section on Implied Directive Language, can be used here. As we first meet our client we can begin by 'matching' his physiology. We might note the slump of his shoulders and then assume a certain position in the chair similar to his. If her legs are straight out in front, I can place mine in a similar manner. As is the case in any of these interactions, they can be overdone. Too rigidly matching or mirroring can have a reverse effect. Clients can sense this as mocking or demeaning and certainly as behavior far removed from genuineness and positive regard.

Matching the physiology of his breathing also can be highly effective. As I match his breathing tempo and then approximate his voice tone, we begin the process of connecting and merging and I haven't spoken a word, yet. You can experiment with this by visiting with someone differently, the only difference being your matching their depth and rhythm of breathing and their voice tone and tempo.

I have learned that when I match clients' physiologies, particularly their breathing, voice tone and posture, I can be far more effective in conveying a high PEGS climate, especially my empathic understanding.

I hope I can write clearly and descriptively about this. A client comes in to see us describing her depressions:

Cl: Yeah, I guess you might call it depression (head bent down and talking slowly in a low voice).

C: [WE COULD NOW BEND OUR HEAD DOWN SLIGHTLY AND TALK IN A LOW VOICE MATCHING THE VOICE TEMPO.] It's that awful depression that brings you in to see me, is that part of it?

As I match her physiology, I can begin to 'lead' her. I might notice, as I begin to talk a little more rapidly in a louder voice, she too may begin to talk this way. As our client begins to experience PEGS and matching physiology we can deepen our therapeutic connection by listening and watching how she represents her world (VAKOG).

THE THREE PHASE COUNSELING PROCESS

Through their years of studying the process of counseling, Carkhuff and his colleagues pointed out three basic phases that counseling follows: Exploring, Understanding, and Acting (Carkhuff and Berenson, 1977).

EXPLORING

I amaze myself each time I work with individuals or groups because I notice a similar process that invariably takes place. As we sit together, individually or in a group, we kick off the sometimes awkward task of getting to know one another — the Exploring phase begins. In the past I would struggle with what to say, how to begin. Now, I generally share what I'm experiencing, usually a feeling of excitement and suspense wondering where we shall be going and what the client brings to our time together. We each continue to explore. I will often ask initially, 'What do you want to get from our being together?' or 'What is your goal in coming here?' These questions prepare us for a solution-oriented process rather than focusing on problems. I get very different kinds of responses than if I had asked, 'What is the problem?' The client most frequently comes from a very vulnerable position, scared and unsure of what will happen and I must respect that. Thus, most frequently we begin with this 'vulnerable position, scared and unsure' (utilizing whatever is presented).

The Exploring phase (I also call it the downward phase) consists of my listening and responding with PEGS to my clients, which helps them explore and struggle with where they are in their world and what is going on in it. One client would hold her head in her hands and ask herself, 'Just what is going on? What is happening to me?' Slowly as she began to grapple with these questions, she started to have a semblance of understanding. Can you stop a moment and listen to yourself recalling when you might have gone through these head-holding explorations?

The Exploring phase can all but shut down unless the client senses PEGS. This opening phase in counseling can be the most delicate stage. The client may be vulnerable, doubting, or confused. He may be filled with anxiety as to what to expect. His fears and expectations can overwhelm. What I say or do in these first few moments can have crucial effects. In empathizing, a level 3 (interchangeable response), for example, may be critical. Any higher level of empathy might prove distracting.

    Cl: I don't know what's wrong. I guess I'm kind of lost.
    C: Sort of really lost and you don't know where to begin but you'd

like to understand, find solutions and move on, is that it?

I really like this response (level 4 or 5) yet the client might be overwhelmed if not confused by this high level, complex exchange. In fact, many clients have never been listened to this carefully and in this manner. It's as if I'm just learning to be a goalie and Wayne Gretzky comes in, 'fakes me out' and sends a vicious slap shot into the net. My response must match where my client is, otherwise I overwhelm and momentarily lose the connection we have.

Cl: I don't know what's wrong. I guess I'm kind of lost.
C: I think I hear the lost part, do I?

Here the counselor's response may seem clearer yet tentative and encourage the client's continuation (a level 3 interchangeable response).

In the Exploring phase, clients often experience a kind of self-diagnostic process which elicits greater clarity that can lead to growing understanding.

During this process my own language patterns become essential. For my words can have a startling impact on the directions my clients take. For example, I find I rarely use the word 'problem' since that presupposes they have a problem. I might better describe their struggles as being with 'issues' or 'situations' or creating 'solutions.'

Clearly this not so subtle change of labels can have quite an effect? There is a difference between having a problem vs. an issue or being in a temporary muddle or simply being 'stuck.' For example, just learning to substitute 'won't' for 'can't' can evoke different perceptions. 'I won't,' presumes I take charge and choose. 'I can't' implies 'It is out of my hands,' 'I have no choice in it.'

UNDERSTANDING

The Exploring phase can be described as necessary but not necessarily sufficient for Understanding (the second phase). Clients in productive Exploring processes participate in a learning process which can result in gaining Understanding. Understanding can result in the 'Ah-ha' insights that can become the foundation for the third phase. Just as Exploring may not be totally sufficient for Understanding, Understanding may not be sufficient in itself for Action. I have been aware, frequently, of clients who seem to have Understanding yet appear completely unable to act on their 'insights.' One young woman once told me, 'I really believe I know *why* I'm depressed, but I still feel just as bad.'

The Understanding phase of counseling should not be interpreted as necessarily gaining 'insight' or realizing the answer to 'why' questions. While this occasionally may happen, more frequently the Understanding phase results in clarification and a special kind of awareness as to what-is-going-on.

Understanding in the counseling process involves the construction of meanings, not necessarily the reasons. Clients so often start with the *why? Why* do I do this? *Why* do you think this is happening? *Why* am I so depressed, scared, lost, etc.? *Why* me?

In my earlier counseling days, '*why*' was an important part of my interactions. If I got lost or didn't know how to respond I would often ask my client '*why?*'

Cl: I'm depressed all the time.
C: *Why* are you depressed?

Now I have trapped myself with this question. My client begins to try to explain the '*why*' of her depression. She begins the mental search for her 'becauses,' because of this, because of that. Her explanation draws upon cause and effect and now we enter a verbal cul-de-sac. *Why* can be a powerful question to ask in the external world yet, in my opinion, is of little use in the internal world of counseling. Understanding is better arrived at through *What, How, Where* and *When*. These questions press toward facts, events, happenings, behavior, and solutions. Clients can learn *how* to change through understanding *what* to do and Hypnocounseling can be at the very heart of this search.

Cl: I'm depressed all the time.
C: All the time?
Cl: Well, not ALL of the time.
C: And now I wonder if you can tell me about those times you DON'T DEPRESS yourself.

This example, although in a condensed form, shows a process of understanding that differs significantly and more helpfully than the '*why*.' The counselor's last response suggests choice; indirectly suggesting the client does it to herself. The use of the verb form of 'depressing' suggests ownership and responsibility. At this point the counseling often can take a dramatic change in direction. In addition, the client can be subtly learning that there are times when she is not depressing herself — exceptions to the rule she formerly held. (Brief therapy, as we will discuss later, focuses on 'exceptions', or times when the complaint is not experienced.)

Understanding occurs in those moments where clients learn there are no simplistic causes and effects. Rather, understanding takes place when clients learn that they must be responsible, that they have choice, and that resolutions are possible and lie within.

ACTING

Exploring and Understanding are necessary but not necessarily sufficient. The figuring out, my self-exploration and growing understanding of my world and its issues, are not enough — what *I do* about it becomes the theme of the Acting phase. Within the therapeutic relationship emerges the directions and the actions I must take.

If, as a counselor, I can be fully with my client, with PEGS and Exploring and Understanding with him or her, I will hear what seem to be appropriate clues for possible actions. In the Acting phase I hear the directions and kinds of actions that fit this client most uniquely. Here, I find help from the eclectic stance of Hypnocounseling; for the deeper my knowledge of other approaches, the more options begin to be opened to us. It is as if I have many different glasses to look through and, therefore, I see a richer and more varied scene. I sense that how he asks for more direction or how she tells me, indirectly, may be signaling for a rational approach (RET or RT). Others signal they tend to be very visual, and imaging might be of value. Here I see the person as the authority for his/her own living. Answers, resolutions and actions to achieve these goals come from the client; my task becomes one of facilitating and providing as many options as I can. I prize choice very highly and make the belief-assumption that both the client and I have choice. We shall illustrate several strategies of the Acting phase in the latter section of the book.

Probably the most critical learning I have made regarding the process of counseling has been its flow and variability. At one time I thought that the process progressed in a certain order, by the numbers so to speak; (1) Exploring, (2) Understanding, (3) Acting. Each time I tried to 'push the river,' to force my map of the process, it invariably resulted in a breakdown.

I try to remember to trust the process, especially when I sense I'm trying 'to fix someone up,' forcing my own agenda, or simply just not listening or acknowledging the individual's uniqueness. I may have some hunches as to what's going on or what clients must do, but ultimately it becomes the clients' responsibility to find their own meaning and their own actions. I am only a facilitator.

The three-phase counseling process becomes distorted whenever I move too slowly or too rapidly away from my client. For example, the Exploring phase may be very brief. Quickly we connect, building a positive, therapeutic relationship, and may even move through the Understanding phase and yet become stalled when called upon to Act. You may notice clients who, it seems, require care and lots of time to work through the Exploring phase and then seemingly skip the Understanding phase to focus almost immediately on plans of Action. There are no fixed blueprints for the counseling process.

For certain individuals, building trust in the Exploring phase may take an inordinate amount of time. When my impatience dominates our counseling, both of us lose. How essential it becomes that I stay with my client and look to him for direction and for feedback as to where we must go next, what we must do next. At the end of the day, if I can trust my client to be able to determine her own pace and direction, we both will learn and grow in positive directions in the process.

In pulling together the core communication levels (1–5) and the three-phase counseling process of Carkhuff *et al.* you may have noted how the levels and phases parallel each other. Clearly, a level 3 response (interchangeable) seems to be most effective in the Exploring or beginning phase of counseling. A level 4 response appears most appropriate at the Understanding phase; a level 5 response is most helpful when approaching the Acting phase. The following example shows appropriate Counselor levels of response (3–5) for each counseling phase: Exploring, Understanding, and Acting:

Cl: I just never seem to know what's going on. He'll say one thing and do another.

C: Yes, its so hard to predict, so confusing. [Exploring phase; a level 3 interchangeable response.]

C: So hard to predict since you rarely know what to expect and this not knowing really tugs at you. Is that part of it? [Understanding phase — with a level 4 additive response.]

C: Realizing how upsetting his unpredictable behavior has become makes you want to think of things you must choose to do. Is that close to it? [Acting phase with level 5: forward thinking.]

It seems important for me to match the appropriate level (3–5) with the particular counseling process phase that we are in.

Perhaps because the process description is simple and very general I have found Carkhuff's model extremely flexible and helpful. Naturally, the three-phase system must not become a Procrustean couch into which both clients and the counseling process must fit themselves. Instead, the system serves as a very general guide as to where we are and what-is-going-on, and this process can support an eclectic stance.

I believe each of us finds our own way of counseling. Ultimately we must, in fact, take a stand. At this point my way (which changes from time to time) is only for me and is in no way meant to convey that it should be yours. My great fear is that when a person, group or nation, has a certain 'right way' they attempt to impose their way on others. And eclecticism can serve as a partial defense against such authoritarianism.

Chapter 6
Strategies

You cannot step twice into the same river.
Heraclitus

The shoe that fits one person pinches another; there is no recipe for living that suits all cases.
Carl Jung

The strategies in this section are representative of countless procedures that counselors and clients can develop cooperatively. The four that I've chosen to emphasize can lend themselves to easy use by the counselor. For the most part, they also can be readily learned by clients and can serve as springboards to other variations that clients/counselors together might construct.

I use these strategies when clients and I seem to be stuck. For example, we shall read of the importance of a specific series of *questions*, which are the root and ground of Brief Therapy (BT). Drawing upon an appropriately constructed strategy, clients can not only come to grips with the BT questions but also can move beyond impasses.

While these approaches may appear to be the mainstays of the Acting phase of counseling, interestingly, I have found them to be helpful in the Exploring and Understanding phases, as well. Therefore, I tend to use these tactics early on in our counseling sessions whenever necessary.

Hypnocounseling, and its high PEGS relationship, as well as its hypno-suggestive language, acts as an adjunct and catalyst to help create strategies that specifically are tailored to clients, i.e., clearly within their perceptual field. This presents me with a delicate issue. If I try to foist a strategy on clients that comes only from me and the clients are not directly involved, I run the risk of the approach failing in several ways. It can serve to confuse or actually turn clients off. Or clients, feeling an inner compulsion to comply, can play the game of agreeing and going along, with little change and growth taking place. In these latter situations my high PEGS have been missing. When clients feel they 'should' comply, for example, I have failed them; they may no longer trust me.

The strategies of Hypnocounseling come from many sources, principally my clients. Strategies are most often a result of the counseling connection that the client and I form. Together we begin to construct a strategy that fits the client in the Acting phase. Additional origins lie in the writing and works of many others as well as the perceptive offerings from countless graduate students, colleagues, and friends who have shared their discoveries with me.

We will examine four specific strategies that clients and I have created: Surrogate Self (SS), Fantasy Relaxation Technique (FRT), Fantasy Door Approach (FDA), and Dials, Meters and Gauges (DMG). I have provided scripts for FRT and FDA that can be audiotaped or read (see Appendices A and B). These strategies can be used with many clients yet must be sculpted to fit each client in unique ways, out of unique contexts.

If I have created a high PEGS therapeutic climate as perceived by my client, then we begin to create a specific intervention with which both of us feel comfortable. At this point, I need to trust my clients; I need their help for I must turn to them for direction, feedback, resources and above all their own desire to change.

When I listen with respect and care, clients listen to themselves (sometimes, sadly, for the first time). As they are helped in this process of listening to themselves, they learn to see, to sense and to hear more clearly those still quiet voices from within. They share such thoughts as, 'I can't believe I said that,' or 'I wonder where that came from' or 'It's amazing, I never realized how important that was.' These discoveries represent insights and surprises that, if treated with care and respect, can be nourished and then translated into directions and goals: what *they* want and what *they* want to change. From these private musings emerge the strategies and actions that, together, we can construct.

SURROGATE SELF — SS (GUNNISON, 1976A)

The use of the 'Surrogate Self' in counseling is a simple Gestalt-like role-playing technique (Perls, 1969) that can be especially effective when the client has begun to see the counselor as a trusted, caring, and understanding person. The importance of building the nourishing therapeutic relationship within the net of hypno-suggestive language cannot be underplayed; otherwise, the counselor becomes a 'gimmick agent' armed with a big bag of tricks that is utilized whenever movement is not taking place ('movement' by the counselor's definition). The counselor becomes a factory worker on a production line, never really making any contact with the person. SS may not be used with all clients although it can become a 'critical incident' in the life of the counseling process when it fits.

I like this strategy because out of desperation a client (Cynthia) and I created and developed it together over a period of several sessions. I am struck by what seemingly resistant clients can do when given the opportunity to take over their own counseling. I have used many variations of SS tailored to fit each client. I like it because it fits the person-centered and utilization approaches (Hypnocounseling) so neatly. In addition, SS demonstrates a strategy that is eclectic and can serve as an excellent bridge to brief therapy (BT).

Clients, because of their misunderstanding and simple lack of knowledge of the counseling process, often play a kind of 'cat and mouse' game, expecting us to 'fix them up.' Many believe we automatically analyze them and will give them our expert interpretations assuming that we know what-is-going-on; thus they, too frequently, sit passively and wait.

A 19-year-old female client (Cynthia) began to argue with me and then would avoid any further discussion. She would often sit for long periods in stony silence waiting for me to pull the strings. I told her what I was experiencing — a kind of frustration, a confusion as to what was happening with me. I honestly told her I was uncomfortable. (When feeling uncomfortable, angry, lost or confused, I often tell the client.) I was beginning to feel angry. I felt lost and told her so. I recall a silence and at this point I believe it was the first time I became consciously aware of my going into an altered state.

It was as if I gave up control — a daydreaming sensation. I distinctly recall feeling a warm numbness and while I did not experience Erickson's blinding flashes of light, her face appeared strangely, as if it were in a cloud. Everything seemed slower: her voice, her movements, as if we had shifted into another time (each of these observations suggesting an altered state). As Rogers (1985) put it,

> I find that when I am closest to my inner, intuitive self, when I am somehow in touch with the unknown in me, when perhaps I am in a slightly *altered state of consciousness* in the relationship, then whatever I do seems to be full of healing. (p. 565, italics added)

These words struck me, and this experience transformed and touched me because I had had similar experiences in counseling. Now I know that when clients and I have created strategies for action, they had invariably emerged when I had experienced this form of self-hypnosis. And 'Surrogate Self' was constructed in and emerged from a similar process.

Nevertheless, I recall believing that my client had within her the answers and resolutions. Yet, I became more confused, wondering: What is going on? What is happening? We had reached an impasse; we were spinning away from each other.

Cynthia had come to counseling at the insistence of two friends and a positive part of her dorm life consisted of these friendships. The 'utilization' of this fact certainly created the spark out of which SS occurred as our strategy of choice.

I made a statement: 'Cynthia, I need your help' (I am continually surprised at the positive response I get in seeking 'their help'). For the first time, I perceived a possibility of cooperation.

When I'm cooperating with my client in creating a strategy, I do not see the whole picture. I experience that 'tunnel vision' of self-hypnosis. I experience a loosening of the bonds, a relaxed trusting of the process, a belief and conviction that the client ultimately holds the answers within. Also, Cynthia seemed to sense we had to utilize the importance of friendships and her ability to find her *own* way, her *own* resolutions. It was as if we had mentally merged; we had begun to construct a strategy together, yet neither of us was aware of that.

I began to imagine a strategy which I shared with Cynthia. It included a very close trusted friend — real or imagined. She responded to my request, 'I need your help,' and began searching for a 'name' she might choose in our role-play. After deciding upon the name 'Anne,' a childhood friend, we began.

Perhaps even more effective than, 'I need your help' is the suggestion 'to pretend.' The word 'pretend' like 'wonder' has hypnotic implications. They are both inward-searching words and 'pretend' can have age-regressing aspects that carry us back to our childhood memories. I will often remind clients of how they used to 'pretend' they could fly or sail ships out of trees, or play house or perhaps on rainy days be on a boat in the house with only two chairs and a blanket.

Pretending, it seems to me, becomes an additional way to carry on in respectful ways even if I sense some degree of client resistance. And so in Cynthia's case I asked her to pretend: 'Let's pretend that Anne is a very close friend *who knows you better than anyone else*. She is your closest and most trusted friend, and you have given her permission to come in and share everything she knows about you. Now, Cynthia, try to imagine that you have just left the room and that you are now Anne sitting in that other chair. From now on, you (Anne) and I will carry on a conversation.'

The name of the client's friend becomes essential and when by mistake I say 'Cynthia,' I apologize and repeat the name Anne, as well as reminding her that the best friend (in this case, Anne) '*Knows her better than she knows herself.*' This pretended fact serves as the key to success. She must pretend herself into a belief that this best friend 'knows her better than she knows herself,' a very crucial injunction. When we pretend something, we can pretend it into 'reality' at another level. A young man who came for relaxation training assured me that he could not be relaxed by me or anybody else. We talked about this in our rational heads and I wondered with him as to why he CHOSE NOT to relax. He objected to this and I said, 'OK, James you win. You WON'T (instead of can't) be relaxed and I believe you. BUT I wonder WHEN you *can* PRETEND to relax, NOW or do you want to wait until the next session? And remember you WILL NOT relax [Pause] BUT you *can* PRETEND to relax [Pause] I WONDER what the first thing you will DO [Pause] if you were pretending to RELAX? [Pause] Just IMAGINE what it would FEEL like to RELAX [Pause] but DON'T relax, just PRETEND' (capitalized words signify Interspersals).

Back to Anne (Cynthia).

This role-playing is difficult, but, surprisingly, if we have built a high-trust relationship, it quickly begins to move very effectively as the client starts to feel comfortable in the role. I continually reinforced the role by calling Cynthia, 'Anne.' I constantly reminded Anne that Cynthia was out of the room and that she had given both of us permission to 'gossip' about her and to answer my questions as truthfully as she (Anne) could. As I started to talk with Anne, I asked Cynthia to change chairs. As she moved to the other chair Cynthia *became* Anne. Sometimes I have asked the client to leave the room and return as the best friend and sit in the other chair. Sometimes, I have asked clients to leave the room by closing the door behind them. When they return by opening the door and entering they become the SS (I learned of the powerful effects that the door had on clients' perceptions to the point that the door-metaphor evolved into the Fantasy Door Approach (FDA) to be discussed later in this section). The changing of geography serves as a helpful pattern interruption. This use of two chairs, common in Gestalt-oriented counseling, helps dramatize the difference and increases the ease of role-playing. The questions and topics Anne and I could deal with are limitless. For best effect, they may be arranged in a hierarchy from the safest to the more crucial. I have found special value in such questions as:

1. 'Anne, I'm concerned and confused about Cynthia right now. I don't know what she expects from me. What is going on with her?' Typical responses to this question have been: 'She doesn't know what to expect from you either?' or, 'She just wants someone to listen to her.' This kind of question often elicits valuable concerns regarding the counseling process and, sometimes, our relationship.

2. 'Anne, as clearly as you can, tell me what you think is most seriously bothering Cynthia. You see, she simply won't talk to me and I was hoping you might give me some clues.' Her response might be, 'She's worried about her father's drinking and she's actually afraid of him,' or 'She thinks she's pregnant.' This rather abrupt question (the-heart-of-the-matter-question) can lead to useful information and, as Anne and I interact, important counseling is going on.

3. 'Anne, I get the feeling that Cynthia expects me to read her mind, and I can't. It seems as though for some reason, trust or whatever, she just will not share with me. What do you make of it?' Quickly the client learns to be Anne and answers in the third person. In response to this question, the client and I learn about trust in me and any other blocks that may be experienced.

4. 'Anne, I need your help. I do care about Cynthia, and I'm not too sure she really believes that. I am concerned. What do you think I should do? How should I behave?' Often I've heard responses such as: 'It's hard for her to believe you care: no one else has,' or, 'Just keep listening to her and don't turn her away.' This is another abrupt question and very powerful in the kind of answers that emerge, each

of which will probably be very important now and in our future counseling sessions.

5. 'Anne, I'm not sure, but what do you think Cynthia expects from me?' Responses to this question have included: 'Tell her what to do,' 'Just listen to her,' 'Give her some answers,' and 'She just wants to talk with someone.' This elicits feedback. Through our discussions of this question and the responses that result, I get much closer to her expectations of me, especially when I follow with 'Anne, what do you sense I should do?'

6. 'Anne, you know Cynthia has never talked about her mother yet constantly mentions her father. Why is that?' This kind of question is most productive, especially in areas where I sense there is a blatant omission. This is the content question, a very real question about the client's world that we had hitherto avoided and yet may promise important implications for our direction. Other questions might be:

7. 'Anne, what do you think Cynthia is feeling about our being in here talking about her?'

8. 'Anne, what do you suppose Cynthia needs right now more than anything else?'

9. 'Anne, what are Cynthia's hopes (or fears) at this point in her life?'

10. 'Anne, what do you think is the major thing keeping Cynthia from growing?'

    As we discuss Brief Therapy (BT), we will note the myriad of special BT questions available and the following are also very effective BT questions to ask with the use of Surrogate Self:

11. 'Anne, what does Cynthia want from counseling? What is her goal in coming here?'

12. 'Anne, what is Cynthia doing when she's feeling good about herself?'

13. 'Anne, what is going on now in Cynthia's life that is working?'

14. 'Anne, what is Cynthia DOING that she likes to do and is making her feel better?'

15. 'Anne, what are those things Cynthia is doing that ARE NOT working out?'

16. 'Anne, when Cynthia is continually doing whatever when will she start DOING something else?'

17. Throughout all of the interactions, Anne must be continually reminded that she knows Cynthia better than Cynthia knows herself. This 'seeding' enables the counselor to ask critical questions. 'Anne, What does Cynthia need to CHOOSE to do NOW? Anne, what is the first thing Cynthia must accept?' When Anne responds, 'I don't know,' I quickly interject, 'You mean Cynthia doesn't know?' I will wait and remind her that she knows Cynthia better than Cynthia knows herself. I will wait and repeat, 'I need your help.' 'Anne, after all, you do have the answers.'

These questions will be discussed more fully in the BT chapter.

These are just a few representative questions that the counselor might ask of Anne. I find that two or three important questions are ample since we both have much to process. After it seemed Anne and I were finished for the day and before I asked Cynthia to return to her chair, I said something like this to Anne: '*Anne, we've really appreciated your help and we hope we might call upon you again if we should need you. Now Anne, you can move back to Cynthia's chair and let's see what we've learned*' (or 'Anne, you can leave the room, get Cynthia and ask her to return').

It is crucial that the client (Cynthia) summarize and otherwise clarify what she has discovered. From this reflecting and processing, clients are more able to see what has been going on and what they must *choose* to do. As the surrogate self 'leaves,' client and counselor continue to work together with the new material that has emerged. The technique is straightforward and simple. It builds from honesty in the relationship. Its value lies in the quick accessibility to important areas between counselor and client that may take too long to discover in the usual counseling relationship. Thus, it can be particularly helpful in those cases where counselors do not have the luxury of time on their side.

As clients concentrate and focus on the role-play, they seem to be far more honest with me, especially in feedback as well as providing more helpful and beneficial suggestions to modify our strategies. Many times clients dramatically change our whole approach. In another Gestalt-switch they role play me (their counselor) and I play them. As you can imagine this brings about many changes.

In my conversations with many surrogate selves, I have gotten important, sometimes painful feedback to me as a person in the relationship; times when I hadn't listened, times when I had inadvertently judged unfairly. I was taught how I had done all of this. I realized how often I had gone on thinking I was doing a great job only to learn how I had been perceived by my client. Thus, the SS exercise provides an excellent opportunity for counselor evaluation by the client.

We have discovered important insights and possible behavioral solutions. What appears to be happening is that the approach provides a safe and objective platform upon which more relevant personal encounters take place. To speculate further, possibly using SS as if one were playing a part on a stage, enables clients to make discoveries that otherwise might not be available. One young woman described her experience as 'weird,' as if she were freed to explore in directions she had never taken. Becoming the 'other person' is a kind of escape from one part of the self to another. The technique of SS sometimes brings on amazing understanding. Perhaps the role-playing within the self (a play within the play) allows an anonymity which permits greater honesty. One male student told me that when he played 'George' he was able to be 'amazingly objective' and discovered things about himself he had not noticed before. He began to realize that 'George' was very important to him; how sad: he had never had a close and trusted friend.

I have noticed times when I have had important questions whose answers might have proved extremely helpful, yet for some reason I had avoided asking. Perhaps they seemed too abrupt or too intrusive; nevertheless, continually I am amazed at the ease with which I can ask these questions and the client, seemingly, so comfortably answers them within the framework of the SS strategy. I believe this occurs because of a form of hypnotic dissociation that emerges when clients attempt to pretend another role. It is as if I can make a split (or dissociate) between me and a role or part I am playing.

Through the use of SS, clients have a chance to plan and shape the direction and ultimate goals of their own counseling, especially when thinking about questions such as, 'Anne, what should I do as a counselor when Cynthia sits with me? What actions should I take?' While the initial response might be highly questionable it still opens unexplored avenues. It is important to emphasize that while the counselor learns from the surrogate, the client learns as well, and often this form of self-discovered awareness is enough in itself.

When counselors go to their clients seeking help with resolutions and tapping in on their creativity, they use a variation on the theme of SS. How many times have we asked our clients, 'If you were I, what would you tell me?' or 'If you were your own counselor/therapist what would be your answer?' or 'Let's switch chairs and you be me (counselor) and I will be you (client).'

Naturally, the greater the ability to be fully in the role of 'Anne' or 'George' or 'counselor,' the greater the success in the technique. Respect, patience, support and modeling on the part of the counselor significantly help clients learn how to role-play SS.

To summarize then, the use of the Surrogate Self as a Gestalt-like role-playing technique assumes that counselor and client have a developing interpersonal climate of trust, caring and honesty. As clients role-play their 'closest friend,' both counselor and clients hit upon highly relevant material that is extremely important in the counseling process. It is a technique especially valuable in cases of client confusion, blocking, or resistance.

FANTASY RELAXATION TECHNIQUE — FRT (GUNNISON, 1976B, 1985A)

FRT emerged as a specific strategy co-developed by Alex, a male college student, and me.

Alex appeared many years ago on a spring afternoon a few days before his final exams. He complained of being 'out of control' and bothered by what he described as 'losing it — a kind of mental block' when taking math exams. As we explored further, he told of his real panic, and his 'not being able to control it.' Furthermore, during a test, Alex felt something kept him from recalling anything from his classes (his mind went blank). He could not understand this because he had done well in all of his other classes, only on math tests had he 'clutched.' Real pressures appeared, not only failing his math requirement thus putting in jeopardy his GPA (grade point average) but also his graduation, for he had only a few days before his final exam in math. This situation, by necessity, proved to be an example of a kind of 'brief therapy' thrust on us both.

Alex explained that his life had become increasingly difficult. Once he began to worry about the test, mental panic built up with such force that he felt powerless and frightened. On previous occasions he had been forced to leave the testing room utterly frustrated, depressed and in shock.

We didn't have the luxury of looking into past history, of understanding the source of this very real anxiety to Alex. I became increasingly frustrated with our lack of time; if we had had many sessions the problem and context would seem to suggest the use of behavioral techniques and/or desensitization. However, several sessions were required to put these techniques into effect.

In that first session, it was as if we had taken an express train through the three process stages of counseling. I was unaware of trying to create high PEGS and 'exploring' the issue as fully as we could.

Alex: And I just don't know *why* this happens.
C: Yeah, and it really spins you around and if you knew WHY then it would be different. Is that it?
Alex: (Pause, shrugging his shoulders.)
Oh, I don't know. I'd almost like to give up. You know I can't even sleep at night. And how can I study for my other exams? Why? [HOW MANY TIMES HAVE I GOTTEN 'HOOKED'? AND ALEX'S COMPLAINTS PRESENTED A PERFECT TIME. I COULD HAVE GOTTEN US BOTH 'HOOKED' HAD I BITTEN ON THE 'WHY?', 'GIVE UP' AND 'CAN'T EVEN SLEEP AT NIGHT' BAITS. FORTUNATELY, AND PERHAPS BECAUSE OF MY DESPERATION OVER THE AMOUNT OF TIME WE HAD, I RESPONDED EMPATHICALLY TO HIS FEELING OF BEING OVERWHELMED. (ANOTHER EXAMPLE OF WHEN AN EMPATHIC RESPONSE CAN BE HIGHLY DIRECTIVE.)]
C: You're overwhelmed and discouraged as well right NOW and, YES, you'd like to know WHY, BUT you're not sure that would help anyway. Is that correct?
Alex: Yeah, I just don't understand... (pause).
C: Well, I understand you block on your math tests. It frightens, depresses and frustrates you until you draw a blank and you WANT to get through all of this SUCCESSFULLY and MOVE ON, is that right?

This is a critical point for us. I think my communication levels (Carkhuff) of 3, 4 and 5 helped. I tried to have Alex focus on some kind of successful solution. (You must understand that all of this took place many years before I had conceptualized Hypnocounseling or encountered Brief-Solution

Therapy.) I also discovered we can trust and draw upon our inner wisdom for creative solutions at certain times and in certain contexts *with* our clients. I had come to believe Alex and I displayed mutual trust — We were *cooperating* with each other as Gilligan (1987) suggests. The counselor is continually 'operating' with the client, and the client is continually 'operating' with the counselor. In a sense, effective counseling takes place when the counselor and client 'cooperate' with each other in 'common-unity.' As Erickson (1980c) put it, the therapeutic relationship between client and counselor '. . . is one of *interpersonal cooperation* based upon *mutually* acceptable and reasonable considerations' (p. 21).

I remember wondering if this would be one of those times when all my 'fancy' knowledge would be useless and that I'd simply 'blow it.' I was lost and a bit angry ('Why did you wait until now to come in?'). That last angry response I knew, if genuinely shared, would be unhelpful and distracting to pursue because of our time limits. However, I did share my sense of feeling lost. At first Alex was a bit unsettled, because to him counselors always knew what to do and were the experts. I tried to summarize and move us toward the Acting phase.

C: Alex, I really need your help now.

I want my clients with me. I want (need?) their help, for in the long run only they can know what works best for them. When asking for Alex's help I had to explain my 'lostness' and how, together, we could 'invent' a solution. Together Alex and I began to review 'what was going on.' We reviewed the events which led up to the impasse.

The more I listened to Alex, the more I felt confused and overwhelmed myself. I began to hear that mix of levels; describing meanings vs. describing things and events that we discussed earlier (Cade and O'Hanlon, 1993). Alex would start to describe facts and events and then add meanings, interpretations and causes. We decided to stay at the 'fact and events' level. This allowed us to explore what was going on, what was happening and what he wanted.

I recall the hard work and cooperation each of us showed. Back and forth it went, exploring so many possibilities of what to do. Finally, Alex said, 'If only I could just *interrupt* these thoughts and feelings.' That seemed to be the way. Steve de Shazer (1985) talks about finding the correct key, or the skeleton key, to open many doors rather than trying to understand the function and construction of the lock. Alex's word 'interrupt' 'keyed' for me. I recall mentally rehearsing Wolpe's (1961) systematic desensitization, a process of interrupting phobias by using relaxation. When discussing this with Alex we realized time was the issue with this approach. Instead of sneaking up on Alex's fear we both decided to go after it directly. With the springboard from Wolpe's work, Alex and I tailored an approach that resulted in FRT.

The first session ended with our focusing on the events and the happenings. There seemed to be no doubt that we had experienced each of the three process phases of counseling; Exploring, Understanding, and Acting. We parted with a goal.

In the second session Alex and I devised a plan to 'interrupt' through relaxation. He learned to imagine his body as separated into three zones: Zone 3 represented the head, neck, shoulders and arms; Zone 2 the trunk of the body down to the hips; and Zone 1 the thighs down to the toes. He was instructed to practice this countdown, 3-2-1, as often as he could. We agreed that if he could 'count himself down' (3-2-1) within ten seconds he would be definitely on track. He described it as a 'relaxing wash' as he counted down from 3 to 1 (see Appendix A, FRT).

Awareness was an additional discovery Alex made. He learned to become aware of his body and what was going on each moment. Thus, in the second session Alex was deeply relaxed and through the count-down procedure he learned to relax himself and practised this many times in the office. When he left, he was able to control his own relaxation and agreed to practice counting down every time he was aware that he was not attending to any special task. Alex counted down dozens of times until he was able to do it quickly and smoothly.

By attending to his body, Alex was learning to switch 'figure and ground' in Gestalt psychology language. The 'figure,' that to which he was attending, no longer had to be the anxious test situation but rather the awareness of his body in the process of relaxing. And the test-panic could drop back into 'ground.'

Also in the second session, after testing the success of his self-relaxation, I asked Alex to describe the specific situation that brought on the test-taking anxiety. As concretely as he could, Alex began describing the walk up the steps and into the building, the long corridor and the classroom at the end, including his own seat, where he would sit to take his exam.

In becoming aware of his body we discovered that a variety of physical cues appeared just prior to his feeling anxious. Alex and I began to realize that if we could discover the earliest physical sensation that preceded his flight into anxiety he could *interrupt* and control that.

Midway in the second session I took Alex on a guided fantasy of the math-testing situation: the stairs, the building, the corridor, the testing room, and his seat. As soon as he became aware of the bodily cues, he was told to interrupt them by counting down.

The client must fantasize the disturbing experience until he discovers the earliest physiological cue that precedes the anxiety situation. As soon as the individual senses the physical cue, relaxation is repeated. In other words, the counselor takes the client back and forth from fantasy to relaxation until the client has discovered the earliest physical cue to the imminent flight into panic or unwanted behavior. It is not uncommon to discover several bodily cues. Each fantasy trip and discovery of another cue must be followed by self-relaxation. Thus, many times the individual will take the same fantasy trip until there is no earlier bodily cue. Awareness of the earliest physiological cue is uppermost in the process. Perls' (1973) admonition, 'Get out of your head and into your body' is very important at this juncture of the technique.

At first, Alex became aware of his stomach tightening, then he became aware of a 'hot pressure' in his head followed by a tingling in his fingers. By fantasizing and then relaxing, Alex discovered tingling in his fingers as the initial cue that became the important stimulus for his response to count down. FRT was helpful since a physical cue (tingling in his fingers in the hand he held his pencil) warned of the impending flight into test-anxiety. Self-relaxation became the response to the tingling of his hands, and the mental block and hysteria were avoided. Tingling became the new conscious stimulus and relaxation (count down) clear elements of behavioral therapy. We were excited. Alex passed his math exam and graduated.

Different aspects of FRT have high transfer value. Once the approach has been learned for one situation, it can be generalized to others quite easily. The client learns that the body is inevitably involved in those experiences seemingly only psychological in nature. By learning this instant relaxation technique the person can transfer it to other anxiety situations.[1]

FRT can be used as an effective pattern interruption. Smokers, seriously committed to stop, can find FRT helpful. They 'walk' themselves through the fantasy trip that leads to their first urge to smoke and identify the earliest physical cue that precedes the act of smoking, often a craving that many describe as a 'pleasurable irritation' localized in the chest or throat. Hypnotic language patterns, particularly suggestion and interspersals involving CHOICE, presuppositions of what will be different in their lives when they become nonsmokers, as well as anchoring strategies can all be piled up as catalysts to augment the effects of the primary strategy of FRT. Between the urge to smoke (the physical cue) and the smoking itself, FRT becomes the pattern interruption, which must be repeated over and over again until the urge subsides.

C: Isn't it a WONDER WHEN you discover you have CHOICE? You can CHOOSE to change. WHEN will you become a NONSMOKER? NOW or SOON? And each time you COUNT DOWN you might want to use that as the SYMBOL and reminder of your NEW NONSMOKING status. Could you not?
[INTERSPERSALS ARE CAPITALIZED PRESUPPOSITIONS, ILLUSION OF CHOICE. NOTICE THE INDIRECT SUGGESTIONS UNDERLYING ALL OF THIS VERBAL ANCHORING.]

Another real advantage is that the technique can be put on an audiotape so that people can practice on their own. I have programmed tapes using

---

1. This explanation of the use of FRT with Alex contains many elements of what I would consider a solid working eclecticism.

FRT to eliminate smoking, to block anxiety, to reduce stress as well as for conditions where pattern interruption seems appropriate. Individuals have found that at first they must use the tape daily; eventually the frequency can be diminished once the client's new habit-ritual has been established.

The self-relaxation aspect of FRT is sometimes helpful for those individuals who occasionally have difficulty going to sleep because of incessant mental activity that is wasteful, inefficient, and counter-productive.

The count-down technique of FRT is not unlike the 'relaxation response' as described by Herbert Benson (1975). He has taken the secrecy and mysticism out of relaxation and has described a sound and empirically-based approach. Benson's thesis is that stress and hypertension are natural outcomes of urban, technological living. The inherent 'fight-flight' syndrome, while a valuable survival kit for our prehistoric ancestors, does not fit the accepted behavioral patterns of industrial societies. One simply does not fight the boss or run away. The frustration of this instinctual reaction brings on stress and anxiety that result in impaired functioning, high blood pressure, heart attacks, and stroke. Benson found that four elements of meditation were highly effective in blocking the dangerous effects of stress: (a) a private place; (b) a relaxed and comfortable body position (a not too comfortable position so as not to fall asleep); (c) a 'letting be,' passive mental set; and (d) a mantra: the use of a word or phrase repeated over and over again, for example, FRT's 3-2-1. Clients who have successfully employed FRT can transfer these learnings to meditation.

FRT typifies an eclectic position in that it is behavioristic and can be an effective approach for changing specific unwanted behaviors. It is a simple technique easily mastered by members of the helping professions. The approach is most similar to desensitization and reciprocal inhibition, yet differs in several significant respects. First, FRT is brief, generally taking only two work sessions. Second, the technique does not utilize a hierarchy of anxiety-producing stimuli, but, like implosive therapy, goes directly to the troublesome stimulus. Third, FRT focuses almost exclusively on the physiological cues that precede the unwanted behavior. FRT's eclecticism is further unveiled in its humanistic, existential (May, 1958) and Gestalt Therapy roots.

FRT is humanistic in that it assumes people are not only reactive but also proactive, capable of experiencing their own becoming and growing. The technique assumes the wholeness of the person. It also points toward self-control through integration of the intellectual, emotional and physiological dimensions. Individuals learn to control and avoid the debilitating flights into their heads. Body awareness serves as immediate feedback without the use of biofeedback equipment. It is Gestalt in the sense that the technique assumes integration and wholeness and depends on the Gestalt concept of awareness as well as figure/ground shifts for its success (Passons, 1975; Perls, 1973). It is existential in its assumption that individuals can choose, control, and assume responsibility for their own behavior.

FRT does not make up the whole counseling process; it is only a subset within the larger process, a strategy in the Acting phase. Its value lies in helping clients learn to cope, control and neutralize highly specific and unsought behaviors that block movement toward growth in the larger sense. The technique interrupts anxiety and helps change behavior, but it does not get into the etiology of the behavior. However, as Eysenck (1964) implies, controlling and eliminating certain anxieties can help the client break out of the vicious circle that so thoroughly entraps. The quick success, for example, of removing a specific block to growth can be intrinsically rewarding and can serve as a spur to continued work. Martin (1972) postulates, 'if a highly specific fear can be identified, its quick relief . . . can be motivating and rewarding even though internalized conflicts underlie the fear' (p. 133).

In summary, FRT is an attempt to bypass flights into panic and anxiety. In addition, FRT can be viewed as *pattern interruption* in that 'counting down' can be seen as an interruption that can give back control to the client. By becoming aware of the earliest physiological cue that precedes the mental panic and subsequent blocking of behavior, the individual immediately responds by relaxing and thus detours mental spinning and confusion. For example, the student who becomes petrified at taking exams first feels the physical cue, quickly relaxes (and can relax as often as desired), and thus 'washes' away not only the physical distress signal but also avoids the flight into mental confusion that would have developed if the process had not been interrupted (see Appendix A — A Script for FRT).

The 'countdown' of FRT can be used to attain a relaxed or meditative state; however, its significance is that it can be used as an instant (less than ten seconds) *pattern interruption*. To my knowledge, the 'countdown' is the only relaxation technique designed to be immediate and available to the client in any situation in life which requires instant interruption — interruption of addictive thinking and behaving.

After experiencing 'action phase' strategies such as FRT, clients benefit by thoroughly reflecting on their experience. Furthermore, counselors can encourage clients to create and modify strategies in ever widening ways so as to use them in many arenas of their lives, thus acquiring even more than independence from their counselors — the ultimate goal of Hypnocounseling.

FANTASY DOOR APPROACH — FDA (GUNNISON, 1982, 1991b)

Sometimes our emphasizing the outer world, our behavior, and our reactions to external events blocks an understanding and appreciation of our inner world. Many of our sensations about the self are part of this inner world, in fact, our inner world is the largest part of that organism we call the self, private and utterly alone. No person can accurately experience another's inner world.

We create our own reality with our language and perceptions, the way we talk to ourselves: it is the template through which we view our world. If we create our reality, we also create our pains, blocks and dilemmas. Following Ellis (1973, 1979) and Epictetus, it is not the external event that causes our difficulties but rather our fantasies about them. We create our own difficulties. Why then not use the same process of fantasy and imagery to let go, change, reinterpret the difficulties and blocks in our living? Fantasy-imagery, more specifically FDA, may be one of many ways to access the nondominant brain hemisphere functions and thus elicit more redefinitions and re-creations of what is going on. The use of Hypnocounseling can effectively bring this about. Aroaz (1985a) takes the position that

> ... conscious, left hemisphere activity is ineffective in the process of human change ... The more one tries and the more effort or will power one uses to achieve a personal goal, the less one succeeds. This is why relaxation [FDA and Hypnocounseling] — the condition in which thoughts can be dealt with gently, peacefully, and nonforcefully — is usually a preliminary to hypnotic change. (pp. 8 and 9)

As befits our model, FDA is also eclectic, based on concepts and ideas from several points of view. It stresses a phenomenological approach with behavioral and Gestalt components (Perls, 1969, 1973), drawing on speculation borrowed from work in fantasy-imagery (Bandler and Grinder, 1975) and right-left brain functions (Galin, 1974; Jaynes, 1977; Ornstein, 1977, 1984).

Fantasy Door Approach is an example of synergic process, which has been described by Coulter (1976) as 'working together,' as of the working together of seemingly disparate ideas or functions that produce a new whole greater than the sum of the parts (Gestalt). Synergy represents the process whereby dichotomous positions transcend and then merge into wider and newer levels of relationship. It clearly reminds me of Bohr's complementarity principle. Thus, FDA may be a technique whereby communication and linkage (synergy) between left-right hemispheres can be improved.

I cannot help but sense the effect of nonlinear (chaos-complexity) and dynamic energizing systems on the construction of most of the strategies that we examine here. The concept of synergy can be found in many approaches, systems, and life phenomena.

FDA, as in the case of so many other techniques, emerges as a joint endeavor of both counselor and client (Gunnison, Shapiro and Bradley, 1982). It seems inconceivable that methods, techniques, or a whole system of counseling could be developed in a one-way vacuum. Together the client and counselor form a cooperative relationship out of which emerges new learnings, new resolutions, and new techniques. This approach emerged when client and counselor knew the direction in which the client wished to move, and what the client wished to change. The counselor's expertise (knowledge of methods, techniques, and models) may be critical; yet it is the world and its parameters, as perceived by the client, that must provide a major focus. Both client and counselor created FDA as an appropriate means toward resolution and change.

Essentially, there are four aspects of FDA. First is the concretizing, or reifying stage. Here the individual is encouraged to make the debilitating issue concrete and to imagine where in the body this would be located. Second, the client is helped to relax through the countdown of FRT (Benson, 1975; Gunnison, 1976b; Jacobson, 1938). The third aspect of the process is a guided fantasy to the door (Shaffer, 1978, 1979; Sheikh and Shaffer, 1979). Doors seem to have a universal appeal. Doors can represent significant changes and can have potent and personal meanings. The final and critical stage is what takes place behind the door. Here the client encounters that portion of the world that has frustrated and inhibited growth; often new awareness, discoveries, and resolutions occur at this juncture.

A young woman, Susan, described a vague panic and uneasiness in her life. In previous work with other helpers many techniques were applied with little success. The nebulous and gnawing feeling persisted; it had begun to affect her whole life. Susan could not concentrate, had difficulty sleeping, and found school work almost impossible. As she put it, 'I was feeling scared and controlled by something vague and indefinable.' Time after time, we tried to close with what was going on, with what was bringing on this fear — nothing. Finally, Susan felt that if she could put form to the vague feeling we might begin to move. In addition, we both wondered where this form might be located in her body. She was soon describing a 'black world, a writhing mass, and a deadly stillness, blackness and blinding white lights' that was located deep in her chest cavity. By concretizing (reifying) her fear, imagining it consisting of form and matter, we were better able to deal with it. Thus, we both began to create the Fantasy Door Approach.

Susan had spoken of 'needing to close all of these feelings out.' We talked of how doors could do that, and a door became her special symbol. FRT helped her to become relaxed, and open-ended suggestions guided her on a fantasy that took her down a path, across a field and stream, and up a hill at the base of which was a large door. It was clear to her that this door-image she owed to Robert Browning's poem, 'The Pied Piper of Hamlin.' In the poem, the town fathers had originally promised to pay the Pied Piper to rid the town of its rats. The town council suddenly reneged and the Pied Piper piped all of the children of Hamlin town into a door at the foot of a hill and they were never seen again. That door became the symbol for the Fantasy Door Approach. Stories, legends and poems can become powerful and useful aids in counseling. Susan was guided through the 'door' into a tunnel that wound deeply into the hill and curved to the right. On her left was another door behind which lay the vague and 'controlling fear,' the 'black void' deep within her chest. It seemed appropriate to stop here. In fantasy, she stood in front of this door imagining what lay just inside. Then she was guided back. She described being aware that something was behind the door and felt both fearful and excited, as if she knew something was about to happen. We decided that during the next session she would finally open the door and fully experience what lay behind it and that she would know what she must do. It seemed important that she take two sessions before finally entering her door. The time interval seemed to help with the intensity and meaning of her experiences as well as giving us more time to ground the suggestion that she would be able to handle the experience and that she would learn a great deal. After her second journey she described her black void as being 'aloneness,' which represented people of all ages and cultures. She claimed to hear 'their voices and their silences.' She seemed to hear about 'their despair and their hopes.' She described how she heard their 'weeping and laughter.' She felt 'connected to them' and yet talked of the sensations of each being utterly alone. And 'I did not close the door after me, so aloneness escaped into the world with me' (Gunnison, 1982, p. 404).

I shall not forget Susan's journey. We were both astounded with the sensitive poetic description of her experience behind the door. Interestingly, her message took the form of the metaphor (FDA) that I have *borrowed* and *tailored* for use in other counseling sessions. I remain continually amazed at the strength and courage people can draw upon when in need.

In a grieving situation FDA seemed to be the method of choice for a young woman named Anne who had cut herself off from any kind of deep feeling. Five months previously, a young male friend and several family members had been brutally and senselessly murdered, and Anne had felt almost nothing. She had become numb to any emotion and became passively reactive to her world, no longer taking initiative. She had not dealt with the deaths and began to feel intolerable terror and anxiety that increasingly filled her waking and sleeping hours: a terror that she might be the next victim.

> Cl: It was a tunnel in which I walked. I could see a small bright light and felt scared and went slowly. Along the way, I met Charles, the friend who had been killed. He was wearing what I pictured him to be dressed in when he died; a white sheet of sorts wrapped around his waist. I looked at him for a moment and then we hugged each other. It was a really meaningful hug; it felt good to hold him. I stared at his face. He was really reassuring and told me to continue on, that he would be there when I returned. I could see a light in the distance. It was a big bright room. I sat in the doorway and relaxed. After a time I started back, it was as if I were watching myself walk back down the tunnel. I felt people all around me. They seemed to

> be reassuring, as well. I felt safe enough and just continued to walk. When I reached the point where Charles had left me, I looked for him. He wasn't there. I sat down and sobbed a good hard cry. This was something I hadn't done at all throughout the past five months. I felt different. I felt so very calm and that everything was all right. I felt ready to leave. (Gunnison, 1982, p. 404)

For another grieving situation a recent client, Rachel, found FDA appropriate and useful. No matter what the technique, it must fit and be appropriate to the person's perceptual field of experience. Rachel entered a cave beneath a special mountain which seemed to have a calming and helping effect. A very special door existed in that cave and through the 'seeding' effects of Hypnocounseling she began to realize that her mother was behind the door and she could open it, go in, and do what she had to do. 'Seeding' in hypnosis and Hypnocounseling comprises an indirect and subtle set of suggestions to help clients move in those directions they desire. Most of the seeding techniques (usually verbal) are drawn from IDL and in Rachel's case mostly consisted of 'yes sets' and presuppositions.

C: And Rachel as you stand before that door NOW, you *can* experience all the feelings, thoughts, that YOU WANT to explore. (Pause) DOORS *can* be very important in most cultures. SOME made of wood, SOME made from metals, SOME made from reeds or cane, AND SOME made from skins or hides (pause) ALL *can* OPEN things up or CLOSE things off (pause) or SHUT things IN or SHUT things OUT (pause) BEGIN or END (pause) those things needing BEGINNING or ENDING (long pause) I WONDER WHEN you will GO behind the DOOR (pause) NOW or when you are READY?

Rachel's imagination and sensitive creativity showed throughout. She went behind the door and rearranged, reconstructed, reperceived herself and her world. She had an opportunity to draw closure and in subsequent informal meetings said, '... I've let go and taken the memories of mother with me ...' (Gunnison, 1989, pp. 157–8).

It seems important to discuss or process the meaning of the fantasy experience for several reasons. In one sense, it simply helps clarify and reinforce the learning. In another sense, it is fascinating to speculate that as the individual verbalizes (left brain function) the imagery (right brain function), synergy results and a new perceptual reorganization occurs. Watzlawick (1978) argues that one purpose of therapy might be to lessen the discrepancy between the two hemispheres. At any rate, whatever is happening, discussion of the personal meaning of the experience seems invaluable. Anne's summary of her interpretation follows:

> My encounter with Charles felt really good to me. It was quite apparent what my fantasy was telling me. I felt good about it. It made me feel like I could finally remember Charles in his life, as he

was, not as the 'death picture' wrapped in sheets as I had made of him in my mind. I also felt like I could allow myself to continue to love him in his death. The people I had felt surrounding me were the identified people I felt were a threat to my life . . . I realize now that there are people in the world who are threatening, they may be around me, but I haven't encountered them. The fears I have are wasted energy because they are unknown to me. It's hard to explain, but since I walked through them, I feel more confident. And I know I must continue just as I pushed myself on at that point in the fantasy. (Gunnison, 1982, p. 404)

Thus FDA focuses on the inner world of the person and consists of four stages: (1) concretizing or reification, (2) relaxation, (3) guided fantasy, and then (4) going through the door. To understand the four stages of FDA and to explain how they work, it seems appropriate to explore the relationship between hypnosis-imagery and right hemispheric functioning.

The process of concretizing or reifying probably helps more for client clarification than anything else. It is not easy for clients to mentally transform a painful and immobilizing emotion into a physical object or thing. It becomes another metaphor, a powerful pattern interruption when a client changes her pain into a dark blob, a searing sphere or whatever other creative image arises. The pattern interruption of concretizing/reifying that results seems to help clients more effectively focus on the disturbing element. At least at the start, it provides something to have behind the door.

The second stage of relaxation is closely related to the guided fantasy of the third stage. Parenthetically, it should be noted that the kind of relaxation or guided fantasy is probably not important (although FRT would clearly be appropriate). It should be a technique of relaxation and guided fantasy appropriate to the counselor's skills and the client's perceptual field. To someone with claustrophobic feelings, relaxing in a cave or tunnel is just as absurd as guiding an individual from the inner city across a wilderness mountain meadow; the experience must fit. I assume that in both relaxation and guided fantasy the individual is experiencing a phenomenon akin to hypnosis.

Sarbin and Coe (1972) and Barber (1985), make a cogent and strong argument regarding the close overlap between guided fantasy-imagery and hypnosis. In fact, they state that it is apparent that the phenomenon we describe as hypnosis is clearly related to and dependent on the subjects' imaginative process. Day (1977) suggests that it is these imaginative processes that are linked to right hemispheric functioning. In addition, Ley (1979) and Jaynes (1977) note that hypnosis, as a state of consciousness, is predominately the responsibility of the right hemisphere as well. Thus, relaxation, fantasy-imagery, and hypnosis merge (synergy?) to access the right hemisphere. We now have another way of viewing change.

The fantasy trip down a path, across a field and stream, and into a tunnel in a hill is a set of guided suggestions; however, what occurs behind the door, within the tunnel, is a production of the individual. It has often been described as having a dream-like quality. There is probably a very real tapping of the right hemisphere. There exists an intriguing possibility that one reason FDA may work in those cases where other more rational methods and talk therapies do not is that the difficulties may involve right hemisphere processing. Methods that tend to be objective, logical, and rational — such as RET, Reality Therapy, and Decision Therapy — involve the left hemisphere; therapeutic techniques such as FDA make contact with the right hemisphere.

Anatomically, the communicating linkage between the two hemispheres consists of a large bundle of interconnecting fibers called the corpus callosum (Ornstein, 1972). A wild hypothesis may be that, just possibly, effective counseling serves in a like manner, as a kind of corpus callosum between the hemispheres. Wholeness, integration, psychological health (whatever the label for psychological well-being) are terms that describe a synergic process (Coulter, 1976) of the two hemispheres. For example, when I have a bodily felt-sensation that things are awry, that something is going on in my world that is vague, undefined, I may be responding to my right hemisphere. How amazing the change when my left processing produces, 'I feel sad, because my friend is leaving.' Now the left hemisphere cogently and helpfully symbolizes the right hemisphere sensation and I feel different. So the hypothesis is that change, therapeutic insight, is a result of synergic, linking processes in both hemispheres.

I have learned that there are many doors in the tunnel. Clients and I have discovered doors that lead to a dream room. Here clients can enter and have an insightful, helpful 'dream.' Something as simple as the door to the 'answer room' was created by one client who then took the answer room and 'door' with him. He later remarked that it was 'fantastic' to be able to sit quietly and go to his answer-room door when faced with situations for which he needed resolutions and answers. At other times clients can construct doors to lead into rooms of the past when they might confront their child.

FDA, as with any counseling strategy, must conform to the clients' needs and world. Those who have the slightest fear of the tunnel, construct or find 'doors' in cottages, cabins and, in fact, one client found a self-standing door just beyond the meadow. Some clients cannot handle fantasy trips down paths, across mountain meadows by beautiful mountain streams. City people, for example, get lost even estranged from the whole process when they are asked to climb a mountain or hike along a woodland path. We must be able to shift quickly to hallways and stairs in buildings, to vacant lots or parks or alleys. Their comfort zones widen and we can be productive again. When strategies become inflexible or coercive, ignoring the need of the client, they become useless.

You might lead into FDA by proposing options. 'Would you like to try something that might help us?' If yes, try to describe it. 'We can go on a fantasy trip down country paths, mountain meadows. Do you like hiking on paths and into mountains?' If not, 'when do you like to get away by yourself and where?' Utilize 'Some people prefer walking in city streets and alleys, others in malls or vacant lots. You'll know which is most helpful and comfortable.' This person-centered and utilization introduction empowers the whole process of FDA.

A fascinating point of departure may be from the client's 'special spot' or his/her 'favorite place.' I find that most clients love to find that 'special place' where they experience wholeness and peace; where they feel safe and empowered. Our 'special spot' can be anywhere and we may find ourselves alone or with special others. I think another gift, besides letting clients learn to relax themselves (FRT), can be the gift of identifying this 'special spot.' It is also important for them to realize that they can return there whenever they wish.

To begin the mental imagery associated with FDA in the clients' own geography (their special place) both comforts and empowers them. Clients, interestingly, feel safe and more hopeful whenever they can be encouraged to construct strategies and actions from their own perceptual fields. Fantasy-imagery, more specifically FDA, may be one of many ways to access the right hemisphere, thus eliciting more synergic redefinitions and re-creations of what is going on.

As with FRT, an FDA script has been prepared for use in Appendix B.

DIALS, METERS AND GAUGES — DMG

Our world is so filled with dials, meters and gauges (DMG) that one has to work hard to find places where they do not exist or intrude. My car is filled with dials and gauges. I can hardly go into any room in my house without seeing at least one kind of meter: a clock, a thermostat on the wall, a radio or TV. All are so commonplace — begging to be used in counseling.

When Danny, a 13-year-old young man, came to see me, he spent time telling me of how much he liked cars and wanted to someday become an auto mechanic. You can be sure the following became a regular part of our counseling: dials, gauges, engines, brakes, carburetors, steering mechanisms. It seemed that in future 'inspections' (sessions), he might want some help in brake and carburetor adjustments. We talked of learning how to use his out-of-control gauge on his own dashboard (forehead). These suggestions, while metaphoric, also served as pattern interruption and rich sources of utilization.

DMG is compatible with person-centered and utilization approaches. The person can construct them and utilize them in their own perceptual fields. For example, Marge responded to my question, How are you doing? with, 'On a scale of 1–10?', thus opening up DMG as a strategy. I recall being in my counselor-trance state and heard this as a useful and compelling metaphor. I cannot say if the 'meter' we constructed came from us or that I had heard or read it somewhere else, but the everyday occurrences of our clients can be utilized in helpful and person-centered ways. I have yet to find clients who have not been interested, motivated and excited about discovering and creating their own gadget.

Marge, a bright middle-aged woman with depression, was referred by a colleague for some 'relaxation and hypnosis.' Notice how, in the following interaction, Hypnocounseling 'seeded' the construction and her discovery of a DEPRESSOMETER. She learned FRT and could count herself down quickly.

C: I need to get clear on this. You say your depression gives you so much pain that your whole body seems to ache. Is that part of it?

Cl: No, it's that I sometimes get a headache but I don't mind, it's the depression that I want to get rid of.

C: OK, so at this point you have this awful depression that can even give you a headache; however, what you WANT most is to get through it? Or do you mean CONTROL it? Is that it? [THIS LAST QUESTION IMPLIES TENTATIVENESS AND SERVES TO CONNECT WITH THE CLIENT, A LEVEL 4 RESPONSE. WHEN CLIENTS CAN DISAGREE OR CLEAR ME UP ON SOMETHING, I FEEL OUR RELATIONSHIP IS GROWING IN HELPFUL DIRECTIONS: 'SEEDING' THE ACTION PHASE. THE INTERSPERSAL CONTROL PROVED SIGNIFICANT.]

Cl: Yeah, CONTROL it? Maybe? Hadn't thought of it that way. Just want to get rid of it.

C: Not sure about CONTROLLING, maybe, BUT you'd sure want to get it behind you, as the garden snake sheds its old NO LONGER useful skin?

Cl: Yeah and the more I talk about it the more depressed I get.

C: Right NOW, how bad?

Cl: On a scale of 1–10?

C: Marge, that's fantastic, do you know you just discovered a METER? Let's call it a 'depressometer.'

Cl: I have a what? [FASCINATING HOW JUST ONE WORD CAN HAVE A HELPFUL IMPACT. A METAPHOR *UTILIZE IT* I COULD HAVE SAID 'LET'S PRETEND YOU HAVE A "DEPRESSOMETER."' (HER ROLLING EYES MIGHT ALSO HAVE MEANT SHE WAS LOOKING FOR A DEPRESSOMETER.) I COULD HAVE SIMPLY ASKED, 'WHAT ARE YOU SEEING RIGHT NOW?' — GOING RIGHT TO HER.]

C: You have a great 'depressometer' and you don't see too many these days. Would you like to learn about it?

Cl: I don't know what you're talking about.

C: Well, half the time I don't either but that's . . .

Cl: Well, what do you mean?

C: OK, Marge. You COULD sink back in your chair. And you could COUNT DOWN, NOW or LATER. As you hold your

C: depressometer or look at it strapped to your wrist (pause). You can even sense the depressometer as warm, cold, smooth or rough (pause). And NOW we can find out whether it has a sound (pause). Do you hear anything? (Pause.) [THIS CLIENT AND I HAD A GREAT RELATIONSHIP. SHE HAD A SENSE OF HUMOR (EVEN THOUGH DEPRESSED) AND WE UTILIZED IT. THIS CLIENT'S INTERRUPTION WAS AN EXCELLENT SIGN OF INVOLVEMENT. FRT YES SETS, TRUISMS ACCESSING — VAKOG.]

C: As you LOOK at the dial (pause) YOU said it had numbers from 1–10 (pause). Is that not true? (Pause.) NOW as you look at your dial on your depressometer, (pause) what does it READ? (Pause.) Does 1 mean little or no depression and 10 off the wall? (Pause.) Or is it reversed?

Cl: 1 is no depression and right now it's about 3. (Slow labored speech.)

C: Oh 3, and you *can* easily SEE the 3 on your DIAL (pause). So 3 means not very much depression (pause). And NOW, MARGE, (pause) I wonder if you could TRY something DIFFICULT (pause) BUT I KNOW you can DO IT (pause) TRY to move it up to a 4 — depressing yourself (pause). That's right, you *can* TAKE your TIME (pause) And let me know WHEN (pause) you've MOVED it up to a 4 (pause). Good! [Pause.] And, I wonder just HOW you did that? (Pause.) Marge, isn't it interesting (pause) that when you learn to climb UP a mountain (pause) you ALSO have learned to climb DOWN? (Pause.) Your *conscious* MIND [pause] knows so much [pause] that your Unconscious mind (pause) KNOWS MORE, of (pause) HOW a faucet CONTROLS the shutting OFF (pause) and the turning ON of water (pause). Your conscious mind might NOT be sure of (pause) the connection of GRAVITY, (pause) FAUCETS (pause) and Depressing, (pause) BUT your Unconscious can know FULL (pause) WELL (pause). There it is. [ILLUSION OF CHOICE — IF THERE BE NO IDIOMOTOR RESPONSE YOU CAN ASK THE CLIENT TO 'PRETEND' LEFT OR RIGHT POCKET. LEFT FINGER TWITCHES (IDIOMOTOR RESPONSE). VISUAL/KINESTHETIC ACCESS — NODS AGAIN. PARADOXICAL INTERVENTION — NODS HER HEAD IN ASSENT. INDIRECT SUGGESTIONS SUCH AS PARABLES OR METAPHORS INVARIABLY ARE MORE HIGH-POWERED THAN DIRECTLY TELLING. SPLITTING PUNS AND PLAYS-ON-WORDS ARE EQUALLY AS POWERFUL. PUNNING.]

Marge and I discussed at great length what she experienced (some clients prefer to keep their experiences private — I certainly respect that). Marge enjoyed sharing what she felt. I encouraged her to reify the depressometer — what it looked like (V), felt like (K) and how she could use it. She was teaching me about this meter intervention DMG. She described the sensation of control of her depression and the growing awareness of choice. She spoke about this choice in terms of responsibility, offering the idea that if she could make herself more depressed, she could *lessen* her depression. Marge was willing to experiment with a homework assignment we discussed. She was able to use her 'depressometer' to test the existence and levels of her depression. I asked Marge if she would try to use her 'depressometer' when depressing rather than be depressed in ways that she had learned throughout her life. Marge promised to 'consult' her depressometer on a regular basis and then make her own adjustments. I was excited and curious and in response to my question, 'How did you raise your depression?' (a paradoxical intervention) she went into great detail describing the visual and auditory images and sounds that depressed her, learning that she depresses herself.

In subsequent meetings, Marge elaborated on her success in choosing and controlling her depression. She found several ways of imaging or fantasizing positive feelings which served as excellent Pattern Interruptions for depression. One of these, she discovered, was her favorite spot; a summer camp she had gone to as a child. Here she felt, 'whole and at peace.'[2]

I hope by now the myriad of combinations and possibilities can be recognized. DMG can be utilized in many different contexts. I have used an 'anxietizing meter.' As in the case of a 'depressometer,' learning begins as you and the client create a context for the 'anxietizing meter.' Hypnocounseling seeds the whole process of utilizing the device in appropriate and necessary ways.

DMG has many unusual elements. First, it's a primary pattern interruption. Second, this interruption forces choice, in a way. A third advantage aids the individual and because of the context elicits the development of responsibility. Fourth, inherent in the DMG process is the vivid sense of control. Individuals don't have to view their symptoms as caused by the habitual patterns of the past. Instead, they find that they have mentally constructed a DMG device that conveys feedback as to their symptoms or debilitating situations. They can 'pretend' themselves into being in a 'new reality,' new perceptions and behaviors.

One middle-aged woman who had used DMG asked if she could use it for 'stopping something.' I was intrigued and agreed to help. She developed her own strategy from which, once again, I have learned. She described a meter from 1 to 10, where 10 represented her 'smoke stack' as she called it and 1 was the goal of nonsmoker status.

She used the meter in gradual steps since she had too often failed in a 'cold turkey' approach. She continually checked her meter and chose to move from 10 to 5. Not being successful, she became more 'realistic' and chose 8 as her goal (she described the number of cigarettes and the frequency of smoking for each point on her meter). Eventually, as she lessened the frequency of smoking, she found it very helpful to pinch her

---

2. Readers might want to try this. Sitting back in a quiet and relaxed state you *can* drift off to *your* favorite place; a place where you feel whole, peaceful and great about yourself — and you can return there as often as you wish.

left hand between the thumb and forefinger each time she felt the urge to smoke (very similar pattern interruption used in FRT for interrupting smoking). The pinch served as kinesthetic awareness that helped her choose to interrupt smoking behavior. Not only is this a form of pattern interruption, but also a form of kinesthetic anchoring involved in her counseling strategy. To me, this was the purest form of Hypnocounseling; wherein this client created her own therapeutic strategy.

In addition, I have found metering to be an important part of brief eclectic therapy; two sessions and the practice time in between seems to be sufficient in most cases. Metering lends itself to Hypnocounseling and the person-centered and utilization approaches. We utilize whatever the client brings — the person's symptoms, the person's pain each become important motivators in his/her context. We assume humans have the inherent tendency to grow, to actualize in the context of their lives and that specific blocks in their growth and development can best be resolved from within as long as people perceive and experience the therapeutic climate (PEGS).

As I begin to observe closely and listen carefully to a client, I usually begin to hear (or rather they are telling me, indirectly) the strategy that I should consider. For example as I listened to Agnes:

Cl: I am depressed all the time and I can't do anything about it.
C: Is it that this depression seems to chain you and control you?
Cl: Yeah, I just don't enjoy things anymore and I can't seem to do anything about it.

Because I want to remain open to clients, I listen for any clues that tell me of the way they view their world and what strategies/theories seem to 'fit.' At this point I think I hear Glasser (1965, 1984, 1985) in this client's attempts to describe her depression. Her admission of no longer enjoying things and feeling powerless reminded me of Glasser's four needs: belonging, power, freedom and fun. Was I, in fact, hearing Glasser? I must test this out with my client for she has the answer. (Again, an example of how eclecticism works in Hypnocounseling.)

C: Sort of means that with the depression you don't have FUN anymore and sort of like you've lost your POWER? Is that it?
Cl: Exactly, I used to at least enjoy reading and being with friends, but now I don't feel like doing anything. [TENTATIVE TESTING OF GLASSER'S NEEDS.]

At this point I hear her talking about 'doing and behaving,' another component of Glasser's work. There appears little, if any, aspects of Glasser's theory or strategies that might conflict in any way with Hypnocounseling or BT. In fact, Reality Therapy and Hypnocounseling are based on the belief that a supportive therapeutic relationship (PEGS) must be built.

You may very well ask, 'OK, so how do we use Hypnocounseling with

Glasser's Reality Therapy, for example?' Let's return to Agnes.

C: Agnes, am I to understand you would like to 'enjoy things' more and feel as if you have some CONTROL of your life?
Cl: I guess so. I just don't know what to do. What do you recommend?
C: I guess it's almost painful and frustrating not knowing 'what to do,' is that it? (Slowly.)
Cl: Yeah, I want out!
C: You mean you want to stop it?
Cl: Well, I've been trying and I can't.
C: (More slowly) So, DEPRESSING yourself has no pay offs — or does it? [USING CLIENT'S LANGUAGE WHENEVER POSSIBLE AND APPROPRIATE. HERE WE USE GLASSER'S 'CONTROL' FRAME. I CHOOSE TO IGNORE THIS QUESTION. NOW, I START SLOWING MY RHYTHM OF TALKING. PACING AND MATCHING NOW WITH INTERSPERSALS.]

Here the Hypnocounseling begins with the interspersal DEPRESSING. I would agree with Glasser that this implies they're doing it to themselves rather than having it done to them as they originally viewed it. The construct of DEPRESSING also acknowledges responsibility and choice. In the language of Hypnocounseling we have already started to 'seed' the idea that clients can have control.

Cl: Oh, I don't know. What do you mean?
C: I remember as a child, if I had tantrums for a while (only for a while) I could CONTROL my parents and teachers so tantrums had a pay off — know what I mean? BUT I don't know if DEPRESSING might have a similar pay off — or not?

Glasser wants clients to believe they have choice and can use this awareness to control their world. I am reminded of the old sailor's comment, 'You can't change the wind, but you can trim your sails.' And furthermore, I might even share this saying with Agnes (if appropriate).

Agnes also talks about 'being with friends' and this might indicate setting up her 'best friend that knows her better than she knows herself' via Surrogate Self.

I hope this is beginning to make sense to the reader, i.e., what I mean by listening to the client to learn where to go in the counseling, what strategies or actions that seem appropriate.

As I reconsider the sampling of strategies in this chapter, I am reminded of the debt I owe to the eclectic position for my development as a counselor. Fantasy Relaxation Technique, for example, shows the influence of the behavioral conditioning approaches. Surrogate Self clearly represents a strong Gestalt tendency with assumptions and questions heavily influenced by Glasser's Reality Therapy.

Perhaps you can pick up the underlying thread (perhaps cable would be more accurate) of Ellis and RET with my emphasis on doing, thinking, acting and the impact that values, beliefs and interpretations have on our perceptions. 'People are disturbed not by things, but by their view of things,' Epictetus, first century AD.

Yes, Hypnocounseling draws from many sources including Alfred Adler. Ellenberger (1970) lamented the fact that much of Adler's work had been unacknowledged and unappreciated: 'It would not be easy to find another from which so much has been borrowed from all sides without acknowledgment than Alfred Adler' (p. 645). Actually Wilder (1959) put it more bluntly: 'The proper question is not whether one is Adlerian, but how much Adlerian one is' (p. xv).

Yes, I would imagine you can sense the influence of Adler (1970) on Hypnocounseling in the brief-therapy-like questions; the stance of encouragement and support, the belief in choice and responsibility and, above all, the belief in growth, health and a positive direction (Gunnison, 1990). Note how Alfred Adler (1970) states this:

> Individual psychology has shown that every individual is seized by the striving for perfection, by the upward striving . . . The striving for perfection is as innate as something which belongs to life, a striving, an urge, a developing, a something without which one could not even conceive of life. (p. 31)

This could have been written by Erickson, Maslow or Rogers — could it not?

No doubt it becomes apparent, at this juncture, that I have borrowed from many sources; however, each strategy, technique, idea has invariably been adapted to fit the template of the individual as well as the major assumptions of the person-centered and utilization approaches.

Chapter 7
Hypnocounseling and Brief Therapy

> *And since you know you cannot*
> *See yourself so well as by reflection,*
> *I, your glass, will modestly*
> *Discover to yourself that of*
> *Yourself which you yet know not of.*
> William Shakespeare

On first stumbling upon the shorter therapies in the 1960s and 1970s, I found approaches that seemed too directive and too blatantly manipulative for me. Often I came away with the sense that these writers were too full of themselves and had a kind of professional arrogance — an occupational hazard. Above all, I did not get the impression that the client was in charge nor served as a source of direction and/or resolution. As in the case of my first experience with hypnosis, I sensed condescension and authoritarianism in the guise of expertise. However, following the advent of the brief therapies influenced by Erickson's works, a more respectful and empowering approach seemed to appear.

For years I have struggled to find ways to shorten the number of counseling sessions. Hypnocounseling, of course, has been a solid attempt to do just that. The strategies created with clients such as FRT, FDA, DMG, SS have each served as 'keys' to shortening resolution times in counseling. I am reminded of Steve de Shazer's (1985) metaphor of the skeleton key. What seems important in counseling is finding the 'key' to the solution. If we have in our counseling kit-bags a 'skeleton key' that opens many doors, we can be far more flexible, thus following the Lanktons' (1983) eighth assumption: 'The person with the most flexibility or choice will be the controlling element in the system' (p. 12). As I model my flexibility, hopefully, it might 'rub off' and be learned by my client who might leave our sessions believing in choice and becoming increasingly more flexible.

Moshe Talmon (1990) wrote a book titled *Single Session Therapy* (SST). His discussions could become the ultimate of brief therapies. Talmon defined SST as one face-to-face meeting between counselor and client with no previous or subsequent sessions within one year. He realized that many clients attend only one session (the average number of sessions being only 3–6). Originally, Talmon assumed that clients drop out of counseling because they are dissatisfied for a number of reasons. A closer examination, however, showed that most clients who drop out after a single session do so because they have accomplished their goals and on the average report as much improvement as those who have stayed the course. I found Talmon's book to be an unusual starting point for learning about the brief therapies.

An interesting idea my wife and I have learned from Talmon's SST is to begin by utilizing the first appointment phone call a perspective client makes. We use this time for pre-session interventions that can have an excellent catalytic effect that can shorten the number of sessions appreciably. We immediately begin 'seeding' and using hypno-suggestive language during the initial phone call. 'When you meet with us for the first time we will want to hear what changes have begun to occur since this phone call.' This helps 'seed' the idea that spontaneous changes can and do occur and that we are most interested in here-and-now changes.

BRIEF THERAPY — BT

It becomes impossible to discuss the brief therapies and ignore the impact that Erickson has had especially on the Brief Therapy (BT) that came out of the work at the Mental Research Institution of Palo Alto, and the Brief Family Therapy Center of Milwaukee. BT can be traced through the writings, among others, of Cade and O'Hanlon, 1993; de Shazer, 1988; O'Hanlon and Weiner-Davis, 1989; Walter and Peller, 1992; Watzlawick, Weakland and Fisch, 1974; and Weiner-Davis, de Shazer and Gingerich, 1987.

BT centers on solutions and resolutions. Focusing on 'the problem' actually could not only maintain the problem but also exaggerate a problem that might not even exist except in the counselor's perception. Instead of seeking diagnoses and causes for problems, BT concentrates on changing the focus from problems to solutions and holds belief and value assumptions comparable to Hypnocounseling. The problem is in our thinking and the solution is in changing our thinking. While this (problem-solution) has been a major theme, it is obvious to me that it is very difficult advice to follow by those who are oppressed and perceive themselves as helpless and hopeless victims. Nonetheless, I believe that in the long run that is all any of us can choose. To move from the horror of my existence, I must choose to think about it differently. I must not forget the profound affirmation that Viktor Frankl (1959) made following his experience in the death camp '... everything can be taken from a man but one thing: the last of the human freedoms — to choose one's attitude in any given set of circumstances, to choose one's own way' (p. 65). How powerful an attitude, to know that I have ultimate choice as to how *I react* to any given situation or event!

BT ASSUMPTIONS

As you read through these assumptions you may want to consider where you stand on each. You may notice parallels among similar assumptions of Rogers and Erickson. Nevertheless, these remain as assumptions of BT distilled from the works of Cade and O'Hanlon, 1993; O'Hanlon and Weiner-Davis, 1989; Walter and Peller, 1992:

1. CLIENTS ARE CAPABLE OF MAKING RESPONSIBLE CHOICES
We assume people are born with the privilege of having choice and can learn to act on those choices in ways which make them aware of the consequences. We can aid clients in their movement toward responsible choice-making by interacting with them at the verbal and nonverbal levels, as if they already are responsible choice-makers. Hypno-suggestive language, especially presuppositions, helps here:
> *Now that you know, deep down, that you are a responsible chooser, how will you deal with that?*
>
> *And as you think of that alternative, which part of you is considering the consequences?*

2. CLIENTS HAVE WITHIN THEMSELVES THE RESOURCES NECESSARY TO CONSTRUCT SOLUTIONS WITH A POSITIVE FOCUS
This assumption represents a basic trust and faith that individuals have a locus of control from within. I treat my clients as if there is *no doubt* that they can construct solutions and change in those positive directions as they define them. And I interact with them *as if* they do:
> *And even NOW you might go back to a time in your life when you got through a difficult situation or accomplished a task that seemed impossible. AND you can take the time to recall that action.*

3. CLIENTS HAVE THE CAPABILITY AND DESIRE TO CHANGE QUICKLY
This assumption seems far removed from the early belief that counseling represented a lengthy, time-consuming process and clients must not be rushed. BT can imply resolutions that move too fast. While I believe clients can change rapidly, I need to caution myself to let them *go as slowly* or as *rapidly* as they need, for they are undergoing new ways of experiencing, thinking and feeling.

They may want to *steep* in all of this newness rather than be quickly *dipped in* and *out*.

4. SOLUTIONS CAN EMERGE FROM EXPLORING EXCEPTIONS
When counselors and clients look for 'exceptions' or times when the problem is not there, solution 'blueprints' emerge. For example, when I ask clients to recall exceptions:
> *And so tell me of those times and places, when you're not confusing*

or guilting yourself.

What are you doing when you're not depressing yourself or anxietizing yourself?

5. YOU CAN'T STEP INTO THE SAME RIVER TWICE (HERACLITUS)
As clients change their perceptions by focusing on the constancy of change, new vistas arise; permanence disappears, little is the same. Change is constant. If our clients learn to accept this, then they will behave as if change were inevitable.

6. WHEN CLIENTS AND COUNSELORS FOCUS ON TINY CHANGES, LARGER CHANGES FOLLOW
Given a simple homework assignment that appears realistic and achievable, clients can begin to believe solutions to larger issues are possible. Clients who have a small success can enlarge upon it. Small steps can lead to great strides. And, as the counselor, you can suggest this when you ask:

And what little thing happened just now?

If you were looking up a steep stairway and your goal was to get to the top, what must you do first?

I have learned to wait, to be patient, as my clients will invariably come up with their answer and I have to be prepared for it. Each part of our 'small change' goes from pennies to silver dollars.

7. BT EQUATES WITH THE 'PERSON-CENTERED' AND 'UTILIZATION' APPROACHES
The counselor must use the client's map of the world and the language and representation of that world. In addition, BT focuses on the person-client as the source for direction and solution, the client becoming the authority and expert at the center of the process. The therapeutic climate (PEGS) focus becomes the bedrock for brief therapy.

8. THE ORIENTATION OF BT EMERGES AS A MAJOR FOCUS ON THE 'PRESENT AND THE FUTURE'
Instead of being oriented to pathology or exploring past causes and history, BT concentrates on what is going on in the here and now and how changes can be made in the future.

Hypnocounseling and BT seem to me to be built on the same bedrock of assumptions so well stated by Rogers (1961):

> If I can provide a certain type of relationship, the other person will discover within himself the capacity to use that relationship for growth, and change and personal development will occur. (p. 33)

9. *Clients tend to represent their worlds on a continuum between things and events (reporting) and meaning (editorializing)*, Cade and O'Hanlon (1993)

As briefly mentioned earlier, by *reporting* the world we describe it as we perceive the 'things and events.' When we *editorialize* we begin the subjective process of ascribing 'meanings and interpretations' to the external world we perceive. The world of events and/or happenings provides us with the backdrop from which we begin the attribution of meanings and values and beliefs. Major dysfunctions occur when we blur these distinctions and we begin to ascribe meanings in unhelpful ways.

For example, assume you and I perceive a person frowning. That is what we *report*; however, what you and I do inside with that frowning, makes all the difference. We start *editorializing* (thinking again) what the frowning means. 'Must mean he doesn't like me.' 'She's in pain.' 'He doesn't approve of what I did.' We could go on *editorializing* ad infinitum. 'Unchecked assumptions' abound and result from not checking our *editorializing* with our *reporting*. We have made 'unchecked assumptions' about the meaning and interpretation of the individual's frown. One way to check this out would be to ask the person what the frown meant.

In one of my classes, a student sitting in front of the class kept dropping her head and it seemed she was starting to cry. Rather than upset the class or embarrass her, I ignored her. I editorialized, thinking she had just left a sad situation or maybe my lecture triggered deep emotion. In conversation with her after class, I asked if she were OK, and said that I had noticed that she had kept her head down and seemed to be crying. At first she gave me a rather startled glance and then smiled and told me that she had gotten something in her eye. We should all get such a break, once in a while!

During my tenure at St. Lawrence University I taught a practicum class in counseling each semester. The counselors-to-be would share their taped counseling sessions and early on there would be continuous discussion as to what certain clients 'meant' by what they verbally or nonverbally communicated. When I would ask the counselor presenting the case, 'Did you ask?', students would look at me as if I were crazy. So I would ask them what they meant by those shocked looks (rolling eyes) I was seeing. Then, many would explain that they felt it would be uncomfortable for them to ask, that they would feel intrusive. We then looked at the two levels and discussed the dangers of their own editorializing and the unchecked assumptions which arose from them.

There appears to be a magic in the air when we see a lush wheat field. Of course, we've forgotten the ponderous and heavy work that precedes the bountiful harvest: the plowing, the planting, and the irrigating. Brief Therapy can have a similar illusion about it. It seems easy to recognize the magical interventions, not realizing the plain hard work required to build the therapeutic relationship, to listen and to plan for the utilization of those resources which our clients bring.

Chaney (1996), in an interview with John Weakland six months before his death, asked, 'What was the most important thing that a therapist needs

to do?' Weakland replied:
> ... really listen to what the client says. REALLY listen. That means a number of things and one of the main things it means is don't get into the business of being so perceptive that you know what the client says or means better than the client does. (p. 20)

In BT, as in Hypnocounseling, the responsibility for outcomes must be placed in the hands of the client. The power of the approach, it seems to me, lies in the set of increasingly narrowing questions that can be answered only by the client. The effectiveness of the process once again depends upon how well I can create the high PEGS climate. This latter condition seems especially important since BT requires a flexibility and trust on the part of the client that generally may not be present at first. We ask clients questions that appear difficult if not impossible for them to answer. They need our support here. These questions, at first, tend to confuse and temporarily block our clients.

The way I ask questions results in very different answers or solutions. Remember, questions are very directing, for example our classic unhelpful question: 'Why are you depressed?'

EXAMPLES OF BT QUESTIONS

Questions represent the 'keel and rudder' of Brief Therapy. For the question has (within its structure) presuppositions and implications that lead toward positive and specific 'events, happenings,' and outcomes. For example, 'What is your goal in counseling or what do you want to change now?' has within it the presuppositions that the client has a goal, can identify it and not only wants change but also can change. How different than, 'Well, what's the problem and why do you have it?' Here the presupposition remains that you have a problem and that finding the cause seems important, all of which goes counter to BT assumptions.

When I ask the questions, 'What is your goal in coming here?' or 'What do you want?' the answer I receive becomes the outline of what the client now must *do*. Not only does the client answer the question but also the answer provides the solution as to what the counselor and client, cooperatively, construct.

As we move from the initial general question, the focus narrows to specific requests for what-is-going-on at the things, events, and happenings level. BT prefers to concentrate on the things-and-events level on the assumption that change here will bring about positive change at the meanings level.

Walter and Peller (1992) describe a delightful example that indirectly symbolizes the process of positive focus and movement. It seems that a strong hitter for the Chicago Cubs had fallen into a long and paralyzing slump. The manager-coach, Jim Frey, noticed the batter watching videotapes of his striking out, grounding and popping out. The player clearly focused on what he had been doing wrong, trying to find the 'cause' for his disastrous slump. Of course, the player was learning and relearning how to bat in unsuccessful ways. As Jim Frey walked by, he stopped and praised the player for his determination and desire to improve for the team and for himself, and, while doling out his sincere praise, he made one suggestion. He recommended that the player return to the team video library and select only those films that featured the player on top of his game, swinging and hitting in a highly successful fashion.

The questions I have adopted (and adapted) can be found in the writings of Cade and O'Hanlon, 1993; de Shazer, 1988, 1991; O'Hanlon and Weiner-Davis, 1989; Walter and Peller, 1992. I call them 'facilitative questions' because they serve as springboards from which we facilitate and tailor questions that specifically 'fit' our clients. The use of the questions can be difficult since there is no order, no template, no outline. The outline or direction must come from the client. How freely can we give over control and choice to our clients? This decision becomes challenging and difficult. For many of us, giving up control may run counter to much of what we've learned.

> ... How do we construct solutions? Very simply: *one*, define what the client wants rather than what he or she does not; *two*, look for what is working and do more of it; *three*, if what the client is doing is not working, then have him or her do something different. (Walter and Peller, 1992, pp. 5–6)

To me, this summarizes BT. We can now turn to the questions that can be generated by the three ways of constructing solutions.

1. In helping clients clarify what they want, I find the following initial kinds of questions helpful: 'What is it you WANT from counseling?'; 'What is your GOAL in coming to counseling?'

    These initial questions suggest that clients have 'wants' and goals. 'What ONE thing would you want to change NOW?' Focusing on ONE thing helps in two ways. First, we can immediately go to one topic rather than be bombarded and confused with a litany of changes. Second, if we can make one small change, then we can expect other changes to occur. One small change can breed success and a positive outcome.
2. When clients tell us what is working, we have cues as to what kinds of observations they can make outside of the session as well as what directions to take: 'What is going on NOW in your life that is working?' or 'What are you doing or what is happening in your life NOW that you like, even enjoy?' or 'What things are going on that are positive in your life, NOW?' Whatever answers I get, I want to reinforce and suggest that clients continue doing those things or being in similar positive situations.
3. If things are not working for clients, it's imperative that we learn in

minute detail exactly what they are doing. Rarely does the client *experience* the problem/issue continuously, and often clients seem to be unaware of this reality. So when exceptions are discovered they represent actions clients can take. The *Exception Question* tends to interrupt patterns of thinking and can change and/or expand modes of representation (VAKOG). The structure of the Exception Question elicits another way of viewing the issue and, for us, new options for homework assignments. The following are examples of exception questions:
- 'What are you DOING when things are working OK?'
- 'What is going on when the unwanted issue doesn't occur?'
- 'What are you doing when the issue seems absent?'
- (As soon as we get an answer we are already in the process of constructing solutions.)
- 'Of those things you're doing NOW which are NOT working out?'
- 'Are you still doing them?'
- 'As you look back NOW, are there things you're STILL doing that are NOT working, NOT helpful?'
- 'OK, instead of continually doing ____ when will you start doing something else ____?'

This is a form of pattern intervention. You are intervening and suggesting that clients interrupt their ineffective pattern of thinking and behaving by doing something else. For example, the counselor asks:

    C: Are there things you are STILL doing that are just not working?
    Cl: I guess I shouldn't go to the pub right after work.
    C: Why shouldn't you be going to the pub, how's that?
    Cl: Well, the kids are home from school and I guess I should be there.

In this case we have an example of the father drawing upon his own awareness to recall a pattern that is not helpful. The counselor doesn't make that judgment. All you and I do is ask the facilitative questions.

In addition, I have found that the following questions seem to help change and tap in on the client's resources and awareness.
1. 'I need to know how we're doing. What things are happening DIFFERENTLY or that you are DOING differently that can tell us we're on course?' Once again we can see the presupposition that things are happening and the client is doing something different as well as the suggestion that the client knows where we're going and how successful we are — an important question for feedback.
2. de Shazer (1988, 1991) devised the 'Miracle Question' which gets at what clients would be doing differently if the issue were resolved.

This question propels us into the future where we can look back to see how the issue had been resolved.

> 'Suppose tonight while you are asleep a miracle occurs and the issue is resolved — gone! How will you know? What will you be doing/feeling differently next morning that tells you there's been a miracle? What will those closest to you notice differently about you?'

3. Invariably, as we move through the counseling process, I also need feedback as to when our counseling should be terminated. Termination of counseling, it seems to me, is a topic that must be confronted systematically in counseling.

> 'What will be happening differently, what will you be DOING differently that will signal to us that our counseling is over?'

or

> 'When and how will you know and feel differently, when it is time for counseling to end?'

These questions do elicit resolutions; however, there are many other variations that can be created to fit appropriately. And when you try, you can discover your own helpful questions.

The BT questions we choose appear laden with assumptions and presuppositions. A primary focus of the questions concentrates on acting, doing, behaving and a new reframing of meanings. In addition, the question must lead to a positive representation. By positive representation, I mean representation of something that *exists*. Our questions can elicit ways in which we represent our world, whether it be in a Visual, Auditory, Kinesthetic, Olfactory or Gustatory mode (VAKOG).

Too often I hear clients say, 'I don't want to feel depressed anymore.' Here, clients try to represent nondepression, yet because of thinking nondepression, they once again become ensnared with depression. The more they try not to represent their depression, the more depressed they make themselves. It is impossible to dwell on negatives, positively.

You can try to comply with the requests, 'Do not think of an elephant' or 'Do not think of the number seven.' You probably will discover that you can VAKOG an elephant or the number seven, but that it becomes impossible to nonelephant or nonnumber seven without thinking of them. You may want to experiment with this by re-examining your own ways of not depressing yourself. Maybe you sense the trap as described above.

C: What do you want out of this counseling?
Cl: I don't want to be depressed anymore.
C: INSTEAD of being depressed what ELSE do you want?
Cl: You mean instead of being depressed?
C: Yes, INSTEAD of being depressed what DO YOU WANT to happen?
Cl: Well, how about if I want to be less depressed?
C: OK, that's at least moving us in a positive direction. And (talking slowly) you must not let me put words in your mouth.

	INSTEAD of wanting less depression, what would you rather have?
Cl:	You mean being happy?
C:	Is that what you want?
Cl:	Yes.
C:	OK, and what is going on or what are you DOING when you're being happy?
Cl:	Well, being with my kids.
C:	What do you DO with your kids when you are being happy?
Cl:	Oh, going on walks.
C:	What else?

Now C wants the client to list behaviors at the 'things and events' level that make the client happy. In addition, you can notice the specific 'things' on the list that clients can do and can practice for homework assignments between sessions. In effect, the client has described, or listed, his own remedies and all we need to do is keep him focusing on his lists. The client can take the time to re-examine his world and see it from a hopeful and positive perspective.

Carol, a middle-aged woman, came to see me because she wanted, 'Some suggestions about my life.'

C:	Carol, what ONE thing would you want to change?
Cl:	I don't want to feel so overwhelmed. [THIS IS WHAT THE CLIENT DOESN'T WANT.]
C:	Yes, I gather that, that's what you don't want. INSTEAD what do YOU WANT?
Cl:	A peaceful home.
C:	I wonder if you can go inside and SEE what that 'peaceful home' would be like? What do you HEAR? What does it FEEL like? [ACCESSING VISUALLY, AUDITORILY, KINESTHETICALLY AND PRESUPPOSING WHAT IT WILL BE LIKE.]
Cl:	What do you mean?
C:	Well, if, with your eyes open or closed, you imagine your home as being peaceful, what would it LOOK like? [ILLUSION OF CHOICE.]
Cl:	It just looks orderly — neat.
C:	So if I were to SEE your peaceful home I would SEE order and neatness.
Cl:	Yes
C:	OK, and are there any sounds that you can HEAR in that peaceful house?
Cl:	*No it's quiet — maybe some music . . .*
C:	Aha! and what kind of music?
Cl:	Probably some soothing classical music.
C:	Should I assume if necessary you could identify that peaceful music? [AND I WILL PUSH HER ON THIS.]
Cl:	Oh yeah.

C: And Carol, can you tell me what you FEEL like in that peaceful home?
Cl: I feel warm, comfortable and at home with myself. [I WILL COME BACK TO THIS AS WELL.]
C: 'Home with myself'; and that means . . . ?
Cl: Oh I don't know, probably relaxed and comfortable with myself. [INCOMPLETE SENTENCES ARE MOST FREQUENTLY COMPLETED BY THE CLIENT.]

In Carol's case our BT questions have not only facilitated exploration on her point, but also have given us cues or clues as to where to go from here. For example:

C: What are you doing at home when you're NOT feeling overwhelmed?
C: What are you DOING, what is going on when there's (order and neatness) (certain kinds of music) and (your feeling at home with yourself)?

We would ask her to be specific and list as many examples as she can. Then we might ask:

C: Carol would you try something? Would you go home today and find some small pockets of order and neatness? and go to those spaces. Could you go home and play some of that peaceful music and enjoy it in your orderly and neat places? In fact could you take a mental tour of your house, now, finding these orderly and neat places as well as where you are feeling at home with yourself? [IN MOVING TOO FAST AND PROVIDING TOO LONG A LIST I CAN END UP OVERWHELMING HER, WHICH WAS HER INITIAL COMPLAINT; THEREFORE, I HAD BETTER PRESENT THE PROGRAM IN THE FORM OF QUESTIONS.]

No one describes this process as being easy. It takes a respectful patience to hang in with clients at this beginning point in the process. However, a lot of learning, I believe, takes place here. Notice how the counselor sticks with the client; suggesting and leading the client into a representation of what they *want* instead of what they *don't want*. Notice the movement from 'meanings' to 'events and happenings' when the counselor asks 'What are *you doing* when you feel happy?'

As the client provides an ever-increasing list of 'events and happenings' that lead toward becoming happier, the counselor receives a blueprint for what the client can do differently now and in the future — specific homework assignments can emerge directly from the client.

In the first session, when the smoke and dust have begun to settle, I try to ask my first BT question. The smoke and dust, however, represent important metaphors in early sessions. They symbolize the natural upheaval experienced by clients in a new experience and in a very different relationship. Clients come to counseling with many unchecked assumptions. It may seem appropriate for me to spend time briefly explaining my expectations, beliefs and goals in counseling. Possibly just describing my values regarding human beings could be helpful. If I have one, discussing my 'creed' of counseling. And then again, possibly just 'doing it' rather than talking about it could be the more beneficial way. It depends on the feedback (verbal/nonverbal) that I get from the client which will determine my choice — for the client continually sends critical indirect and direct feedback to me and my task becomes, as Erickson would say, 'observe, observe, observe' and Rogers would say, 'listen, listen, listen.'

I try to imagine that my client and I have only one session together. By thus shifting from an attitude of fragmented and serial sessions to a holistic attitude of one session we can expect therapy to start right away.

Clients enter a strange and difficult relationship in which they suddenly realize they are expected to be the experts in control of their lives and some never do. It becomes very hard for them to imagine that they have within themselves the resources and the potential to solve their own issues or problems. I find all of this to be most unsettling for clients because their universe of expectations and assumptions has been turned on edge. And when I can utilize this confusion, disbelief and resistance, clients find their own momentum and eventually we both learn to have a greater trust in the process.

When this happens we begin the process of settling in with each other. This is also the time when clients decide if they are the appropriate 'customer' for counseling. As Cade and O'Hanlon (1993) put it, 'Who wants help, with what or for whom?' (p. 52). For example, I recall a young man who sat with me one day, stating 'I need counseling and you have the answers.' After some discussion it became clear that he was not the 'customer' for the kind of counseling I would provide. He patiently listened to me explain my values and goals in counseling. He was not interested. I gave him several names of counselors whose style I felt would be more comfortable with him.

To help with these kinds of issues, I designed my 'Creed of a Counselor.' It consists of a single sheet that I give to each client. It serves as an outline of what counseling means to me. This creed is served as an excellent springboard for discussion. It represents my attempt to answer common questions and concerns that clients often ask; however, it is always in the process of revision. I have included my first creed which is meant to be compared with the latest version.

CREED OF A COUNSELOR

Clients seek us out. They seek us out for very private and painful reasons. We must be able to tell them what we can do, what we can offer. If only for the ethics of the situation, people must have the right to know beforehand our personal values and our objectives. The following creed is an attempt to share my values, beliefs, and goals with that person who sits with me.

1. I will not agree to help you go off the edge. I will not agree to help you become a robotized normal and adjusted person. I will not help you stay and wallow in the cesspool of your own making. All of these go against my values. I will help you to grow, to become more productive, *by your definition*. I will help you to become more autonomous, more resistant to enculturation, more loving of yourself, more excited, sensitive, and full, more free to continue becoming the authority for your own living.
2. I cannot give you your dreams or 'fix you up,' simply because I cannot.
3. I cannot make you grow or grow for you. You must grow for yourself.
4. I cannot take away your loneliness or pain.
5. I will not sense your world for you, evaluate your world for you, or tell you what is best for you in your world, for you have your own world.
6. I cannot convince you of the crucial choice of choosing the scary uncertainty of growing over the safe misery of not growing.
7. I want to be with you and know you as a rich and growing friend, yet I cannot get close to you when you choose not to grow.
8. When I begin to care for you out of pity, when I begin to lose trust in you, then I am toxic, bad, and inhibiting for you, and you for me.
9. Believe me, my helping is conditional; I will be with you, I will hang in there with you as long as I continue to get even the slightest hints that you are still trying to grow.
10. If *you can accept* all of this, then perhaps we can help each other.

I do believe we have responsibility *to* our clients not *for* them (for they must be responsible for themselves) by telling them who we are and how and where we propose to take them. Could you clearly explain to your clients your approach, your goals, your views of the counseling process and the counseling relationship?

I can still stand by much of that earlier creed, written some years ago. However, I also believe that it should be undergoing constant revision.

As I have mentioned previously, continual revision of creeds seems imperative. Recently my wife and I deleted our #9 statement since it seemed redundant. We replaced it with a sentiment that included a real need to speak to client commitment, hence the change:

9. WE BELIEVE that we cannot help you if you CHOOSE NOT to help yourself. We have to TRUST YOUR COMITTMENT to *ACT*, to *CHANGE* and to *GROW*.

My wife, Patricia, and I have a small private practice in which we do 'dual counseling.' We like this approach for several reasons. It offers the client a male and female point of view and it allows for what we call 'dialoguing.' Here, Patricia and I will often talk with each other (client listening), wondering about what's happening, where we're going. We often discuss possible directions and consequences, as well. The result of all of this is a not so subtle pattern interruption. We excuse ourselves and carry on a conversation in the client's presence. As you can imagine, clients frequently gain new ideas, reframe, and sense new possibilities and choices as they listen to our discussions of them.

We have recently worked up a creed that is given out to clients at the first session. With the help of our discussions of the creed with clients we mutually discuss as to whether or not we are suited for each other. If we do not work together we try to do our best to seek appropriate referral. Occasionally clients prefer to choose to work with just one of us. However, when they have the choice, they do value our 'dual' relationship for counseling. We find ourselves continually modifying, creating and dramatically changing our strategies to be more in harmony with our client. Nevertheless, in terms of movement in our present use of BT, the Creed seems to be invaluable.

OUR CREED FOR COUNSELING

We believe that we must be able to tell you who we are and what we can and cannot do for you. You have the right to know beforehand, our beliefs, values, and our goals and expectations that we have for counseling. What follows is our attempt:

1. WE BELIEVE that YOU should rest assured that CONFIDENTIALITY and TRUST remain at the corner stone of our counseling with YOU.
2. WE BELIEVE in helping YOU to grow, to become more productive, more autonomous, more sensitive and loving of yourself and others, more excited, and freer to continue living your life more fully.
3. WE BELIEVE that if YOU can sense us as honest, caring, respectful, and empathic; YOU can accept our help, to help YOU grow and change in directions YOU choose.
4. WE BELIEVE that we cannot give you your dreams nor 'fix you up,' nor take away your emotional hurt, nor make you grow — for YOU must do all of these for yourself.
5. WE BELIEVE that we cannot tell YOU what is best for YOU, nor sense your world for YOU, nor evaluate your world — for YOU have your own world.
6. WE BELIEVE that we cannot convince YOU of the crucial choice of choosing the scary uncertainty of growing over the safe misery of not growing.
7. WE BELIEVE that YOU have choice and can choose responsibly, and that YOU are the expert and authority for your own life.
8. WE BELIEVE that YOU have the experiences and resources necessary to bring about resolutions and positive changes as QUICKLY as YOU wish.
9. WE BELIEVE that we cannot help you if you CHOOSE NOT to help yourself. We have to TRUST YOUR COMMITMENT, to ACT, to

CHANGE and to GROW.
10. ULTIMATELY, WE BELIEVE that YOU can change, and that YOU can learn how to focus on positive solutions, rather than problems — and, above all, you can learn that changing your thinking can change perceptions, feeling states, and behavior.

We can continually use this creed to gauge our progress

In counseling, the discussion of the creed elicits so much. The client not only experiences a new openness and sharing, new goals and purpose, but also a new way of thinking about counseling and therapy. This is the realization that counseling involves creativity, responsibility, participation, and client direction and control. It provides the realization of hope on the part of clients, that they are in charge and that they, in fact, can change. There comes the beginning awareness that the way we think is what causes our problems and that we can learn to change the way we think.

As counselors in this initial stage we begin to create the high PEGS climate through all three stages listed by Carkhuff — Exploring, Understanding, Acting. Sadly, but realistically, emergence of PEGS is not like pushing the 'on' button nor putting the process-gear in 'forward'; rather, it is our respectful, empathic and accepting attitude that comes from deep within us.

The Exploring phase provides an ideal opportunity to begin to ask the first BT questions. (While we are focusing on BT as our primary strategy, it very well may be that you might observe and hear issues that simply do not lend themselves to BT and, naturally, you will drop back into your observing and hearing mode and look and listen for other directions and other cues.) As responses to the BT questions occur, they hold within them the ground plan for Exploring, Understanding and Acting.

The Understanding phase rarely ever appears as a separate process. Invariably Exploring, Understanding and Acting are inextricably intertwined. As clients struggle to answer BT questions, the process helps to clarify and understand the issues. Strategies such as Surrogate Self, for example, not only help in understanding what is going on but also assist in clarifying and understanding.

George

I spent two sessions (Exploring and Understanding phases) helping George construct his goal, helping him learn what he wanted. He was quick to tell me what he *DIDN'T* want, and like most clients he found it difficult to put into positive focus what he *DID* want.

As we settled in with each other, I learned of his painful sadness and depression as a result of his wife having left home. In addition, I learned something else equally important. He called himself 'an alcohol-abuser' and three years ago he had stopped drinking entirely. I tucked this information away in my 'closet.'

Often in counseling, as I listen carefully, I hear events, experiences or happenings that may have real impact and yet at the moment might be irrelevant or even deflecting. I have a metaphorical 'closet' in which I can hang up all sorts of information for possible future use. This closet is easily accessible because the door remains open. And you can imagine I 'closeted' the alcohol-abuser and the 'three years of not drinking' business. I choose to remember and store in my closet all accomplishments, no matter how small or even trivial. Later we can return to these facts as evidence of action, accomplishment and self-discipline, traits often forgotten when clients feel 'helpless and hopeless' (the two h's go together and I frequently notice them at some juncture in counseling).

I used to take notes until a client once challenged me, telling me that he questioned if I were even listening because I appeared so busy. He also expressed a certain anxiety or uneasiness, wondering what I was writing about. At first, I felt defensive and was about to argue for the importance of reports in the center where I worked. Soon it dawned on me that note-taking could be reframed. Since then, I have called them *our* notes. Clients and I often use them cooperatively as an integral part of our counseling process. For example, I told George that I liked to write things down so I could remember them and so that he could read them over, check them for accuracy, relevancy and make whatever corrections were necessary. They really became his notes. It was suggested that he refer to them whenever he wanted and to make whatever corrections or discoveries he deemed appropriate. We talked about my 'closet' and what he believed should be put in it.

In counseling there should be few secrets and this truth sometimes becomes difficult to explain to clients. Whatever I say, whatever I do, should be open and fair game to clients (another rationale for a Creed). The client remains my teacher, and I try to become the best and most respectful student I can be. I observe, listen, ask questions and take whatever surprise quizzes my client throws at me.

As George began to 'teach' me of his world, his perceptions and his feelings, I tried my best to fully understand him. My levels of empathic response were my attempts to convey to him that he was worthy of being listened to, that I was learning what he was teaching me. And so my questioning began, invariably assuming that he had the answers.

In responding to my question, 'What is your goal in counseling?' like many clients at first, George responded with wishes and complaints, not to be confused with goals and wants. 'I want my wife to stay with the family. She has her own apartment,' and 'She's always hanging out with people I don't trust,' and 'All she does is go to these women's meetings.' I responded by acknowledging his feelings of loss (wishes) and his anger and frustration (complaints) and then said:

> *George, INSTEAD of wishing she would stay and INSTEAD of worrying about her hanging out with people you disapprove of, what do YOU want?*

George still struggled with this question and subsequent solution-focused questions that I asked. However, I had some important information for the 'closet' and for our notes. He responded to this question, 'George, what things are going on that are important and positive to you, THESE DAYS?' He re-emphasized the importance that the two children had in his life while complaining that his wife did not seem to care for them, that they seemed hurt by her absence. In addition, George spoke of the new closeness and support he was experiencing with two of his friends. It was this clue that pointed us in the direction of Surrogate Self (SS).

HYPNOCOUNSELING AND SURROGATE SELF (SS) AS A SCAFFOLDING FOR BRIEF THERAPY: AN EXAMPLE OF MIX AND MATCH

I asked George if he would try SS, explaining the procedure and, hopefully, what we might accomplish. Hypnocounseling served as a catalyst.

C: And, George, I am impressed with the special friends you have. And I wonder if you and I might ask for their help. [IDL.]

George: Sure, I guess. [UNCERTAIN STILL.]

C: Well I wonder if you can imagine a friend that you trust and respect, a friend that *knows you better than you know yourself.* You may want to notice how you could relax, NOW, as you recall that special friend. [INTERSPERSAL CAPITALIZED.]

After some time discussing this, George 'invented' a friend he called Max who had similar characteristics of both of his 'buddies.' In the Surrogate Self experience sometimes clients identify with an actual friend. Often, however, it's an invented person who combines certain characteristics of a good friend in their lives, perhaps because it's too threatening to have an actual person who knows them better than themselves. As mentioned earlier, this distinct form of dissociation allows the counselor extraordinary leeway in asking questions that ordinarily would be seen by clients as inappropriate.

C: Max, it must be difficult if not a bit confusing to be asked to help a friend out this way. Is that part of it? [LEVEL 4 RESPONSE.]

Max (George): Yeah (hesitantly).

C: MAX, we really appreciate your helping GEORGE and me out this way. And *you KNOW George better than HE KNOWS HIMSELF* (pause.)

There is no intent to elicit trance; however, if George (Max) chooses to go into a light trance, then naturally, we would utilize it. 'Max' did not seem to be totally there with me so I suggested PRETENDING.

Max: Yeah, but I don't know what to do.

C: Well, Max, if it seems difficult, you can always CHOOSE to PRETEND. [INTERSPERSALS.] Maybe you can recall times as a

	child you used to PRETEND all sorts of things. [AGE REGRESSION.] Some people CHOSE to pretend GAMES, others CHOSE to pretend ACTING out roles in a play. [ILLUSIONS OF CHOICE AND TRUISMS.] I don't know how or when you, Max, can CHOOSE to PRETEND.
Max:	Yeah (a kind of sheepish smile as his eyes roll and he slowly blinks). [OBSERVING.]
C:	That's right, Max, the smile and the blinking of your eyes MIGHT be telling me [FEEDBACK THE OBSERVATION], that you can be relaxing and enjoying it, NOW. [GIVE CHOICE (ILLUSION OF CHOICE).] If you want to, or maybe not. [OBSERVING THIS AND GIVING MAX (GEORGE) THIS FEEDBACK.]
Max:	Unh, Unh.
C:	Yes, am I noticing that your breathing is changing, deeper, more slowly and rhythmically?
Max:	Yeah. [THE 'I-NEED-YOUR-HELP' CAN BE MOST POWERFUL.]
C:	Max, there are some questions I need to ask about George because you're here AND *you know George better than he knows himself,* would you answer them? I need your help, here.
Max:	Sure, I guess.
C:	I appreciate that and I know George does . . . (pause).
C:	With your eyes OPEN or CLOSED (leaning forward) Max, what does George WANT to do now — and remember you know him better than he knows himself.
Max:	He wants to get on with his life.
C:	What does he DO to get on with his life? [BT QUESTION.]
Max:	'I' have to focus on the kids and my friends. [SLIPS BACK TO GEORGE.]
C:	(Interrupting) Max, you mean HE (George) has to focus on the kids and friends? [QUICKLY INTERRUPT WHEN THIS OCCURS.]
Max:	Oh, yeah.
C:	Tell me, how and what George has to do to focus on the kids and his friends? [FOCUSING ON EVENTS AND HAPPENINGS (HOW AND WHAT — BT).]
Max:	Well, he shouldn't worry so much about her and should focus more on the kids.
C:	And how can he do that?
Max:	Just be there when the kids come home and play with them.
C:	What can he do to stop worrying about his wife?
Max:	Get into this new job, do things with his kids that they like.
C:	Hold it, so I can jot this down in OUR notes. [TAKING NOTES SO WE WILL REMEMBER.]
C:	Max, what's going on in George's life when he's NOT worrying or focusing on his wife? [EXCEPTION QUESTION.]
Max:	Yeah, he's with his buddies and his kids; starting to get ready

	for the fishing season.
C:	So let's see, George doesn't worry when he's spending time with his buddies and his two kids; the excitement and getting ready for fishing. What does he like to do?
Max:	Him? George? or all of them?
C:	I see, what does George like to do? Can you be specific, Max? [SLIPPING BACK TO GEORGE.]
Max:	He likes to hunt and fish. He likes taking his kids fishing and hiking although 'my' daughter doesn't enjoy fishing.
C:	(Interrupting) you mean George's daughter?
Max:	Oh yeah. She's hanging out at school more with her friends, now. [VAGUE.]
C:	I guess that's pretty natural, isn't it?
Max:	Yeah!
C:	George might find it difficult, however, [PRESUPPOSITION] he knows — THINGS CHANGE (pause). And I wonder WHEN George will begin to realize he can't CONTROL people — and expect them to do what HE wants. What do you suppose that would mean to George?
Max:	I guess he'd have to realize he has to let go of Carole (wife).
C:	What is there about George's letting go of Carole?
Max:	'I' know . . . [AGAIN, CORRECTING THE INTERACTION.]
C:	(Interrupting) Max, you mean that George knows something important?
Max:	Yeah, he can't force her home and he has to let go.
C:	How will George do that? It's got to be difficult but we do know that he can do it. Do we not? (Wait for a response.) After all, Max, he remembers the courage and self-discipline it took to kick over his 'alcohol abusing' and be healthy for three years now, without a drink — what an incredible accomplishment! [RESPONDING AT THE 'THING AND EVENTS' LEVEL.]
Max:	Yep (now sighs and shifts in the chair).
C:	Max, when you just sighed and moved like that — you must know what George is going through right now.
Max:	Yeah.
C:	Max, you tell me you know WHAT George has to do but I need to know HOW he does it.
Max:	I don't know.
C:	You mean George doesn't know HOW?
Max:	No! I don't know. Can't you tell him how or at least help him?
C:	I'd sure like to try — but first it would help if you could tell me what George needs to do to let go.
Max:	I don't know — it's like I can't seem to stop worrying about her — I . . . [WHEN IT GETS UNCOMFORTABLY CLOSE — CLIENT SLIPS OUT OF THE SS MODE.]
C:	(Interrupting) — Wait a minute Max, you mean George can't

Max:	seem to stop worrying about her? [CORRECTING THE SLIP.] Yeah!
C:	That reminds me of a STORY. [METAPHOR.] Once upon a time a young lad left his people to search for the special Medicine Man at the peak of a distant mountain. After days of arduous travel he stumbled upon the old man with magical knowledge. The old man did not get up nor move but rather watched carefully and quietly. The young man was too tired to say anything and just stood there overwhelmed and scared, yet, oddly and peculiarly excited. [METAPHORS HAVE MEANING AND MAYBE NOT THE MEANING WE INTEND, BUT CLIENTS WILL MAKE THEIR OWN CONSTRUCTIONS OF MEANING THAT EMERGE FROM THEIR OWN PERCEPTUAL FIELDS.] Finally the Medicine Man said: 'There are two kinds of worries, young warrior, GOOD kinds and BAD kinds. BAD worries are those about which you can do NOTHING and GOOD worries are those about which you CAN do something — you CAN CHOOSE! You can learn how to think differently. To worry about the weather is a BAD worry, because you can do nothing about controlling or changing it. BUT you can change it into a GOOD worry by thinking about choices and ways to survive; clothing, shelter, etc. The young man smiled, relieved, and with respect turned back to his tribe having learned an important lesson that day — NOW Max, I wonder how you would share the meaning of that story with George? What does it mean for George?
Max:	Well, I guess it means he can't worry about Carole because there's nothing he can do except at least be decent to her.
C:	So, for George, are you saying that he has made Carole a bad worry?
Max:	Yeah.
C:	How or What does he do about BAD worry — about Carole?
Max:	Guess he's got to let her go knowing she's gonna do what she's gonna do.
C:	It's almost like I hear you saying that George trying to control Carole is a really BAD worry. Is that it?
Max:	Yeah — there's nothing he can do about that. It's up to her now.
C:	Max, it will be fascinating to hear from George what he will be doing differently and how others will be seeing him differently. I'll check with you (if you can be here) and George in the next session. [BT QUESTION.]
Max:	OK.
C:	One other thing, Max, when and how will you and George know and feel differently? When will we all know when our counseling is over? [BT QUESTIONS.]
Max:	I think he'll be different with Carole not badgering or

	questioning her all the time. George will probably spend more time and do more fishing with the kids.
C:	Is that when you and George think counseling will be ending?
Max:	I don't know.
C:	You mean he (George) doesn't know.
Max:	Yeah, not yet.
C:	Max, can I take some time to put all of this down in George's and my notes? And I need your help here.

It seems so crucial to write down these notes for relevancy, accuracy and importance. In fact, George will be asked to take them home, review them and change whatever seems necessary.

I must now thank Max, respectfully, and ask if he would be willing to return should George and I need him.

It should become clear how Hypnocounseling elements and SS can serve as a catalyst and support for Brief Therapy and the solution-focused questions.

Yes, it's hard work. I must create the climate. I must carefully observe and listen, picking up whatever cues I perceive and then utilize, utilize, utilize.

Non-conclusion

THE NON-CONCLUSION

Something olde
Something new
Something borrowed
Something blue

With the exception of 'blue' (and I'm not sure whether that fits), Hypnocounseling represents *borrowing* from *olde* models; the combining of Rogers' person-centered approach with Erickson's utilization approach and Carkhuff's core condition levels and the three-phase counseling process. Thus, Hypnocounseling is a *new* approach to counseling as a result of *borrowing* from the *olde*.

The secret is, there is no secret. The conclusion is, there is no conclusion.

Conclusions provide an ending; Hypnocounseling has no ending. Open systems, expanding and dynamic systems, each are continually emerging. When I try to identify, clarify, explain these systems they are no longer open. I have closed them down.

Hypnocounseling is the glue that binds the primary strategy to the client. Hypnocounseling, with its emphasis on the therapeutic relationship, the belief in people and its utilization and hypno-suggestive language, provides a substructure for positive change and growth.

Remember, counseling is neither fixing up nor changing clients. Rather, it is providing a therapeutic environment in which the counselor assists the client in 'fixing' and 'changing' themselves.

It might be appropriate to take stock by reflecting on the following questions and issues:
1. What was the one or more specific points you took away from this book that were helpful and meaningful to you?
2. If you were to rewrite this book, which part(s) would you change?
3. With which one or several positions in this book do you disagree? And why?

4. If you were to try, I wonder with which of the strategies you would begin? With which strategies do you feel most comfortable?
5. What is your own primary strategy or approach? (Adlerian, the Brief Therapies, cognitive-behavioral, eclectic, Freudian, Gestalt, Jungian, RET, RT, etc.?) Can you begin to construct ways Hypnocounseling can be used to increase the effectiveness of your approach?
6. And isn't it comforting to know that you don't have to stand exam on this. But, if you did, how do you think you would do?
7. Now that you've read through the text, what do you think clients would say about the approach and strategies?
   a. Would they be comfortable with them?
   b. Would you be helped if your counselor-therapist used these methods?

THE GARDENERS

The gardener has a deep and
   sustaining belief in *growth*.

She does not force, nor pull,
   nor stretch the plant.

He sows the plant in spots
   exposed to the warming rays of the sun,
   but not too much to *burn* the leaves.

She waters the plant with
   a caressing spray,
   but not too much to *drown* the roots

He fertilizes the plant with
   a gentle spreading,
   but not too much to *rot* the roots.
            H. Gunnison

Gardeners know their limits — knowing intuitively that there comes a time when they must step back and trust the plants to grow for themselves.

APPENDIX A

A SCRIPT FOR FRT

This script can act as a guide and you may find yourself constructing other phrases, words, and intonations that seem more appropriate to you. You may have someone read this to you or you may audiotape the script yourself or by someone else. Being aware of Pacing-Matching, you can read the script slowly Matching the person's breathing and speaking only at the time of exhalation. When recording the script you can be aware of this Pacing-Matching by reading very slowly in time with your relaxed and comfortable breathing and in that case you would be 'leading' the listener.

After pacing and matching someone's breathing, you have made a special kind of connection. For example, a person in panic will be breathing in rapid shallow breaths and as you pace with your parallel rapid breathing and speaking, you connect. Notice how quickly you can 'lead' the person into calmness by slowing down your breathing and slowing and lowering your voice rhythm and tone. Try it and observe what happens.

See how well in all of your taping and/or reading of the scripts you can be aware of Implied Directive Language (IDL); the use of words such as can, might, will, perhaps, which allow for tentativeness and permissiveness. Remember, words in 'CAPS' represent Interspersals so you must raise or lower your voice and change rhythm — a kind of nonverbal emphasizing, setting the words off from the rest of the sentence. In addition, I have included 'directions' should you be reading this to someone. If in experiencing any of these tapes you feel the slightest discomfort or anxiety you can always open your eyes, get up and, if you deem it helpful, seek out professional help.

In the left-hand column you will find the script.	In this column you can look for messages or comments from me as well as identification of hypno-suggestive language patterns.
And NOW (slowly) you *can* find a QUIET place to sit or lie down, UNCROSSING your legs (pause). You *can* BEGIN to go DEEP INSIDE and you *may* ALLOW what you are EXPERIENCING RIGHT NOW (pause) to just CONTINUE (long pause).	IDL (in italics). Presupposition. IDL.
Many people notice their breathing CHANGING (pause).	Truisms and Yes sets. Begin your pacing soon, as you observe their tempo of breathing. Presupposition.

AND I WONDER WHEN you *can* sense your OWN breathing, SLOWLY — more DEEPLY (pause) and DEEPER.

You *might* want to be aware of how COM-FOR-TABLE and RELAXED you *can* feel — NOW (long pause). That's right.

Be mindful of your Pacing.

When your eyes get HEAVY (pause) and you *can* know, you *can* close them, but NOT TOO rapidly (pause). Only as slowly or as rapidly as seems RELAXING.

Presupposition.
Now you could slowly close or open your *own* eyes (a kind of non-verbal embedded command).

Most people find they *can* RELAX and IMAGINE BEST with their eyes closed (pause) NOW (pause).

Truism.

Some people *can* keep their eyes open. BUT YOU WILL know which is BEST for you (pause) open or CLOSED.

Truism.

You *might* want to remind yourself that you CAN BE in charge of YOU (pause) and NOW with your eyes CLOSED or open, you *can* begin to IMAGINE your body separated into three zones: (pause).

Illusion of choice.
You might want to describe this with your hands showing imaginary horizontal lines.

You *might* want to imagine zone THREE: (short pause) as your HEAD, your NECK, your ARMS. That's right. PLEASANTLY RE-LAX-ING (pause) and TWO, (short pause)
the whole TRUNK of your body ALL the way DOWN to your hips (pause).
And ONE: your thighs all the way DOWN to your TOES — YES (pause).
And NOW we *can* begin this PLEASANT, (short pause) COMFORTING, (short pause) and RELAXING PROCESS.

As you carry on, you may find yourself adding or deleting pauses. In fact, you may find yourself constructing different words and phrases; adding or deleting Interspersals and IDL. Remember, this is your guide.

(Pause) THREE: And you *can* become aware of your scalp muscles RELAXING and LETTING GO at the BACK of your head, at the SIDES of your head, (pause) relaxing those muscles around your ears, and letting go of TENSIONS at the FRONT of your head.

Remember, slowly continue Pacing the breathing and *practice* talking and *talk during the exhalation periods.*

THIS letting go *can* proceed DOWN the front of your FACE to your JAW (pause). Sometimes it's surprising to notice how often our Jaws feel tense AND YOU *can* be aware of LETTING GO (pause)

Truism.

letting your jaw just RELAX (pause). You *might* even be interested in noticing (pause) that in the FUTURE when your JAW feels TENSE (pause) it can be a SIGN that the rest of you is TENSE (pause) AND you *can* be surprised at how QUICKLY you *can* COUNT DOWN (pause).
Isn't it a wonder that as your jaw lets go, the REST of you *can* REST (pause) and NOW as your head begins to feel RELAXED (pause) you *can* notice your NECK (pause). Most people are RARELY aware (pause) of how THEIR HEAD seems to be in BALANCE on their NECK (pause) soooo, COM-FOR-TABLY. And as you find yourself MOVING or adjusting your neck in RELAXING WAYS (pause) you *can* be aware of how your RIGHT shoulder was tense and NOW BECOMES SO RELAXED (pause) and I don't know how RAPIDLY or SLOWLY those WAVES of RELAXATION will WASH down your entire right arm to your fingertips. And like an electrical current (pause) the tension can EXIT from EACH of your fingertips, dispersing harmlessly in the air (pause). In the same manner, you can be AWARE of how your tension can LEAVE your LEFT shoulder (pause) NOW or SOON? The tension moves DOWN your LEFT ARM and OUT your finger-tips like an electrical current — harmlessly dispersing in the AIR (pause) FOLLOWED by those WAVES of RELAXATION (pause).
Can you NOT FEEL IT? (Pause.) THREE (pause). You *can*, experience your HEAD, NECK, SHOULDERS, and ARMS in the PROCESS of RE-LAX-A-SHUN. (Pause) Yes. (Pause) And now, TWO: (pause) You *can* become aware of RELAXING your chest, (pause) AWARE of how your breathing has ALREADY CHANGED, (pause) SLOWER, DEEPER, and More Rhyth-mi-cal. (Pause) You *can* be AWARE of HOW your STOMACH MUSCLES, (pause)

. . . your HIP MUSCLES, ALL just LET GO (pause) Notice (pause) how the top part of your BACK *can* begin to RELAX (pause) SLOWLY or RAPIDLY,

. . . DOWN between your shoulder blades (pause) RELAXING and just LETTING GO all the way DOWN to your rump — your hips (pause) and NOW the whole TRUNK of your body *can* experience this comfort of RE-LAX-A-SHUN (pause). And finally, ONE: (pause). You can be aware of how the tension in your right thigh *can* turn into LETTING GO (pause).

Presupposition.

Erickson was a master of puns and word play.

Presupposition.
Truism feedback.

Analogy sometimes can be effective in heightening the experience.

Illusion of choice.

Presupposition.

Continue slowly, check in, pace the rhythm of breathing.

Illusion of choice again — must be presented slowly — still maintaining the Pacing and Matching.
Presupposition.

You *may* want to attend to that letting BE experience NOW (pause) and notice how it *can* gently WASH down your right thigh (pause) to your KNEE (pause) RELAXING and COMFORTING as those WAVES *can* WASH the tension (pause). All the way DOWN (pause) your right SHIN (pause) CALF (pause) and that tension LEAVES through your feet and toes (pause) into the air and onto the ground (pause). Your LEFT thigh *can* RELAX (pause).

Not only Visual, but also Kinesthetic accessing.

SENSATIONS of QUIET and PEACE *can* develop THROUGHOUT your ENTIRE BODY (pause) and carry DOWN to your left KNEE (pause). Letting be and letting go of your SHIN and CALF of your LEFT LEG (pause) and the Gentle RELAXING *can* move DOWN into your left foot (pause). While the tension escapes HARMLESSLY (pause) and NOW (pause) you can be aware of BOTH legs and feet in the comfortable STATE of (pause) RELAXASHUN (pause).

You MAY want to REVIEW (pause) and NOW go back and COUNT DOWN THREE, TWO, ONE (pause). You can take a few moments to STEEP (pause) and LUXURIATE in this experience (pause) as TEA BAGS (pause) STEEP in WARM Water (pause). When you are READY (pause) you can AROUSE yourself.

Slowly here.

Analogy.

Presupposition.

That's right (pause) stretching, changing your breathing and becoming more alert (long pause). Being fully here, NOW. [SLOWLY, TAKE YOUR TIME.] NOW, [READING THIS IN YOUR REGULAR, NATURAL VOICE] you will begin to take over control of your own relaxing.

We can begin again. Only this time I shall say, THREE: and you will be able to relax yourself; head, neck, shoulder, and arms. When you sense being in the process of relaxing, signal by nodding or telling me. Remember we are not talking about total relaxation, but rather the sense of the body in the process of relaxing. Then I will say, TWO: signal me when you feel the Trunk of your body relaxing and then I will say ONE: after you experience relaxing the lower parts of your body to your toes, you can then arouse yourself, move around, and open your eyes. OK, are you READY? THREE: [TAKE YOUR TIME AND WAIT UNTIL YOU GET THE SIGNAL] TWO: [THE SAME. WAIT UNTIL YOU GET THE SIGNAL BEFORE MOVING ON TO ONE] . . . ONE: OK — FINE. Now YOU *can* take over. When I repeat the request to COUNT DOWN you *can* begin relaxing your entire body. And when you have finished, you *can* signal me. OK — READY?

COUNT DOWN [When the individual is aroused you make the following direct suggestions and requests.]

Now, that *can* be a gift to yourself. If you choose to practice this as often as possible, you *can* learn how to count down with your eyes open, while standing or walking. You can choose to repeat the count down as often as you wish, sometimes 5–10 times. Thus, FRT can be a powerful pattern interruption. Speaking before large groups I count down many times until I feel relaxed and ready. Counting down can interrupt many unwanted experiences. Some people even find that counting down can interrupt their need to smoke, to binge, to anxietize or depress themselves. It can be an ally should you practice and choose it to be. Oh yes, and you *might* try an experiment NOW. Try counting down on the exhalations of a deep breath. Exhaling can be experienced as having a natural relaxing quality. You might consider the goal of 'counting down' in TEN seconds or less, by taking a very deep breath and slowly exhaling while saying to yourself THREE, TWO, ONE. (Go ahead, try it, see what you think. You have a powerful and efficient tool should you be inclined to pick it up, practice it, and use it.)

APPENDIX B

A SCRIPT FOR FDA

Prior to beginning FDA, clients should be helped to relax and focus. Any deep relaxation strategy will suffice. I use Fantasy Relaxation Technique (FRT) because I have often presented it as a 'gift' to clients to take with them into their lives regardless of the presenting issue. (You may notice I rarely use the word 'problem'. I prefer to speak of *issue(s), being stuck, or temporarily arrested* as well as *resolution(s)* and *solution(s)*. These indirect-suggestion-words/phrases help change the direction of the client's mind set and thinking.) Presume now that your client can be relaxing comfortably sitting, reclining, or lying thus. The same script directions apply as in the Fantasy Relaxation Technique. Italicized words represent IDL just as capitalized words represent Interspersals (changing voice volume, tone, and tempo). Parentheses ( ) should not be read to the client; they stand for directions and/or comments from me. Remember, speak SLOWLY to Pace-Match client breathing. Hypnocounseling throughout will 'seed' and augment the primary strategy, FDA.

In the left-hand column you will find the script. Do NOT read aloud the contents of the (brackets) since they contain certain instructions.	In this column you can look for messages or comments from me as well as identification of hypno-suggestive language patterns.
You may PERMIT (pause) what YOU are EXPERIENCING right NOW (pause) just to CONTINUE — That's right. (Long pause.) [AND REMEMBER AT THE BEGINNING TALK SLOWLY — GIVE THE CLIENT TIME TO MAKE THE SHIFTS.]	Presupposition with IDL.
You might be CURIOUS (pause) about just how COM-FOR-TABLE (pause) you can BE — NOW (long pause).	Presupposition with IDL.
It is NOT necessary (pause) for you to go into TOTAL RE-LAX-A-SHUN (pause) NOW. (Long pause) That's right (pause).	Interspersals can begin their impact.
And *as* you sit, recline, or lie THERE (pause) COMFORTABLY (pause) you *can* be AWARE (pause) of HOW your Breathing IS CHANGING (pause). Feelings of LETTING GO. DEEP-DEEP Relaxation (pause). And you *can* CHOOSE to close your EYES or keep them OPEN (pause). Now or later (pause) and you *may* find yourself ready to BEGIN a very SPECIAL JOURNEY (pause).	Illusion of choice. Presupposition, IDL. Presupposition. Illusion of choice.

Even NOW you *can* be AWARE (pause) of walking DOWN a certain path (pause). Maybe one you've walked before (pause) or one that's different (pause). Cool and shade? (Pause.) Or WARM and bright? (Pause.)	Illusion of choice.
And it may be none of these (pause) only you *can* know (pause). That's right, NOT too fast NOW (pause). I don't know what you are FEELING NOW (pause). I don't even know what SOUNDS you HEAR, now (pause). As you continue DOWN this SPECIAL path (pause) you CAN SEE a friendly STONEWALL (pause) FRIENDLY (pause). You *might* even want to TOUCH the stones, (pause)	Accessing. Representational Systems, with Presuppositions. VAKOG.
... sensing their warmth, coolness (slow — stretch this out) coarseness, smoothness (pause) softness, hardness (pause) AND NOW NOTICING many other THINGS (long pause).	
Yes (pause) just beyond the stone wall (pause) you *can* SEE a (softly and slowly) beautiful — mountain — MEADOW (pause). And as you LOOK (pause) for the opening in the STONE wall (pause). You *can* BECOME even MORE FOCUSED (pause). I wonder when will you CHOOSE to ENTER the meadow? (Pause.) NOW (pause) or in a MOMENT (pause) NOW (pause).	Illusion of Choice, Presupposition.

Presupposition.

Illusion of Choice. |
| I wonder (pause) as you MOVE OUT into the BEAUTIFUL mountain meadow (pause) *CAN* you (pause) NOW — FEEL (slowly softly) the warmth — of the sun (pause) beating DOWN on your HEAD, NECK and shoulders? (Pause.) | Slowly, still Pacing. |
| WARMING throughout? (Pause.) Many people feel the WARMTH of the sun (pause) as EMPOWERING (pause). Others, feel a WARMTH that CLEANSES (pause). Some people feel the WARMTH as (pause) FULFILLING and REASSURING (pause). You *might* ATTEND to what YOU feel NOW (pause) keeping THOSE positive feelings (pause) for as long as you wish (pause). You *can* even find an EAGER comfort (pause) as you BEGIN the SLOW WALK — through the meadow (pause). LOOKING ahead you *might* even notice a very SPECIAL TREE (pause) SOMEWHERE in the middle of the meadow (pause). | Long Pauses between each Truism.

Notice the string of suggestions that follow throughout the fantasy trip. |
| Now I don't KNOW (pause) if it's tall or short (pause) if it has leaves or needles (pause). In fact, I really don't know (pause) if you SEE that tree, NOW (pause). You *can* walk up to it (pause). You *may* want to just LOOK at it (pause) CAREFULLY (pause). You *might* want to TOUCH it (pause) respectfully (pause). And if you *choose* to (pause) you MIGHT | Illusion of Choice.

Accessing Representational Systems (VAK). |

even TASTE the trunk (pause) with your tongue (pause) and you'll KNOW (pause) if that's appropriate (pause) for you, or NOT. A TREE *can* be (pause) an important symbol to many people. (pause) And many people *can* sense a symbolic (pause) MESSAGE (pause). You *can* take a few moments NOW (pause) to LISTEN carefully (pause) to HEAR that SPECIAL Message (pause). It *may* be advice (pause) It *may* be empowering (pause). It may be COMFORTING and REASSURING (pause). You will know when you hear it (pause) and you might not (pause). You *can* take some time NOW to HEAR to LISTEN (long pause) ——————————————— YES.

Truisms.

Presupposition.

Illusion of Choice.

When suggesting shifts in the fantasy, give lots of time, 5–10 seconds is not too much.

(Pause) and NOW you *can* move on across the meadow (pause) taking that message from the TREE. (pause) and isn't it interesting to REALIZE (pause) you *can* come back to your TREE (pause) anytime you CHOOSE (pause). As you continue across the meadow to the opposite side (pause) swinging your arms (pause) *can* you not FEEL (pause) the tops of the tall grasses TICKLING your fingertips? (Pause.) You *can* find an opening (pause) across the way in the FRIENDLY stone wall (pause). As you approach the PATH beyond (pause) you *can* take time to FEEL the sun's WARMTH (pause) that *can* give you (pause) a feeling of PERSONAL POWER and COMPETENCE (pause). *Can* you not feel that, NOW? (Long pause.) You may carry on through to the PATH (pause). The CALMNESS you can FEEL NOW (pause) KNOWING and ANTICIPATING what's to happen (pause) behind A SPECIAL DOOR (long pause). Down this new PATH (pause) that *can* lead to a pure and bubbling MOUNTAIN stream (pause) beyond which you *can* SEE a CLEARING (pause). That Stream that you *might* NOTICE (pause) goes DOWN to an ENDLESS Sea (pause) and you *can* kneel and PARTAKE of those refreshing and EMPOWERING WATERS (pause) only if you want to (pause) or NOT (pause). Again you *can* return to this mountain stream (pause) whenever you want to sample of the WATERS (pause). There are times to KNOW (pause) and TIMES NOT TO (pause). NOW are TIMES to know. Crossing the stream and I don't know how (pause) BUT YOU *Can* know (pause). Beyond the stream (pause) you *can* see the clearing NOW (pause) and beyond you *can* SEE a beautiful symmetrical HILL (pause) at the BASE of which is an extraordinary

Empowering language.

Presupposition — starting the 'seeding' of what's behind the door.

Illusion of Choice.

and SIGNIFICANT GREAT DOOR (long, long pause). A DOOR you *can* always recognize (pause). And NOW you *might* take a moment to go up to the GREAT DOOR (pause) SEE it CLEARLY (pause) taking your time (pause) and NOW TOUCHING the door (pause) feeling, sensing its COARSENESS — SMOOTHNESS (pause) its unique TEXTURE (pause). I don't KNOW if there are sounds or certain SMELLS (pause) at the Great Door (pause). You *can* even notice the SPECIAL construction (pause). I wonder WHERE the LATCH or KNOB is or some other kind of Hardware — to let you in? (Long pause.) You can KNOW (pause) and I don't know if your RIGHT hand or your LEFT hand will ultimately OPEN the door (pause) behind which you *can* find that UNUSUAL and COMFORTING HALL. That's RIGHT, your (LEFT or RIGHT) hand (pause). As you stand before the Great Door (pause) ready to enter (pause) you *can* know of the HALLWAY, that CURVES to the RIGHT (pause) and the special DOOR to the ROOM (pause) in which you will do those THINGS that YOU WANT to do — that you CHOOSE to do (pause). And NOW you *can* OPEN the GREAT DOOR (pause) and GO within to the HALLWAY (pause). There is COMFORTABLE indirect lighting HERE (pause) with your favorite color (pause.) And you may NOTICE (pause) off the HALLWAY (pause) MANY doors (pause) a DREAMING door, (pause) a MEMORY door, (pause) even a SOLUTIONS door (pause). And THEN you can FIND (pause) your CERTAIN and SPECIAL door (pause). As you walk down the corridor (pause) you *can* find YOUR certain special DOOR (pause). *Can* you not? (Pause.) You *can* LOOK now at your CERTAIN and SPECIAL DOOR (pause).

VAKOG

Presupposition

Notice any twitch, slight movement (ideomotor response) in either hand. Observe, observe, observe and mention which hand.

[AT THIS POINT YOU EXPLORE THE PURPOSES OF THIS JOURNEY. WHAT THE INDIVIDUAL MIGHT FIND IN THE ROOM BEHIND THE SPECIAL DOOR — PURPOSES, LEARNINGS, RESOLUTIONS AND ANSWERS, STRESSING THAT WITHIN THE ROOM THERE IS EVERYTHING NEEDED TO ACCOMPLISH WHATEVER THE INDIVIDUAL WANTS.]

And GO IN when you are READY (pause). I don't know if you will close the special DOOR or leave it ajar (pause). I will wait in the HALLWAY (pause). When you are done and ready to return (pause) you *can* tell me (pause). My best wishes go with you as you NOW ENTER (pause).

[GENERALLY I HAVE FOUND THAT CLIENTS WILL REMAIN BEHIND THE DOOR FOR AS LONG AS SEEMS APPROPRIATE, PERHAPS ONE, FIVE OR TEN MINUTES OR MORE. YOU CAN 'CHECK IN' FROM TIME TO

[TIME AND CAN REMIND THEM THAT THEY CAN TALK TO YOU AT ANY TIME, SHOULD THEY HAVE ANY QUESTIONS OR OBSERVATIONS. I WOULD NOT PROCESS NOR DISCUSS THEIR EXPERIENCE UNTIL THEY HAVE FULLY RETURNED TO THEIR WAKING STATE.

WHEN THEY ARE READY TO RETURN, BE CAREFUL TO RETRACE YOUR STEPS IN THE SAME ORDER AS WHEN YOU ENTERED. GIVE THEM THE OPPORTUNITY TO GO BACK SLOWLY OR RAPIDLY AND TALKING TO YOU WHENEVER THEY WISH.]

And when you're READY (pause) You *can* leave the ROOM (pause). Will you close the DOOR behind you (pause) or NOT? (Pause.) You *can* turn toward the Great Door (pause). Will you close the Great Door? (pause) or will you leave it open? (Pause.) You *can* feel the warmth of the sun as you cross the clearing (pause).

Down to the mountain stream (pause). Crossing it to the PATH (pause) AND Now you *can* see the mountain meadow AHEAD (pause) finding your WAY through the Stone Wall (pause). Crossing the Mountain meadow you *can* SEE and FEEL and HEAR your special TREE (pause). As you say good-bye (pause) you *can* continue on through the stone wall (pause) and move up the path (pause) until you are back in your familiar spot, HERE (pause) sitting or lying THERE (pause) where you *can* be relaxed and refreshed and excited about your discoveries. HERE and NOW (pause). You *may* wish to enjoy your sense of COMFORT AND STEEP in it (pause) as TEA BAGS STEEP in WARM WATER (pause) AND then when READY you *can* stretch, open your eyes and be HERE FULLY (pause and wait).

> You may even ask, 'Do you want to return slowly or rapidly?'
>
> VAK.

Whether or not you discuss the client's experience is better left to them. We must be very respectful of the client at this time because they have had a rare and insightful experience that cannot be pushed.

This becomes another of those critical times when they teach us of the how, the what, and the when of their experience. So as they learn, so do they teach us. For many this can be a significant growing and learning experience.

There are many other doors. I have had clients go through the 'dreaming door' and dream a dream whose subject and purpose has been suggested by the client. A 'Solution door' can be available when you and your client are blocked, and at a loss as to where to go, as to possible resolutions.

The door is a universal symbol begging to be used.

APPENDIX C

REACTIONS TO GUNNISON'S ARTICLE ON THE SIMILARITIES BETWEEN ERICKSON AND ROGERS[1]
CARL R. ROGERS

Rogers and Erickson had no direct contact with each other's work. Whatever similarities exist developed independently. Rogers stresses his reliance on an intuitive relationship to the client's inner core and discusses the basis for this intuition. He also relies on a fundamental directional tendency which exists in every person. He trusts the client to choose his or her own goals. In these respects he sees some similarities between himself and Erickson, confirming Gunnison's points and going beyond them.

I am profoundly impressed by the similarities that Gunnison found between my work and that of Milton Erickson. I never had direct personal contact with Erickson, except a very slight acquaintance when we were both undergraduate students at the University of Wisconsin. Nor have I read any appreciable proportion of his writings. This may seem strange, but many years ago I concluded that though I respected him for what I heard about his work, hypnosis was not my path into therapy. I was not really aware of the fact that his work went so far beyond hypnosis itself. Neither has Erickson ever had personal contact with my work. I do not know how well-acquainted he was with my writings.

I mention these things to indicate that whatever similarities exist developed quite independently — certainly not out of close contact or thorough knowledge of each other's writings. The similarities are therefore real and not simply derivative.

I believe that a lengthy quotation from my most recent writing will confirm many of Gunnison's points. I have just completed a chapter for Kutash and Wolf's (1986) *Psychotherapist's Casebook* in which I first describe the person-centered approach to therapy and then illustrate it by analyzing a single recorded interview. In my description I review the three conditions reported by Gunnison. Then I add 'one more characteristic.'

I described above those characteristics of a growth-promoting relationship which have been investigated and supported by research. But recently my view has broadened into a new area which cannot as yet be studied empirically.

When I am at my best as a group facilitator or a therapist, I discover another characteristic. I find that when I am closest to my inner, intuitive self, when I am somehow in touch with the unknown in me, when perhaps I am in a slightly altered state of consciousness in the relationship, then whatever I do seems to be full of healing. Then simply my *presence* is

---

[1.] Reprinted from the *Journal of Counseling and Development*, 63, 565–6, May 1985. ACA. Reprinted with permission. No further reproduction is authorized without written permission of the American Counseling Association.

releasing and helpful. There is nothing I can do to force this experience, but when I can relax and be close to the transcendental core of me, then I may behave in strange and impulsive ways in the

> ... relationship, ways which I cannot justify rationally, which have nothing to do with my thought processes. But these strange behaviors turn out to be *right*, in some odd way. At those moments it seems that my inner spirit has reached out and touched the inner spirit of the other. Our relationship transcends itself, and has become a part of something larger. Profound growth and healing and energy are present.
>
> This kind of transcendent phenomenon is certainly experienced at times in groups in which I have worked, changing the lives of some of those involved. One participant in a workshop puts it eloquently. 'I found it to be a profound spiritual experience. I felt the oneness of spirit in the community. We breathed together, felt together, even spoke for one another. I felt the power of the "life force" that infuses each of us — whatever that is. I felt its presence without the usual barricades of "me-ness" or "you-ness" — it was like a meditative experience when I feel myself as a center of consciousness. And yet with that extraordinary sense of oneness, the separateness of each person present has never been more clearly preserved.'
>
> I realize that this account partakes of the mystical. Our experiences, it is clear, involve the transcendent, the indescribable, the spiritual. I am compelled to believe that I, like many others, have underestimated the importance of this mystical, spiritual dimension.
>
> In this I am not unlike some of the more advanced thinkers in physics and chemistry. As they push their theories further, picturing a 'reality' which has no solidity, which is no more than oscillations of energy, they too begin to talk in terms of the transcendent, the indescribable, the unexpected — the sort of phenomena which we have observed and experienced in the person-centered approach.
>
> The person-centered approach, then, is primarily a way of being which finds its expression in attitudes and behaviors that create a growth-promoting climate. It is a basic philosophy rather than simply a technique or a method. When this philosophy is lived, it helps the person to expand the development of his or her own capacities. When it is lived, it also stimulates constructive change in others. It empowers the individuals, and when this personal power is sensed, experience shows that it tends to be used for personal and social transformation.
>
> When this person-centered way of being is lived in psychotherapy, it leads to a process of self-exploration and self-discovery on the part of the client, and eventually to constructive changes in personality and behavior. As the therapist lives these conditions in the relationship, he or she becomes a companion to the client in this journey toward the core of self. (Rogers, 1986)

In this same chapter I give a recorded instance of an intuitive response that has no rational connection with what is being said. I discuss it in these terms.

> This was the kind of intuitive response which I have learned to trust. The expression just formed itself within me, and wanted to be said. I advanced it very tentatively, and from her initial blank and puzzled look, I thought that perhaps it was completely irrelevant and unhelpful, but her next response shows that it touched something deep in her.
>
> I have come to value highly these intuitive responses. They occur infrequently (this is the first one I have captured in a recording) but they are almost always helpful in advancing therapy. In these moments I am perhaps in a slightly altered state of consciousness; indwelling in the client's world, completely in tune with that world. My nonconscious intellect takes over. I know much more than my conscious mind is aware of. I do not form my responses consciously, they simply arise in me, from my nonconscious sensing of the world of the other. (Rogers, 1986)

When I use the term 'nonconscious' mind or intellect, I am referring to the fact that 'mind' covers much more territory than 'brain,' a view held by Barbara Brown (1980), among others. What I mean is perhaps best illustrated from the field of biofeedback. If you ask me to raise the temperature of the middle finger of my right hand, my conscious mind is completely baffled. It cannot possibly do it. Yet if you show me a needle that indicates the temperature of that finger and ask me if I can make it move upward, I find that I can do it. How do I make all the analyses and discriminations necessary to accomplish this end? It is completely inexplicable if we limit ourselves to the conscious mind. But the nonconscious, organic mind is quite capable of the task.

Used in this sense, the nonconscious mind is very different from the Freudian 'unconscious.' It also seems to be different from Erickson's 'unconscious,' which appears to be more similar to my term 'the actualizing tendency.' I suspect, however, that Erickson would have found the concept of the nonconscious mind congenial. For me, at any rate, this concept helps to explain how I can know and relate to the inner core of my client without any conscious knowledge of that core. It seems that Erickson had a very great gift for this kind of mysterious communication.

To take up another point, I share Erickson's liking for the power of the metaphor, although we differ in the particulars. I am always encouraged when a client in therapy begins to use metaphors, because I believe that the client can express him- or herself much more readily and deeply through a metaphor than through exact words. So when a client begins to speak of 'this heavy bag that I am carrying around on my back' or speaks of the fear of 'walking into darkness — out of the light and into the darkness,' I feel sure that progress will be made, and I am eager to respond on the metaphorical level. For myself, I believe that metaphors generated by the client will be more powerful than metaphors that I generate. I do use my own metaphors in some intuitive responses, however, and this seems close to Erickson's approach.

One other quotation from this same recent chapter will confirm another of Gunnison's comparisons. It has to do with the nature of trust in psychotherapy.

> ... practice, theory and research make it clear that the person-centered approach is built upon a basic trust in the person. This is perhaps its sharpest point of difference from most of the institutions in our culture. Almost all of education, government, business, much of religion, much of family life, much of psychotherapy, is based upon a distrust of the person. Goals must be set, because the person is seen as incapable of choosing suitable aims. He or she must be guided toward these goals, since otherwise the individual might stray from the selected path. Teachers, parents, supervisors must develop procedures to make sure that the individual is progressing toward the goal — examinations, inspections, interrogations are some of the methods used. The individual is seen as innately sinful, destructive, lazy, or all three. This person must be constantly watched over.
>
> But the person-centered approach depends upon the actualizing tendency which is present in every living organism — the tendency to grow, to develop, to realize its full potential. This way of being trusts the constructive directional flow of the human being toward a more complex and complete development. It is this directional flow that we aim to release. (Rogers, in press)

Although I am sure that there are many differences in Erickson's approach and my own, and perhaps a paper should be written on those, they may not be as important as the similarities. If in our work we both rely on the fundamental directional tendency of the client-patient, if we are intent on permitting the client to choose the directions for his or her life, if we rely on the wisdom of the organism in making such choices, and if we see our role as releasing the client from constraining self-perceptions to become a more complete potential self, then perhaps the differences are not so important as they might seem.

REFERENCES

Brown, B.E. (1980). *Supermind.* New York: Harper & Row.
Rogers, C.R. (1986). A client-centered, person-centered approach to therapy. In I. L. Kutash and A. Wolf (Eds.), *Psychotherapist's casebook: Theory and technique in practice.* San Francisco: Jossey Bass.

References

Adler, A. (1970). On the origin of the striving for superiority and of social interest. In H.L. Ansbacher and R.R. Ansbacher (Eds.), *Superiority and social interest* (pp. 29–40). Evanston, IL: Northwestern University Press.
Allport, G.W. (1962). Psychological models for guidance. *Harvard Educational Review. 32*, 373–81.
American Psychological Association, Division of Psychological Hypnosis. (1993). Hypnosis. *Psychological Hypnosis, 2* (3).
Aroaz, D.L. (1985a). *The new hypnosis.* New York: Brunner/Mazel.
Aroaz, D.L. (1985b). The new hypnosis: The quintessence of client-centeredness. In J.K. Zeig (Ed.), *Ericksonian psychotherapy volume 1: Structures* (pp. 256–65). New York: Brunner/Mazel.
Aspy, D.N. (1967). Counseling and education. In R.R. Carkhuff (Ed.), *The counselor's contribution to facilitative processes.* Urbana, IL: Parkinson.
Aspy, D.N. (1969). The effect of teacher-offered conditions of empathy, positive regard and congruence upon student achievement. *Florida Journal of Educational Research, 11* (1), 39–48.
Aspy, D.N. (1972). *Toward a technology of humanizing education.* Champaign, IL: Research Press.
Atkinson, G.E. (1983). Case studies of hypnosis as a viable technique and tool in counseling (Doctoral dissertation, University of Northern Colorado, 1983). *Dissertation Abstracts International, 44* (2-B), 600.
Azar, B. (1996). Influences from the mind's inner layers. *The APA Monitor, 27,* 1, 25.
Bandler, R. and Grinder, J. (1975). *Patterns of the hypnotic techniques of Milton H. Erickson, M.D.* (Vol. 1), Cupertino, CA: Meta Publications.
Bandler, R. and Grinder, J. (1979). *Frogs into princes: Neuro-linguistic programming.* Moab, UT: Real People Press.
Bandler, R. and Grinder, J. (1982). *Reframing: Neuro-linguistic programming and the transformation of meaning.* Moab, UT: Real People Press.
Barber, T.X. (1985). Hypnosuggestive procedures as catalysts for psychotherapies. In S.J. Lynn and J.P. Garske (Eds.), *Contemporary psychotherapies: Models and methods.* Columbus, OH: Chas. E. Merrill.
Beahrs, J.O. (1982). Understanding Erickson's Approach. In J.K. Zeig (Ed.), *Ericksonian approaches to hypnosis and psychotherapy* (pp. 58–84). New York: Brunner/Mazel.
Benson, H. (1975). *The relaxation response.* New York: William Morrow.
Berenda, C.W. (1957). Is clinical psychology a science? *American Psychologist, 12,* 725–9.

Berman, J.S. and Norton, N.C. (1985). Does professional training make a therapist more effective? *Psychological Bulletin, 98*, 401–7.
Bohr, N. (1958). *Atomic theory and human knowledge*. New York: John Wiley.
Bois, J.S. (1978). *The art of awareness* (3rd ed.). Dubuque, IA: Wm. C. Brown.
Bourland, D. Jr. (1966). A linguistic note: Writing in E-Prime. *General Semantics Bulletin, 5*.
Bozarth, J.D. and Brodley, B.T. (1986). Client-centered psychotherapy: a statement. *Person-Centered Review, 1*, 262–27.
Briggs, J. and Peat, F.D. (1989). *The turbulent mirror*. New York: Harper, and Row.
Brodley, B.T. (1986, September). Client-centered therapy — What is it? What is it not? Paper presented at the meeting of the Association for the Development of the Person-Centered Approach, Chicago, IL.
Brodley, B.T. (1988, May). Person-centered therapies and client-centered therapy. Paper presented at the meeting of the Association for the Development of the Person-Centered Approach, New York, NY.
Brown, J. (1996). Where two worlds meet. *New Scientist, 150*, 26–30.
Buckley, P. and Peat, F.D. (1996). *Glimpsing reality: Ideas in physics*. Toronto: University of Toronto Press.
Cade, B. and O'Hanlon, W.H. (1993). *A brief guide to brief therapy*. New York: Norton.
Capra, F. (1975). *The tao of physics: An exploration of the parallels between modern physics and eastern mysticism*. Boulder, CO: Shambhala Publications.
Carkhuff, R.R. (1969). *Helping and human relations* (Vols. I and II). New York: Holt, Rinehart and Winston.
Carkhuff, R.R. and Berenson, B.G. (1977). *Beyond counseling and therapy*. New York: Holt, Rinehart and Winston.
Cassidy, D.C. (1992). *Uncertainty: The life and science of Werner Heisenberg*. New York: W.H. Freeman.
Cerio, J.E. (1983). The use of hypnotic elements and audio recordings with the fantasy relaxation technique. *Personnel and Guidance Journal, 61* (7), 436–7.
Chachere, M.L. (1969). *Great men of physics: The humanistic element in scientific work*. Los Angeles, CA: Tinnon-Brown, Inc.
Chaney, S. (1996). An interview with John Weakland by S. Chaney. *The Milton H. Erickson Foundation Newsletter, 16, 1*, 1, 5, 19–20.
Cheek, D.B. (1995). Why did the fathers of psychoanalysis abandon hypnosis? *Hypnos: Swedish Journal of Hypnosis in Psychotherapy and Psychosomatic Medicine, 22*, 4, 211–15.
Cline, B.L. (1965). *The questioners: Physicists and the quantum theory*. New York: Thos. Y. Crowell Co.
Combs, A.W. (1965). *The professional education of teachers: A perceptual view of teacher preparation*. Boston: Allyn and Bacon.
Combs, A.W., Richards, A.C. and Richards, F. (1976). *Perceptual psychology: a humanistic approach to the study of persons*. New York: Harper and Row.
Coulter, A.N. (1976). *Synergetics: Adventure in human development*. Englewood Cliffs, N.J.: Prentice-Hall.
Dafler, R.E. (1996). A response by Dafler. *Advances: The Journal of Mind-Body Health. 12* (2), 42–51.
Dawes, R.M. (1994). *House of cards: Psychology and psychotherapy built on myth*. New York: Free Press.
Day, J.H. (1977). Right hemisphere language processing on normal right handers. *Journal of Experimental Psychology, 3*, 518–28.
de Shazer, S. (1985). *Keys to solution in brief therapy*. New York: Norton.
de Shazer, S. (1988). *Clues: Investigating solutions in brief therapy*. New York: Norton.
de Shazer, S. (1991). *Putting difference to work*. New York: Norton.

Dupré, J. (1993). *The disorder of things: Metaphysical foundations of the disunity of science.* Cambridge, MA: Harvard University Press.
Dyson, F. (1992). *From Eros to Gaia.* New York: Random House.
Ellenberger, H.F. (1970). *Discovery of the unconscious.* New York: Basic Books.
Ellis, A. (1973). *Humanistic psychotherapy: The rational-emotive approach.* New York: Julain Press.
Ellis, A. (1979). The practice of rational-emotive therapy. In A. Ellis and J. Whiteley (Eds.), *Theoretical and empirical foundations of rational-emotive therapy.* Momterey CA: Brooks/Cole.
Erickson, E.M. (1962). Observations concerning alterations in hypnosis of visual perceptions. *The American Journal of Clinical Hypnosis, 5,* 131–4.
Erickson, M.H. (1980a). The use of symptoms as an integral part of hypnotherapy. In E.L. Rossi (Ed.), *The collected papers of Milton H. Erickson* (Vol. 4, pp. 212–23). New York: Irvinton.
Erickson, M.H. (1980b). Deep hypnosis and its induction. In E.L. Rossi (Ed.), *The collected papers of Milton H. Erickson* (Vol. 1, pp. 139–67). New York: Irvington.
Erickson, M.H. (1980c). A brief survey of hypnotism. In E.L. Rossi (Ed.), *The collected papers of Milton H. Erickson* (Vol. 3, pp. 3–12). New York: Irvinton.
Erickson, M.H. (1980d). Hypnosis: A general review. In E.L. Rossi (Ed.), *The collected papers of Milton H. Erickson* (Vol. 3, pp. 13–20). New York: Irvington.
Erickson, M.H. (1980e). Hypnotism. In E.L. Rossi (Ed.), *The collected papers of Milton H. Erickson* (Vol. 3), (pp. 21–5). New York: Irvington.
Erickson, M.H. (1980f). Indirect forms of suggestion in hand levitation. In E.L. Rossi (Ed.), *The collected papers of Milton H. Erickson* (Vol. 1, pp. 478–90). New York: Irvington.
Erickson, M.H. (1980g). The indirect forms of suggestion. In E.L. Rossi (Ed.), *The collected papers of Milton H. Erickson* (Vol. 1, pp. 452–77). New York: Irvington.
Erickson, M.H. (1980h). The interspersal hypnotic technique for symptom correction and pain control. In E.L. Rossi (Ed.), *The collected papers of Milton H. Erickson* (Vol. 4), (pp. 262–78). New York: Irvington.
Erickson, M.H. (1980i). Hypnosis: Its renaissance as a treatment modality. In E.L. Rossi (Ed.), *The collected papers of Milton H. Erickson* (Vol. 4, pp. 52–75). New York: Irvington.
Erickson, M.H. (1980j). An experimental investigation of the possible antisocial use of hypnosis. In E.L. Rossi (Ed.), *The collected papers of Milton H. Erickson* (Vol. 1, pp. 498–530). New York: Irvinton.
Erickson, M.H. (1980k). Self-exploration in the hypnotic state. In E.L. Rossi (Ed.), *The collected papers of Milton H. Erickson* (Vol. 1, pp. 427–36). New York: Irvington.
Erickson, M.H. (1980l) Autohypnotic experiences of Milton H Erickson. In E.L. Rossi (Ed.), *The collected papers of Milton H. Erickson* (Vol. 1, pp. 111–12). New York: Irvington.
Erickson, M.H. and Rossi, E.L. (1975). Varieties of double bind. *The American Journal of Clinical Hypnosis, 17,* 143–57.
Erickson, M.H. and Rossi, E.L. (1979). *Hypnotherapy: An exploratory casebook.* New York: Irvington.
Erickson, M.H. and Rossi, E.L. (1981). *Experiencing hypnosis: Therapeutic approaches to altered states.* New York: Irvington.
Erickson, M.H., Rossi, E.L. and Rossi, S.I. (1976). *Hypnotic realities: The induction of clinical hypnosis and forms of indirect suggestion.* New York: Irvington.
Erickson, M.H. and Zeig, J.K. (1980). Symptom prescription for expanding the psychotic's world view. In E.L. Rossi (Ed.), *The collected papers of Milton H. Erickson on hypnosis.* (Vol. 4, pp. 335–7). New York: Irvington.

Erikson, E.H. (1968). *Identify: Youth and crisis.* New York: W.W. Norton.
Evans, R.I. (Ed.). (1975). *Carl Rogers: The man and his ideas.* New York: E.P. Dutton.
Eysenck, H. (1964). The outcome problem in psychotherapy: A reply. *Psychotherapy, 1,* 97–100.
Farson, R. (1975). Carl Rogers: quiet revolutionary — Introduction. In Evans R.I. *Carl Rogers: The man and his ideas.* New York: E.P. Dutton.
Field, M. and Golubitsky, M. (1992). *Symmetry in chaos.* Oxford: Oxford University Press.
Frankl, V. (1959). *From death camp to existentialism.* Boston: Beacon Press.
Frankl, V. (1965). *The doctor and the soul.* (2nd ed.). New York: Knopf.
Frankl, V. (1969). *The doctor and the soul.* London: Souvenir Press.
Frankl, V. (1970). *Psychotherapy and existentialism:* London: Souvenir Press.
Freedman, D.H. (1991). A chaotic cat takes a swipe at quantum mechanics. *Science, 253,* p. 626.
Freedman, D.H. (1994). Quantum consciousnesss. *Discover, 15,* 6, 89–98.
Freiberg, P. (1996). Answers are often closer than we think: People keep perceiving even when they're unconscious. *The APA Monitor, 27,* 24.
Galin, D. (1974). Implications for psychiatry of left and right cerebral specialization, *Archives of General Psychiatry, 31,* 572–83.
Gell-Mann, M. (1994). *The quark and the Jaguar.* New York: W.H. Freeman.
Gilligan, S.G. (1982). Ericksonian approaches to clinical hypnosis. In J.K. Zeig (Ed.), *Ericksonian approaches to hypnosis and psychotherapy* (pp. 87–103). New York: Brunner/Mazel.
Gilligan, S.G. (1987). *Therapeutic trances.* New York: Bruner/Mazel.
Gilmore, R. (1995). *Alice in quantumland: An allegory of quantum physics.* New York: Springer-Verlag.
Glasser, W. (1965). *Reality therapy: A new approach to psychiatry.* New York: Harper and Row.
Glasser, W. (1984). *Take effective control of your life.* New York: Harper and Row.
Glasser, W. (1985). *Control theory: A new explanation of how we control our lives.* New York: Harper and Row.
Gleick, J. (1987). *Chaos making a new science.* New York: Viking.
Goerner, S.J. (1994). *Chaos and the evolving ecological universe.* Langhorn PA: Gordon and Breach Publishers.
Goldstein, K. (1939). *The organism.* New York: American Books.
Gordon, D. and Meyers-Anderson, M. (1981). *Phoenix: Therapeutic Patterns of Milton H. Erickson.* Cupertino, CA: Meta Publications.
Gribbin, J. (1984). *In search of Schrödinger's cat: Quantum physics and reality.* New York: Bantam.
Grinder, J. and Bandler, R. (1981). *Trance-formations: Neuro-linguistic programming and the structure of hypnosis.* Moab, UT: Real People Press.
Grinder, J., DeLozier, J. and Bandler, R. (1977). *Patterns of the hypnotic techniques of Milton H. Erickson, M.D.* Cupertino, CA: Meta Publications.
Gunnison, H. (1975). Creed of a counselor. *Personnel and Guidance Journal, 54,* 143.
Gunnison, H. (1976a). The Surrogate Self. *Personnel and Guidance Journal, 54,* 523–4.
Gunnison, H. (1976b). Fantasy relaxation technique. *Personnel and Guidance Journal, 55,* 199–200.
Gunnison, H. (1982). Fantasy door approach: Merging the left-right hemispheres. *Personnel and Guidance Journal, 60,* 403–5.
Gunnison, H. (1985a). The uniqueness of similarities: Parallels of Milton H. Erickson and Carl Rogers. *Journal of Counseling and Development, 63,* 561–4.
Gunnison, H. (1985b). Group work with athletes. *Journal for Specialists in Group Work, 10* (4), 211–16.

Gunnison, H. (1987). Comparisons of values and beliefs of M.H. Erickson's utilization approach and C.R. Rogers' person-centered approach. In S.R. Lankton (Ed.), *Ericksonian Monographs No. 2: Central themes and principles of Ericksonian therapy* (pp. 15–31). New York: Brunner/Mazel.
Gunnison, H. (1989). Rachel, remorse and hypnocounseling. *Psychotherapy Patient*, 5, 147–60.
Gunnison, H. (1990a). Adler, Erickson and hypnocounseling. *Individual Psychology*, Vol. 46, 4, pp. 411–22.
Gunnison, H. (1990b). Hypnocounseling: Ericksonian hypnosis for counselors. *Journal of Counseling and Development*, 68, 450–3.
Gunnison, H. (1990c). Merging the fantasy door approach with hypnocounseling. Paper presented to: Fifth European Congress of Hypnosis. University of Kanstanz, Federal Republic of Germany.
Gunnison, H. (1991a). Hypnocounseling: A person-centered approach. Paper submitted to the Second International Conference on Client-Centered and Experiential Psychotherapy. University of Sterling, Scotland, U.K.
Gunnison, H. (1991b). Merging the fantasy door approach with hypnocounseling. *Hypnos: Swedish Journal of Hypnosis in Psychotherapy and Psychosomatic Medicine*, XVIII, 153–62.
Gunnison, H. and Renick, T.F. (1985a). Bulimia: Using fantasy-imagery and relaxation techniques. *Journal of Counseling and Development*. 64, 79–80.
Gunnison, H. and Renick, T.F. (1985b). Hidden hypnotic patterns in counseling and supervision. *Counselor Education and Supervision*, 25 (1), 5–11.
Gunnison, H., Shapiro, J. and Bradley, R.W. (1982). Inside the creative process of counseling: Vocational decision-making takes place. *Personnel and Guidance Journal*, 60, 361–3.
Haley, J. (Ed.) (1967). *Advanced techniques of hypnosis and therapy: Selected papers of Milton H. Erickson, M.D.* New York: Grune and Stratton.
Haley, J. (1973). *Uncommon therapy: The psychiatric techniques of Milton H. Erickson, M.D.* New York: W.W. Norton.
Haley, J. (1985). *Conversations with Milton H. Erickson, M.D.* (Vols. 1–3). New York: Triangle Press.
Hansen, J.C., Stevic, R.R. and Warner, R.W. Jr. (1982). *Counseling: Theory and Process* (3rd ed.). Boston: Allyn and Bacon.
Havens, R.A. (1985). *The wisdom of Milton H. Erickson*. New York: Irvington.
Hawking, S. (1993). *Black holes and baby universes*. New York: Bantam.
Heisenberg, W. (1958). *Physics and philosophy*. New York: Harper and Row.
Heisenberg, W. (1971). *Physics and beyond*. New York: Harper and Row.
Herbert, N. (1987). *Quantum reality: Beyond the new physics*. Garden City, New York: Anchor Press.
Honner, J. (1987). *The description of nature: Niels Bohr and the philosophy of quantum physics*. Oxford: Clarendon Press.
Jacobson, E. (1938). *Progressive relaxation* (2nd ed.). Chicago: University Chicago Press.
James, W. (1893). *Psychology: A brief course*. New York: Henry Holt.
Jaynes, J. (1977). *The origin of consciousness in the breakdown of the bicameral mind.* Boston: Houghton Mifflin.
Jeans, J. (1945). *Physics and philosophy*. New York: Macmillan Co.
Johnson, W. (1946). *People in quandaries: The semantics of personal adjustment*. New York: Harper and Row.
Kirsch, I. (1997). Suggestibility or hypnosis: What do our scales really measure? *International Journal of Clinical and Experimental Hypnosis*, 45, 212–25.

Kirsch, I. and Lynn, S.J. (1975). The altered state of hypnosis: changes in the theoretical landscape. *American Psychologist, 50*, 846–58.

Korzybski, A. (1941). *Science and sanity: An introduction to non-Aristotelian systems and general semantics* (2nd ed.). Lancaster, PA: Science Press.

Kuhn, T.S. (1970). *The structure of scientific revolutions.* Chicago: University Chicago Press.

Lambert, M.J., Shapiro, D.A. and Bergin, A.E. (1986). The effectiveness of psychotherapy. In S.L. Garfield and A.E. Bergin (Eds.), *Handbook of psychotherapy and behavior change* (3rd. ed., pp. 157–212). New York: Wiley.

Lankton, S.R. (1980). *Practical magic: A translation of basic neuro-linguistic programming into clinical psychotherapy.* Cypertino, CA: Meta Publications.

Lankton, S.R. (1982). The occurrence and use of trance phenomenon in nonhypnotic therapies. In J.K. Zeig (Ed.), *Ericksonian approaches to hypnosis and psychotherapy* (pp. 132–43). New York: Brunner/Mazel.

Lankton, S.R. and Lankton, C.H. (1983). *The answer within: A clinical framework of Ericksonian hypnotherapy.* New York: Brunner/Mazel.

Leva, R.A. (1987). *Psychotherapy: The listening voice: Rogers and Erickson.* Muncie, IN: Accelerated Development.

Lewin, R. (1992). *Complexity: Life at the edge of chaos.* New York: Macmillan

Ley, R.G. (1979). Cerebral asymmetries, emotional experience and imagery: Implications for psychotherapy. In A.A. Sheikh and J.J. Shaffer (Eds.), *The potential of fantasy and imagination.* New York: Brandon House.

Lloyd, D. and Rossi, E.L. (1992). *Ultradian rhythms in life processes.* New York: Springer-Verlag.

Lopez, F.G. (1987). Erickson and Rogers: The differences do make a difference. *Journal of Counseling and Development, 65*, 241–3.

Lorenz, E.N. (1993). *The essence of chaos.* Seattle: University of Washington Press.

Lovelock, J.E. (1982). *Gaia, a new look at life on earth.* Oxford: Oxford University Press.

Lustig, H.S. (1982). Understanding Erickson and Ericksonian techniques. In J.K. Zeig (Ed.), *Ericksonian approaches to hypnosis and psychotherapy* (pp. 455–61). New York: Brunner/Mazel.

Martin, D.G. (1972). *Learning-based client-centered therapy.* Monterey, California: Brooks/Cole.

Martin, J.L. (1981). *Basic quantum mechanics.* Oxford: Oxford University Press.

Maslow, A.H. (1970). *Motivation and personality* (2nd ed.). New York: Harper and Row.

Maslow, A.H. (1971). *The farther reaches of human nature.* New York: Viking.

May, R. (1958). *Existence.* New York: Basic Books, Inc.

May, R. (1961). *Existential Psychology.* New York: Random House.

Murdoch, D. (1987). *Niels Bohr's Philosophy of Physics.* Cambridge: Cambridge University Press.

Norcross, J.C. (1987). Introduction: eclecticism, casebooks and cases. In J.C. Norcross (Ed.), *Casebook of eclectic psychotherapy.* New York: Brunner/Mazel.

O'Hanlon, W.H. (1987). *Taproots: Underlying principles of Milton Erickson's therapy and hypnosis.* New York: W.W. Norton.

O'Hanlon, W.H. and Martin, M. (1992). *Solution-oriented hypnosis.* New York: Norton.

O'Hanlon, W.H. and Weiner-Davis, M. (1989). *In search of solutions: A new direction in psychotherapy.* New York: Norton.

Oppenheimer, R. (1965). Analogy in science. In F.T. Severin (Ed.), *Humanistic viewpoints in psychology* (pp. 213–16). New York: McGraw-Hill.

Ornstein, R.E. (1977). *The psychology of consciousness.* New York: Viking Press.

Ornstein, R.E. and Thompson, R.F. (1984). *The amazing brain.* Boston: Houghton Mifflin.

Overholser, L.C. (1985). *Ericksonian hypnosis: A handbook of clinical practice*. New York: Irvington.
Passons, W.R. (1975). *Gestalt approaches in counseling*. New York: Holt, Rinehart and Winston.
Patterson, C.H. (1985). *The therapeutic relationship: Foundations for an eclectic psychotherapy*. Monterey, California: Brooks/Cole.
Patterson, C.H. and Hidore, S.C. (1997). *Successful psychotherapy: A caring, loving relationship*. Northvale, NJ: Jason Aronson.
Penrose, R. (1989). *The Emperor's New Mind*. Oxford: Oxford University Press.
Penrose, R. (1994). *Shadows of the mind: A search for the missing science of consciousness*. Oxford: Oxford University Press.
Perls, F.S. (1969). *Gestalt therapy verbatim*. Lafayette, CA: Real People Press.
Perls, F.S. (1973). *The gestalt approach and eyewitness to therapy*. Palo Alto, California: Science and Behavior Books.
Peterson, D.R. (1995). The reflective educator. *American Psychologist, 50*, 975–83.
Pickover, C.A. (1994). *Chaos in wonderland: Visual adventures in a fractal world*. New York: St. Martin's Press.
Pierce, R. (1966). An investigation of grade point average and therapeutic process variables. Unpublished dissertation, University of Massachusetts, reviewed in Carkhuff, R.R. and Berenson, B.G. (Eds.), *Beyond counseling and therapy*. New York: Holt, Rinehart and Winston.
Pool, R. (1989). Quantum chaos: Enigma wrapped in a mystery. *Science, 243*, 893–5.
Remen, R.N. (1996). All emotions are potentially life affirming. *Advances: The Journal of Mind-Body Health, 12* (2), 23–8.
Rogers, C.R. (1951). *Client-centered therapy*. Boston: Houghton-Mifflin.
Rogers, C.R. (1957). The necessary and sufficient conditions of therapeutic personality change. *Journal of Consulting Psychology, 21*, 95–103.
Rogers, C.R. (1959). A theory of therapy, personality and interpersonal relationships, as developed in the client-centered framework. In S. Koch (Ed.), *Psychology: A study of a science. Formulations of the person and the social context* (Vol. 3, pp. 184–256). New York: McGraw-Hill.
Rogers, C.R. (1961). *On becoming a person*. Boston: Houghton Mifflin.
Rogers, C.R. (1962). The interpersonal relationship: The core of guidance. *Harvard Educational Review, 32*, 416–29.
Rogers, C.R. (1977). *Carl Rogers on personal power*. New York: Dell.
Rogers, C.R. (1978). The formative tendency. *Journal of Humanistic Psychology, 18*, 1–24.
Rogers, C.R. (1980). *A way of being*. Boston: Houghton Mifflin.
Rogers, C.R. (1985). Reaction to Gunnison's article on the similarities between Erickson and Rogers. *Journal of Counseling and Development, 63*, 565–6.
Rogers, C.R. (1986a). Rogers, Kohut, and Erickson: A personal perspective on some similarities and differences. *Person-Centered Review, 1*, (2), 125–40.
Rogers, C.R. (1986b). Client-centered approach to therapy. In I.L. Kutash and A. Wolf (Eds.), *The psychotherapist's casebook*. San Francisco: Jossey-Bass.
Romer, A. (1960). *The restless atom*. Garden City, New York: Anchor Books.
Rosen, S. (1979). Foreword. In M.H. Erickson and E.L. Rossi, *Hypnotherapy: An exploratory casebook* (pp. ix–xiii). New York: John Wiley.
Rosen, S. (Ed.) (1982). *My voice will go with you*. New York: W.W. Norton.
Ross, P.J. (1981). Hypnosis as a counseling tool. *British Journal of Guidance and Counseling, 9* (2), 173–9.
Rossi, E.L. (Ed.) (1980). *The collected papers of Milton H. Erickson* (Vols. 1–4). New York: Irvington.

Rossi, E.L. (1993). *The psychobiology of everyday healing.* New York: W.W. Norton.
Sacerdote, P. (1982). Erickson's contribution to pain control in cancer. In J.K. Zeig (Ed.), *Ericksonian approaches to hypnosis and psychotherapy* (pp. 336–45). New York: Brunner/Mazel.
Sarbin, T.R. and Coe, W.C. (1972). *Hypnosis: A social psychological analysis of influence communication.* New York: Holt, Rinehart and Winston.
Schofield, W. (1964). *Psychotherapy: The purchase of friendship.* Englewood Cliffs, NJ: Prentice-Hall.
Scroggs, K.A. (1986). Ericksonian approaches within family therapy. *Individual Psychology, 42* (4), 506–20.
Searle, J. (1984). *Minds, brains and science.* Cambridge, MA: Harvard University Press.
Secter, I. (1982). Seminars with Erickson: The early years. In J.K. Zeig (Ed.), *Ericksonian approaches to hypnosis and psychotherapy* (pp. 447–54). New York: Brunner/Mazel.
Seligman, M.E.P. (1996). A creditable beginning. *American Psychologist, 51,* 1087.
Severin, F.T. (1965). *Human viewpoints in psychology.* New York: McGraw-Hill.
Shaffer, J.T. (1978). Psychofeedback: The use of guided fantasy as a creative therapeutic process. Unpublished MS, Well-Being Center Inc.
Shaffer, J.T. (1979). In A.A. Sheikh and J.T. Shaffer (Eds.), *The potential of fantasy and imagination.* New York: Brandon House.
Sheikh, A.A. and Shaffer, J.T. (1979). *The potential of fantasy and imagination.* New York: Brandon House.
Skinner, B.F. (1948). *Walden II.* New York: MacMillan Company.
Smith, D. (1982). Trends in counseling and psychotherapy. *American Psychologist, 379,* 802-809.
Stapp, H.P. (1993). *Mind, matter, and quantum mechanics.* Berlin-Heidelberg: Springer-Verlag.
Stein, D.M. and Lambert, M.J. (1984). On the relationship between therapist experience and psychotherapy outcome. *Clinical Psychology Review, 4,* 127–42.
Stein, J. (Ed.). (1984). *Random house college dictionary.* New York: Random House.
Stern, C.R. (1985). There's no theory like no-theory: The Ericksonian approach in perspective. In J.K. Zeig (Ed.), *Ericksonian psychotherapy Vol. I: Structures* (pp. 77–86). New York: Brunner/Mazel.
Stevens, B. (1970). *Don't push the river it flows by itself.* Lafayette, CA: Real People Press.
Stewart, I. (1989). *Does God play dice?* Oxford: Basil Blackwell Ltd.
Stewart, I. and Golubitsky, M. (1992). *Fearful symmetry.* Oxford: Basil Blackwell Ltd.
Strupp, H.H. and Hadley, S.W. (1979). Specific versus nonspecific factors in psychotherapy. *Archives of General Psychiatry, 36,* 1125–36.
Szent-Gyoergyi, A. (1974). Drive in living matter to perfect itself. *Synthesis,* Spring, 12–24.
Talmon, M. (1990). *Single session therapy.* San Francisco: Jossey-Bass.
Teller, E. (1969). Niels Bohr and the idea of complementarity. In M.L. Chachere (Ed.), *Great men of physics: The humanistic element in scientific work* (pp. 77–97). Los Angeles, CA: Tinnon-Brown Inc.
Thut, I.N. (1957). *The story of education.* New York: McGraw-Hill.
Truax, C.B. and Carkhuff, R.R. (1967). *Toward effective counseling and psychotherapy.* Chicago: Aldine.
Tuchman, B.W. (1978). *A distant mirror: The calamitous 14th century.* New York: Alfred A. Knopf.
Vaihinger, H. (1925). *The philosophy of 'as if,' a system of the theoretical practical and religious fictions of mankind.* New York: Harcourt, Brace.

VanKaam, A.L. (1958). Assumptions in psychology. *Journal of Individual Psychology, 14*, 22–8.
von Foerster, H. (1984). On constructing a reality. In P. Watzlawick (Ed.), *The invented reality* (pp. 41–61). New York: W.W. Norton.
von Glasersfeld, E. (1984). An introduction to radical constructivism. In P. Watzlawick (Ed.), *The invented reality* (pp. 17–40). New York: W.W. Norton.
Waldrop, M.M. (1992). *Complexity: The emerging science at the edge of order and chaos.* New York: Simon and Schuster.
Wallas, L. (1985). *Stories for the third ear.* New York: W.W. Norton.
Walter, J.L. and Peller, J.E. (1992). *Becoming solution-focused in brief therapy.* New York: Brunner/Mazel.
Watzlawick, P. (1978). *The language of change.* New York: Basic Books.
Watzlawick, P. (1984). *The invented reality.* New York: W.W. Norton.
Watzlawick, P. (1985). Hypnotherapy without trance. In J.K. Zeig (Ed.), *Ericksonian psychotherapy Vol. 1: Structures* (pp. 5–14). New York: Brunner/Mazel.
Watzlawick, P., Beavin, J.H. and Jackson, D.D. (1967). *Pragmatics of human communication: A study of interactional patterns, pathologies, and paradoxes.* New York: W.W. Norton.
Watzlawick, P., Weakland, J. and Fisch, R. (1974). *Change: Principles of problem formation and problem resolution.* New York: Norton.
Weiner-Davis, M., de Shazer, S. and Gingerich, W.J. (1987). Building on pretreatment change to construct the therapeutic solution: An exploratory study. *Journal of Marital and Family Therapy, 13*, 359–63.
Weitzenhoffer, A.M. (1976). Foreword In Milton Erickson, E.L. Rossi and S.J. Rossi (Eds.), *Hypnotic realities: The induction of clinical hypnosis and forms of indirect suggestion* (pp. xii–xix). New York: Wiley.
Wheeler, J.A. (1994). *At home in the universe.* Woodbury, N.Y.: American Institute of Physics Press.
Wilder, J. (1959). Introduction. In K.A. Adler and D. Deutsch (Eds.), *Essays in individual psychology* (pp. xv–xvii). New York: Grove Press.
Wolberg, L.R. (1955). *The technique of psychotherapy.* New York: Grune and Stratton.
Wolpé, J. (1961). The systematic desensitization treatment of neuroses. *Journal of Nervous and Mental Diseases, 132*, 189–203.
Yam, P. (1997). Bringing Schrödinger's cat to life. *Scientific American, 276*, 124–9.
Yapko, M.D. (1985). The Ericksonian hook: Values in Ericksonian approaches. In J.K. Zeig (Ed.), *Ericksonian psychotherapy Vol. 1: Structures* (pp. 266–81). New York: Brunner/Mazel.
Zeig, J.K. (Ed.) (1980). *Teaching seminar with Milton H. Erickson, M.D.* New York: Brunner/Mazel.
Zeig, J.K. (Ed.) (1982). *Ericksonian approaches to hypnosis and psychotherapy.* New York: Brunner/Mazel.
Zeig, J.K. (1985). *Experiencing Erickson.* New York: Brunner/Mazel.
Zeig, J.K. (Ed.) (1985a). *Ericksonian psychotherapy volume I: Structures.* New York: Brunner/Mazel.
Zeig, J.K. (Ed.) (1985b). *Ericksonian psychotherapy volume II: Clinical applications.* New York: Brunner/Mazel.
Zukav, G. (1979). *The dancing Wu Li masters.* New York: William Morrow.

Index

acceptance (see unconditional positive regard)
'acting' 125, 126, 129, 171
actualizing tendency/actualization 24, 37, 39
Adler, A. 82, 155, 195
Allport, G.W. 30, 195
altered states 14, 17, 20
American Psychological Association (APA) 2, 33, 84, 195
American Society for Clinical Hypnosis 3
amnesia (hypnotic) 88
analogies 99
analogue marking 92
anchoring 85, 101, 140
anxietizing meter 153
Aroaz, D.L. 143, 195
Aspy, D.N. 2, 195
Atkinson, G.E. 85, 195
attitudes 8, 11
authenticity (see congruence)
autohypnosis 14, 17, 18, 20
Azar, B. 50, 195
Bandler, R. 14, 16, 85, 92, 93, 95, 97, 100, 143, 195, 198
Barber, T.X. 90, 147, 195
Beahrs, J.O. 25, 97, 195
Beavin, J.H. 120, 203
behaviorism 30, 32, 64
Benson, H. 141, 144, 195
Berenda, C.W. 57, 195
Berenson, B.G. 112, 113, 118, 123, 196
Berman, J.S. 2, 196
biofeedback 26, 141
bodily cues/felt sensation 119, 122, 148
Bohr, N. 60, 65, 66, 67, 69, 71, 196
Bozarth, J.D. 7, 196
Bradley, R.W. 85, 105, 143, 199
breathing 122

Brief Therapy (BT) 90, 125, 129, 134, 157–73
   assumptions 159–62
   questions 162, 165, 167
Briggs, J. 59, 60, 62, 196
Brodley, B.T. 6, 7, 196
Brown, J. 64, 193, 194, 196
Buckley, P. 68, 72, 196
'butterfly effect' 61
Cade, B. 51, 97, 102, 138, 158, 159, 161, 163, 168, 196
Capra, F. 66, 67, 69, 70, 72, 74, 196
Carkhuff, R.R. 2, 8, 110, 111, 112, 113, 118, 123, 127, 137, 196, 202
Cassidy, D.C. 72, 196
Cerio, J.E. 85, 196
Chachere, M.L. 66, 196
Chaney, S. 161, 196
chaos 54–64
Cheek, D.B. 81, 196
choice 45, 75, 79
CIPAR (clarifying, identifying, predicting, acting responsibly) 52
client resistance 132
Cline, B.L. 68, 72, 73, 196
Coe, W.C. 147, 202
Combs, A.W. 2, 24, 34, 35, 196
communication 16, 46
complementarity, principle of 68, 69, 75, 79
concreteness 112, 147 (see also specificity of expression)
congruence 7, 8, 16, 42, 85–8, 112, 116–19
constructivism 49, 50, 54, 79
core conditions (see PEGS)
Coulter, A.N. 143, 148, 196
creationism 48
creed of a counselor 168, 170
Dafler, R.E. 112, 196
Dawes, R.M. 2, 196

Day, J.H. 147, 196
de Shazer, S. 138, 157, 158, 163, 164, 196, 197, 203
DeLozier, J. 16, 198
dependency (of client) 9
'depressometer' 153
deprivation 25
determinism 30, 52, 55, 76
diagnosis 30, 158
dials, meters and gauges (DMG) 130, 149, 153
directivity 11, 83 (see also nondirective)
dissociation 101
Dupré, J. 64, 197
dyslexia 13
Dyson, F. 69, 197
eclecticism 23, 53, 105–28, 141, 143
editorializing 161
Einstein, A. 49, 60, 65, 71, 73
Ellenberger, H.F. 155, 197
Ellis, A. 85, 108, 143, 197
empathy 8, 16, 38, 46, 83, 88, 93, 112, 118, 121–2
Epictetus 155
epistemology 47–56
Erickson, E.M. 82, 197
Erickson, M.H. 4, 8, 13, 14, 16, 18, 19, 21, 60, 83, 86, 89, 92, 96, 99, 100, 102, 110, 138, 159, 191, 193, 194, 197
   tentative assumptions of 44
   hypno-suggestive language of 90
   directive approach of 9
   utilization approach of (see utilization approach)
Erikson, E.H. 32, 198
Evans, R.I. 33, 198
exceptions 125, 164
'exploring' 123, 124, 126, 129, 171
Eysenck, H. 142, 198
facial expressions 122
fantasy door approach (FDA) 130, 133, 142–9, 186
fantasy relaxation technique 85, 130, 136–41, 149–50, 154, 181
Farson, R. 11, 198
Field, M. 58, 198
Fisch, R. 158, 203
Frankl, V. 5, 102, 158, 198
free will 75, 78, 79
Freedman, D.H. 65, 75, 198
Freiberg, P. 49, 198
Freud, S. 81, 107, 108
   'unconscious 27
fully functioning person 23
Galin, D. 143, 198
Gell-Mann, M. 62, 64, 198
gender stereotypes 50

General Theory of Relativity 73
genuineness (see congruence)
gestalt/therapy 14, 49, 90, 107, 108, 133, 139, 141, 143
gestures 122
Gilligan, S.G. 25, 101, 103, 138, 198
Gilmore, R. 57, 66, 76, 198
Gingerich, W. J. 158, 203
Glasser, W. 108, 153, 198
Gleick, J. 58, 61, 198
Gloria 22, 84
Goerner, S.J. 58, 60, 198
Goldstein, K. 24, 198
Golubitsky, M. 58, 64, 198, 202
Gordon, D. 22, 99, 198
grand unified theory 76
Gribbin, J. 65, 68, 71, 74, 198
Grinder, J. 14, 16, 85, 92, 93, 95, 97, 100, 143, 195, 198
growth/growth principle 7, 13, 23, 27
Gunnison, H. 3, 5, 6, 15, 21, 22, 83, 85, 86, 130, 136, 143, 144, 145, 146, 147, 191, 198, 199
Hadley, S.W. 2, 202
Haley, J. 7, 15, 21, 99, 103, 199
Hansen, J.C. 86, 199
Havens, R.A. 86, 199
Hawking, S. 66, 69, 72, 76, 77, 199
Heisenberg, W. 57, 60, 65, 66, 68, 71, 74, 78, 199
   uncertainty principle 65, 68, 70–2, 76
Heraclitus 129
Herbert, N. 65, 68, 71, 199
Hidore, S.C. 111, 112, 201
holism 53, 74
hypnocounseling
   definitions of 89
hypno-suggestive
   approaches 90
   language 85, 88, 90, 93, 103
hypnosis 3, 14, 26, 47, 50, 81, 86
   definitions of 86
   history of 81
hypnotic
   induction 88
   language 90, 140
   patterns 22, 84
   phenomena 87
   suggestion 84, 101 (see also hypno-suggestive)
   trance 15, 17, 18, 84, 87
'illusions of choice' 100, 183
imagery 85
implication 96
implied directive language (IDL) 91–3, 96, 104, 122, 173, 181, 186

indirect suggestion 101
inherent growth 7
internal frame of reference 38, 40
internal maps 44
interpersonal relationship 2, 15
interspersals 92, 132, 140, 173, 186
introjection 39, 44
intuition 18, 20
Jacobson, E. 144, 199
James, W. 38, 77, 78, 199
Jaynes, J. 143, 147, 199
Jeans, J. 68, 70, 75, 76, 199
jokes 21, 99
Jung, C.G. 25, 58, 82, 129
kinesthetic awareness 153
Kirsch, I. 87, 88, 199, 200
knowledge 47, 53
    constructed 47, 49–50
    discovered 47, 48–9
    revealed 47–8
Koch, S. 33
Kuhn, T.S. 66, 73, 200
Kutash, I.L. 191, 194
Lambert, M.J. 2, 200, 202
language
    body 122
    empathic 122
    figurative 21
    hypno-suggestive 85, 88, 90–3, 103
Lankton, C.H. 4, 16, 22, 44, 46, 83, 84, 85, 91, 96, 97, 100, 101, 102, 157, 200
Lankton, S.R. 4, 16, 22, 44, 46, 83, 84, 85, 91, 93, 96, 97, 100, 101, 102, 157, 200
Lao-Tzu 1
left brain function 146
Leva, R.A. 3, 200
'levels of communication' 113
Lewin, R. 59, 200
Ley, R.G. 147, 200
linearity 58
Lloyd, D. 63, 200
Lorenz, E.N. 58, 61, 200
Lovelock, J.E. 200
Lynn, S.J. 87, 88, 200
manipulation 11, 22, 82, 83,
Martin, D.G. 142, 200
Martin, J.L. 66, 67, 200
Martin, M. 89, 92, 101, 103, 200
Maslow, A.H. 24, 32, 61, 200
matching 95, 93, 122, 181, 183
May, R. 57, 200
meditation 89, 141
metaphor 20–1, 26–7, 45, 51, 54, 69, 89, 99, 102, 145, 150, 193
Meyers-Anderson, M. 22, 99, 198
mind/body problem 75

miracle question 164
Murdoch, D. 68, 200
Neuro-Linguistic Programming (NLP) 14, 93
Newton, C. 48, 49
Newtonian physics 57
nonconscious 18, 20, 23, 26
nondirective 9, 11, 12 (see also directivity)
    client-centered approach 4
    counseling 1, 6
nonjudgmental (see unconditional positive regard)
nonrepetition 92
Norcross, J.C. 109, 200
Norton, N.C. 2, 196
O'Hanlon, W.H. 51, 89, 92, 97, 99, 101, 102, 103, 138, 158, 159, 161, 163, 168
Oppenheimer, R. 57, 79, 200
Ornstein, R.E. 143, 148, 200
Overholser, L.C. 99, 201
pacing 95, 122, 181, 183
paradigm change/shift 60, 66 (see also Kuhn, T.S.)
paradoxical intervention 102–3, 152
Passons, W.R. 141, 201
pattern interruption 103, 142
Patterson, C.H. 23, 109, 111, 112, 201
Peat, F.D. 59, 60, 62, 72, 196
PEGS (positive regard, empathy, genuineness, specificity) 8, 15–18, 25, 27, 43, 53, 83, 86, 87, 88, 90, 113, 116–19, 122–3, 129, 137, 153, 162, 171 (see also empathy, concreteness, congruence and unconditional positive regard)
Peller, J.E. 158, 159, 162, 163, 203
Penrose, R. 66, 72, 75, 76, 201
Perls, F.S. 93, 108, 130, 140, 141, 143, 201
person-centered approach 1, 6, 12, 31, 91, 149, 153, 155, 160
Peterson, D.R. 2, 201
phenomenal field 36, 38
phenomenology 1, 34, 54, 79
Pickover, C.A. 59, 201
Pierce, R. 2, 118, 201
Planck, M. 60
Poincaré, J.H. 33, 59, 60
Pool, R. 64, 201
positive regard 8, 15, 88, 111, 118 (see also unconditional positive regard)
posthypnotic amnesia 88
presupposition 96, 101, 159, 182, 184, 186–8
Procrustes 7

Proust, M. 63
psychoanalysis 31, 108
psychological trauma 25
quantum mechanics 49, 54, 65–8, 73, 77
racism 54
Rational Emotive Therapy 85, 90, 107–8, 148
Reality Therapy (RT) 107, 108, 148, 153–4
reductionism 58
reframing 97, 98
regression 132
relaxation 13, 147
Renick, T. F. 22, 83, 199
representational system 93, 95
respect (see unconditional positive regard)
responsibility (for/to) 27
Richards, A.C. 24, 34, 35, 196
right brain function 146–8
'right-wayism' 105–8
Rogers, C.R. 1, 3, 7, 10, 11, 15, 16, 17, 20, 22, 23, 33, 36, 64, 65, 83, 110, 111, 112, 131, 159, 191, 193, 194, 201
Romer, A. 67, 69, 201
Rosen, S. 21, 22, 27, 99, 201
Ross, P. J. 85, 201
Rossi, E.L. 4, 5, 7, 8, 13, 14, 15, 16, 18, 19, 21, 25, 63, 86, 92, 96, 99, 100, 102, 103, 197, 200, 201, 202
Rossi, S.I. 8, 13, 21, 86, 92, 96, 99, 197
Sacerdote, P. 25, 27, 202
Sarbin, T.R. 147, 202
Satir, V. 93
Schofield, W. 111, 202
Scroggs, K.A. 90, 202
Searle, J. 75, 202
Secter, I. 7, 202
self 13, 39, 41–3
   as a tool 13
   actualization 23, 24, 64
self-hypnosis 13, 16, 131–2
Seligman, M.E.P. 80, 202
Severin, F. T. 57, 202
Shaffer, J.T. 144, 202
Shakespeare, W. 157
Shapiro, D.A. 2, 200
Shapiro, J. 85, 143, 199
Skinner, B.F. 64, 78, 108, 202
Smith, D. 1, 202
Snygg, D. 24, 34
socialization 25
specificity of expression 8, 112, 119
splitting 101
Stapp, H.P. 65, 66, 68, 73, 77, 78, 202
Stein, D.M. 2, 202
Stein, J. 83, 202

stereotypes 54
Stern, C.R. 7, 202
Stevens, B. 19, 202
Stewart, I. 48, 59, 60, 64, 202
Strupp, H.H. 2, 202
surrogate self (SS) 130–1, 135–6, 173
symbolization 36, 37, 41
syntropy 23, 63
systematic desensitization 85, 138
Szent-Gyoergyi, A. 23, 63, 202
Talmon, M. 157, 158, 202
Teller, E. 69, 70, 202
therapeutic relationship 23, 83, 90
three phase counseling process 123
Thut, I.N. 47, 202
Truax, C.B. 2, 202
truisms 96
Tuchman, B.W. 62, 202
Twain, M. 1
uncertainty principle 65, 68, 70–2, 76
unconditional positive regard 15, 45, 85, 118–19
unconscious 23, 25, 26, 99, 193
understanding 124, 125, 126, 129, 171
utilization 4, 91, 160
   approach 8, 12, 20, 27, 31, 90, 131, 153, 155, 149
Vaihinger, H. 32, 203
VAKOG (visual, auditory, kinesthetic, olfactory, gustatory) 94, 119, 123, 164–5, 187, 189
values 4, 5, 11
VanKaam, A.L. 57, 203
voice 122
von Foerster, H. 50, 203
von Glasersfeld, E. 49, 51, 203
Waldrop, M.M. 59, 203
Wallas, L. 99, 203
Walter, J.L. 158, 159, 162, 163, 203
Watzlawick, P. 11, 90, 120, 146, 158, 203
Weakland, J. 158, 161, 203
Weiner-Davis, M. 99, 158, 159, 163, 203
Weitzenhoffer, A.M. 3, 203
Wheeler, J.A. 66, 72, 203
Wolberg, L.R. 84, 203
Wolf, A. 191, 194
Wolpé, J. 85, 138, 203
Wordsworth, W. 4
Yam, P. 67, 203
Yapko, M.D. 15, 203
yes-sets 96
Zeig, J.K. 4, 7, 8, 11, 13, 16, 18, 197, 203
Zukav, G. 65, 67, 69, 203